A MODEST COLLECTION

A MODEST
COLLECTION

*Private Libraries
Association*

1956–2006

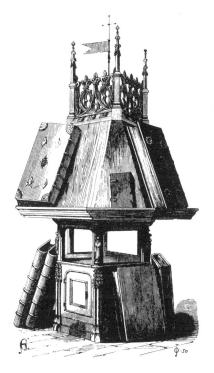

PRIVATE LIBRARIES ASSOCIATION

PINNER MMVII

Text © Private Libraries Association
and the Authors, 2007

Published by the Private Libraries Association
Ravelston, South View Road, Pinner,
Middlesex HA5 3YD, England

1,100 copies (of which 400 for sale)
ISBN 978 0 900002 67 0

A CIP catalogue record for this book is
available from The British Library

Etchings (greatly reduced)
on half-title and page 87 by Jules Chevrier,
from *Les Amoureux du Livre*, 1878

Wood-engraving on title-page
by Orlando Jewitt, from
*Some Account of Gothic Architecture
in Spain*, 1865

Printed in Great Britain by
Henry Ling Limited, at the Dorset Press
Dorchester, DT1 1HD

Edited, designed, and typeset in Sabon by
David Chambers

CONTENTS

ILLUSTRATIONS

Liber Amicorum

David Chambers

HERE, IN THE GUISE OF THE STORY of our Association, is an account of friendships between its members over the past fifty years. They have all been collectors with widely different interests, from countries across the world, united by a love of books and the need to be surrounded by them at the end of a day's work, and in the years of retirement. The aim of the society has been to bring together such enthusiasts and to offer them books and essays in the journal that will lead them further into the bibliophilic quagmire. The enormous range of their interests has added edge to our publications, but our need has been to deal in sufficient depth with the subject in hand, to give purpose to its text, and yet to interest other members whose collections have moved in quite different directions. A number of future essays for the journal will, in fact, be derived from some of the brief essays in this present volume.

The first three of the chapters which follow are reprinted from *The Private Library*, Autumn and Winter 1980 and Spring 1981, with some necessary amendments to allow for the passage of time.

In the preparation of this volume our thanks are due to John Byrne and Paul Nash for reading the text with such great care, and for their extensive corrections which have prevented many errors, both textual and typographic, that would otherwise have escaped into print. The mistakes that remain are mine, of course, for which my apologies.

Fifty years ago we were, it seems, half a century younger. Philip Ward was eighteen, just starting his career in librarianship, and filled with the youthful excitement that has stayed with him ever since. I was getting married in 1956, but joined the Association the following year. Now we hope that the younger minds amongst our members will drive us forward into the next half century. To my sorrow, indeed, two of our contributors, Claude Cox and Len Weaver, have died whilst this volume has been in preparation.

There remain to be thanked in this account of our activities all those members who have worked so hard to carry its affairs to successful conclusion, some, but not all, serving on the Council. To attempt to name them all here would now be an impossible task, but their part should not be forgotten.

Not all our contributors have wanted portraits of themselves to be included, and, indeed, some of the photographs have had to be limited in size so as to improve the quality of reproduction. The style and extent of the essays has varied considerably, but there has been little editing, for the individuality of the pieces seemed part of their attraction. Where space was left at the end of a particular essay this has often been filled with some apt engraving or drawing relevant to the character of the collection concerned.

A book for, and about our friends . . .

THE OFFICERS

HON. PRESIDENT
Dr R. Regensburger, 1956–60
D. J. Foskett, 1961–63
Dr Desmond Flower, 1963–64
Percy H. Muir, 1964–65
J. Rives Childs, 1965–68
Sir Arthur Elton, 1968–71
Raymond Lister, 1971–74
Ruari McLean, 1974–77
Douglas Cleverdon, 1977–80
Dr Glyn Tegai Hughes, 1980–83
William B. Todd, 1983–86
John Russell Taylor, 1986–89
Peter Eaton, 1989–92
Iain Bain, 1992–95
Robin de Beaumont, 1995–98
B. C. Bloomfield, 1998–2001
Colin Franklin, 2001–4
Lynne Brindley, 2004–

HONORARY VICE-PRESIDENT
Frank Broomhead, 2001–

HON. CHAIRMAN OF COUNCIL
A. E. Ward, 1956–61
D. J. Foskett, 1961–63
Council members, 1963–66
David Chambers, 1966–

HON. SECRETARY
Philip Ward, 1956–60
Antony Wilson, 1961–64
Bob Forster, 1964–73
Frank Broomhead, 1973–2001
James Brown, 2002–6
Stan Brett, 2006–

11

HON. MEMBERSHIP SECRETARY
Philip Ward, 1956–60
G. S. Geall, 1960
Antony Wilson, 1961–64
Juliet Standing, 1964–65
R. T. Standing, 1965–66
R. D. Pratt, 1966–69
Peter Hall, 1969–76
Anthony Pincott, 1976–78
John Allison, 1978–

for NORTH AMERICA/USA
Harold Berliner, 1976–77
Bill Klutts, 1977–

for CANADA
Alan J. Horne, 1995–

for AUSTRALASIA
Cyril Wyatt, 1998–

for INSTITUTIONAL LIBRARIES
David Chambers, 1969–70
James Wilson, 1971–77
Frances Guthrie, 1977–91
Richard Goulden, 1992–2005
Richard Faircliff, 2005–

HON. PUBLICATIONS SECRETARY
David Chambers, 1960–

HON. EDITOR *NEWSLETTER*
Frank Broomhead, 1974–2001
David Chambers & Rachel Allison, 2002–

HON. TREASURER
G. W. Sheldon, 1956–58
A. E. Ward, 1958–60
Antony Wilson, 1961–63
R. Guy Powell, 1964–67
R. D. Pratt, 1967–68
Basil Savage, 1969–71
Stanley Brett, 1972–78
Anthony Pincott, 1978–81
Norman Waddleton, 1981
John Paton, 1982–88
A. A. Leith, 1988–90
Derek White, 1991–2000
Dean Sewell, 2000–

HON. EDITOR *THE PRIVATE LIBRARY*
Roderick Cave, 1957–59
Philip Ward, 1960–65
Roderick Cave, 1965–66
Roderick Cave and Geoffrey Wakeman, 1967–68
John Cotton, 1969–78
David Chambers, 1979–93
David Chambers, Paul W. Nash & Stephen E. Smith, 1994
David Chambers & Paul W. Nash, 1995–

HON. EDITOR *EXCHANGE LIST*
Philip Ward, 1956–58
J. D. Lee, 1958–60
J. K. Power, 1960–61
Geoffrey Hamilton, 1961–63
Walter Broome, 1963–87
Peter Bond, 1988–91
Richard Goulden, 1991–2004
Jim Maslen, 2004–

I

THE FORMATIVE YEARS
1956–1961
Philip Ward

I WAS EIGHTEEN, and keen to apply to my growing personal library the professional skills I was acquiring at the National Central Library (now part of the British Library). A private library can only benefit from proficiency in classification, cataloguing, awareness of reference and bibliographical resources, and other disciplines which a librarian masters in the course of training.

But in 1956 there were no societies for 'private librarians', and even now the direction which the PLA has taken favours the collector of fine books as opposed to the 'books-for-use' owner, a tendency offset to some extent by a wide-ranging Exchange List. After being encouraged by my father and mother, without whom the Association would have faltered early on, I suggested the formation of a 'Private Library Association' in a letter to *The Observer* which appeared on 6 May 1956. Membership was initially confined to those with a library of more than 500 books. The aims would be 'to help readers in the organization, cataloguing and fuller enjoyment of their personal collections' and 'to cover every subject field by voluntary organized specialization, and to record locations for loans' (this latter feature was quickly dropped). My family was astounded by the national response, with an average of thirty-four letters a day to answer – and indeed we followed up with a second letter to *The Observer* a year later, with similar success. Each correspondent was sent a questionnaire on his library to help in the preparation of a Constitution and in the compilation of a register of members' special interests.

So it was that a nervous youth rose at 6.30 p.m. on 8 June 1956 in Room 4 of St Ermin's Hotel, Westminster – in the presence of W. Thomson Hill of *The Times* and only twelve others – and launched the society which changed its name there and then to 'The Private Libraries Association'. After earlier discussions in

Cambridge, Dr Reinhold Regensburger had agreed to become founding President, and it is excellent to be able to record here that after his death his widow, Maria, maintained the marvellous Regensburger library of world civilization to its former standards. My father, A. E. Ward, a chartered secretary with vast corporate experience but all too little spare time, was cajoled into becoming founding Chairman, and G. W. Sheldon of Rochester became Treasurer.

*

Private Libraries

Sir,—May I mention in your columns the proposed establishment of a Private Library Association, its membership being limited at first to those individuals who possess a personal library of more than 500 books in all, and a monthly rate of acquisition of at least two books.

The basic aims would be :—

To help readers in the organisation, cataloguing and fuller enjoyment of their personal collections;

To cover every subject field by voluntary organised specialisation, and to record locations for loans.

In order that I may estimate the potential membership of such an association, I ask any interested reader to write direct to me. Comments and criticisms will be welcomed,—Yours, etc.,

P. WARD.

28, Parkfield-crescent,
North Harrow, Middlesex.

*

Letter to *The Observer*, 6 May 1956

I agreed to become Secretary, not realizing then how many thousands of hours the job was to take up over the next five years.

Roderick Cave, B. S. Cron, and N. R. Fearey were appointed to the Council; Mr Fearey soon dropped out, but Brian Cron remained a long-term Council member valued for his shrewdness and dry sense of humour. Roderick Cave was long a tower of strength, co-author of *Simplified Cataloguing Rules* (exemplifying the 'books-for-use' philosophy dominant in earlier years), editor of *The Private Library* from its first appearance in 1957 to October 1959 and from 1965 to 1968, and one of the original

Opposite: Cover, *PLA Quarterly*, vol 1, no 1, 1957

P L A
QUARTERLY

VOLUME ONE   1957   NUMBER ONE

CONTENTS

Editorial

PRIVATE LIBRARIES ASSOCIATION

Hon. Secretary:

Philip Ward, 28 Parkfield Crescent, North Harrow, Middlesex

Hon. Editor:

Roderick Cave, 12 Roundwood Way, Banstead, Surrey

team which conceived, compiled and produced the annual *Private Press Books* from 1959. It was Roderick Cave, a professional librarian who moved on to teach Library Science in the West Indies and elsewhere, who, in turn with Malcolm Pinhorn, for so long maintained the Central Collection of Book Jackets at a time when so many were discarded. Nowadays collectors and librarians alike tend to be aware that dust-jackets have their own bibliographical value, and sometimes display facts about the author, or an illustration, that cannot be found anywhere else in the book. The CCBJ, which in 1962 found a place in St Bride Printing Library, was the earliest general British collection of jackets to be formed, and the PLA was the first body to undertake the work.

The subscription that members were asked to pay was one guinea, a figure that remained constant for many years, while postage in Britain was still reasonably cheap. A figure of three guineas was asked from institutions such as public and university libraries, and from booksellers and publishers. Subscriptions remained the only regular source of revenue for a few years, until the *PLA Quarterly* (January 1957–May 1958) began to earn subscription and advertising revenue, and the first modest publications appeared. A great deal of time was spent, therefore, in publicizing the existence and aims of the Association internationally and nationally, both by writing articles about its work, and by taking out advertisements, many of them by exchange. The leaflet 'An Account of the Private Libraries Association' was issued by the new Honorary Secretary, Antony Wilson, who took over early in 1961, since I was finding the secretarial duties too onerous when combined with the editorship of *The Private Library*, which I had undertaken from the January 1960 issue.

This 'Account' described the PLA as 'an international society of private book collectors – collectors of rare books, fine books, single authors, reference books on special subjects, and above all collectors of books generally for the simple pleasures of reading and ownership'. Later, 'Visits are organized on request to famous libraries, printing firms, binderies, and other places, and after each Annual General Meeting there is an Annual Lecture delivered by an eminent authority'. The visits, including the annual excursion to Peter Eaton's book-mansion, Lilies, north of Aylesbury, began with Waddesdon Manor in 1959, and have subsequently given great pleasure to many members. I edited the *Exchange List* for the first ten issues, from October 1956 to April 1958. From no. 11 it was taken over by David Lee from his home in Bingley, and John Power edited it 1960–61. Another librarian, Geoffrey Hamilton, later took over, and Walter Broome, yet another librarian, served as Honorary List Editor for twenty-four years until his death in 1987. There is an obvious advantage in being able to rely on chartered librarians for accurate cataloguing of this sort.

The Exchange Scheme – operated in conjunction with the Members' Handbook – was praised by *Books and Bookmen* in its first year of operation, the Editor writing: 'There is nothing so dead as a private library which, having been assembled, stands as a monument to one person's changing taste'.

The regulations of the Exchange Scheme were established in 1956. They called for a duplicated newsletter of five sections (Free offers, Exchange offers, Sale offers, Wants, and Notes and queries), often accompanied by news of members' activities, new books on books, exhibitions, lectures, and visits. The principle of marking members' identity by number rather than by their full address, to protect the list from being used by non-members who had not paid their subscriptions, was at a certain point neutralized by a policy of printing in full the addresses of members who contributed to that particular list. The object of the change was to save members the trouble of looking up their members' handbook, which was in any case rarely up to date. The *Exchange List* originally appeared six times a year. Later editions could not keep to this rigid schedule, and we found it necessary (also to save on postage and envelopes) to issue the List quarterly, to coincide with the appearance of *The Private Library*. As an early editor of both, I must add a word of praise to all my successors who will admit, despite their modesty, that standards of production and presentation have steadily risen until there is virtually no improvement possible at the current level of financing.

In 1959 David Lee produced statistics to show how the Exchange Scheme was working. Using as a basis the ten *Exchange Lists* numbered 8–17, he found that of the 435 free offers, 212 sale offers, 184 wants, and 59 exchange offers, 170 free offers had been satisfied as opposed to 48 sale offers, 18 wants, and 4 exchanges. The figures, he warned, were not wholly accurate as not all transactions had been reported. Nowadays the system is different, for the List Editor has direct contact only with the seller/offerer, but not with the buyer/recipient. In 1959 David Lee wrote 'it would seem that the Exchange Scheme is a success and is here to stay. Members in general seem to be pleased – only one letter of complaint (and that justified) has so far reached the List Editor'.

The first *Members' Handbook*, which I edited – and marked CONFIDENTIAL to encourage booksellers to join as associate members! – was dated 1958–59 and consisted of the addresses and collecting interests of the first 172 paid-up members. Among the distinguished names were those of the Corvo specialist Donald Weeks; the Casanova specialist J. Rives Childs (who also wrote for us on Ange Goudar, Restif de la Bretonne, and Henry Miller); the eminent Founding President (and Member no. 1) Reinhold Regensburger, who wrote on 'The Book as Still Life'; the bookbinder Roger Powell; Fr Brocard Sewell; Ronald Doig, whose *Earl Grey's Papers* was one of the first monographs published by the PLA; Peter Opie, the great authority on children's games and children's literature; and Denis Duveen, the collector of books on alchemy and early chemistry.

Internationalism has always been a feature of the PLA, to the point where special Hon. Membership Secretaries had to be recruited for North America and Australasia. But even in the first two years there were members from not only the USA and Canada and all parts of the British Isles, but also from Venezuela, Austria, Eire, France, South Africa, Sweden, and Australia.

In 1958–59, Roderick Cave and I were appointed as a special sub-committee to draw up simplified cataloguing rules for general use in private libraries. Though it was based on the current edition of the *Anglo-American Cataloguing Rules*, the emphasis was on restructuring complex and eliminating often unnecessary rules for practical application to collections varying from a few hundred to twenty thousand books.

Quite unexpectedly the *Simplified Cataloguing Rules* caught on, and within a couple of years we had heard of four institutional libraries who had adopted the code, though that was expressly not our intention. The first impression sold out in three weeks, the second in two months, and the third was also exhausted.

The journal had at first been called the *PLA Quarterly*, but after six issues this was changed to *The Private Library*. Articles have ranged over the whole field of book collecting, though had to be relatively short in extent in these early sixteen- or twenty-page issues. Douglas Foskett, our second President, wrote a series of articles on classification for private libraries, in which he surveyed the schemes likely to be of value in personal collections, and I wrote a special article on the Regensburger Decimal Classification, one of the few devised for complex and comprehensive libraries owned and housed in one home. Philip Beddingham wrote four pieces on bookplates which were subsequently issued as a booklet, *Concerning Bookplates*, in 1960. Inserts connected with articles were enclosed with some of these early issues; 'The Dolmen Press, a selection of designs & title pages MCMLX' in April 1960; 'St Albert's Press' in July 1960; 'The Signet Press' in January 1961; 'The Miniature Press' in April 1961; a page from the Stanbrook Abbey *The Path to Peace* in January 1962; and 'Puffing Billy' from the Allenholme Press in October 1962.

The Private Library regularly printed reviews of new private press books, and in 1958, following the publication by Tom Rae of *The Book of the Private Press*, Roderick Cave proposed a new annual, *Private Press Books*, which he and Rae would edit. The first volume, covering 1959, was issued in 1960. John Ryder wrote: 'I think the establishment and continuation of this project is about the most useful contribution to private press literature to date'. As we know, the annual has continued, offering not only the indispensable bibliography which is now more ambitious in covering so many more countries, but also specimen illustrations and title-pages, a review of the literature of private printing, and of course an index. David Chambers (who joined with the third volume) and Peter Hoy are among the many who have ensured the present high reputation enjoyed by *PPB*, including in later years, Philip Kerrigan and Paul W. Nash.

A Society of Private Printers within the PLA was formed, and has produced several important collective publications in its own right. The durable friendships that have been made through the PLA – one thinks of that amiable correspondent, Alice Taylor, and the compulsive contributor to the Exchange List, Robert Scott – will always constitute a major pleasure of life.

Though I continued to edit *The Private Library* for a short time after leaving England for a long-term library development career in Libya (1963–71), my close links with my eldest 'child' ended in 1963. I had founded my publishing firm The Oleander Press in my spare time in 1960, and that too celebrated a special anniversary in 1981. After four years with the National Central Library, I had spent two years at Holborn (now part of Camden) Public Libraries, several months in Middlesex County Libraries, and three years as Chief Cataloguer at Wimbledon Public Libraries. I felt that my future lay overseas, with the Third World, and in fact I was to spend eleven years in Libya, Malta, Egypt and Indonesia before returning to England late in 1974, to make a professional job of the greatly expanded Oleander Press, helped by my wife and two daughters. Our credo, expressed in our book *The Small Publisher* (1979) is exactly the same as the credo informing the founding and early years of the PLA.

Briefly described, this view of life is that – in E. F. Schumacher's now well-known phrase – small is beautiful. A private library will be smaller than a public library, but will not necessarily be inferior, for it represents the personality of an individual. A small press or a small publishing house (using outside printers) will similarly be of a scale very different from that of a large commercial publisher or a university press, but for that very reason it will find its individuality easier to cherish and sustain. The book collector assiduously purchasing, reading and cataloguing his Gogmagog or Brewhouse Press books neatly complements the press owners in their pursuit of standards. A private library of a few choice manuscripts or a mass of well-loved paperbacks will, in their very diversity, promote independent thought and a vital culture.

An association of private libraries, necessarily diverse in size and subject-matter, becomes an instrument of civilization in a society threatened by the more easily accessible mass media. Marshall McLuhan warned against the enemies of the book in *The Gutenberg Galaxy*, but the threats are even greater today than they were when the PLA was founded half a century ago. The founder salutes, in conclusion, the splendid team of honorary officials who maintain the spate of activities with undiminished enthusiasm.

2

ESTABLISHMENT
1961–1967
David Chambers

FOLLOWING PHILIP WARD'S retirement as Secretary in January 1961, a committee was set up to consider the future programme of the Association. There was a lot of work to be divided amongst the remaining members of the Council, for much of the daily affairs had been in Philip's care. Antony Wilson joined the Council as Secretary, and also handled membership; John Power took over the *Newsletter*, while my work as Publications Secretary extended to the production of new pamphlets as well as their sale. Our budget for 1961 was estimated at £566, split over the journal £200, postage £90, publicity £35, *Exchange List* £10, *Earl Grey's Papers* £30, *Private Press Books* £170, and miscellaneous £31. This was to be covered by subscriptions (at a guinea) £250, advertising £68, sales of *Private Press Books* £200, *Simplified Cataloguing Rules* £15, *The Private Library* £50. (In 2005 our total income was about £18,000.)[1]

Over the next seven years the subscription was kept at a guinea, and the slow but steady rise in the cost of printing was balanced by a similar rise in membership. In August 1957 there were about 130 members, in 1964 about 400 members, 550 in 1967.

The journal was edited by Philip Ward from 1960 to the Summer issue of 1965, when Roderick Cave resumed the editorship until the end of 1967, with Geoffrey Wakeman as joint editor during this last year. In 1960 the journal totalled 56 pages; for 1961 and 1962, 72 pages; for 1963 to 1965, 80 or 88 pages; and for 1966 and 1967, 96 pages. Articles had plainly to be relatively short throughout this period, but a wide range of subjects was covered. D. J. Foskett's series on 'Classification for Private Libraries' was completed over five issues, and there were other

---

1. But see the extracts from the Retail Price Index, p. 378.

series on bookshops in various provincial towns, and on contemporary private presses. One issue, Spring 1967, was devoted almost entirely to Count Potocki of Montalk's press, and since then we have on a number of occasions given up entire issues to single subjects in this way. Rigby Graham's articles were concerned with private presses and bookbinding in various guises – we were long in disfavour for limiting his 'Bookbinding in Human Skin' to matters relating to bookbinding alone but the subject seemed to need some judicious editing. An index to volumes 1–6, 1957–65, compiled by Frank Tapson, was issued in 1966, and to the whole of the first series, volumes 1–8, 1957–67 compiled by Joyce Post, in 1977. The six issues of the first volume were printed by The Stanley Press Ltd, Dewsbury, but thereafter the John Roberts Press took over, and though they were more expensive the results were elegant enough to justify the extra cost. (In 1970 we moved to William Clowes, to W. S. Maney in 1979, and then in 1998 to the St Edmundsbury Press.)

As well as the journal we also published a number of pamphlets on specific subjects. *Private Press Books* was issued annually. Several pamphlets had been published between 1956 and 1960: *Simplified Cataloguing Rules*, 1959, typewritten and duplicated, had gone into three impressions; *The Twelve by Eight Press*, 1959; *Concerning Bookplates*, 1960. These had all been sold to members, but *Earl Grey's Papers*, by Ronald P. Doig, seemed to me to have perhaps too narrow an interest to be sold in large numbers in this way, so I suggested it be issued free to members, and that in future we should issue such pamphlets as part of the subscription. This was agreed and so started a long series of members' pamphlets and books. *Earl Grey's Papers* was the first thing I had seen through the press; Iain Bain subsequently designed a good many of our publications, and I learned and stole a lot from his skilled example.

During 1963 we issued *Concerning Booklabels*, a long essay by Philip Beddingham with two shorter ones by Will Carter and Reynolds Stone, printed at the Stellar Press, and H. M. Nixon's *The Development of Certain Styles of Bookbinding*. The last was taken from his lecture at the A.G.M. in 1962, and though the reproductions of the bindings were small, four to the octavo page, the essential details still came out – but it must be admitted that if we had been able to afford full-page illustrations the effect would have been a great deal better.

Anne Renier's essay on Victorian annuals, *Friendship's Offering*, was issued in 1964, elegantly designed by Iain Bain. This was at a time when the originals could be bought in good condition for five or ten shillings apiece, and my own collecting, and doubtless that of many others, was spurred on by her enthusiastic essay.

In addition to his essays for the journal, Rigby Graham wrote a long essay, *Romantic Book Illustration in England, 1943–1955*, which we published in 1965. Designed by Iain Bain, with twelve illustrations, it again made a considerable impression on the approach of collectors (and the dealers) to the artists of the period, and itself now fetches a good deal more than the 10s. 6d. at which it was issued.

We had asked Iain to write a pamphlet on Dibdin, whose books were then still priced modestly enough, but he in turn persuaded E. J. O'Dwyer to write it for us, though the design of the book, published in 1967, was Iain's. For this we stretched ourselves somewhat, binding it in paper boards with a dust-jacket, and were very pleased with the result.

One other publication of this period was the Cockerell issue of the *Journal of the William Morris Society*, of which we bought 500 copies for £50, issued to members in 1965.

The *Exchange List* was taken over by Walter Broome in 1963 and he ran it until 1987 with never failing accuracy and promptitude. In the early days a list of specialist collectors had been kept, and books likely to be of particular interest to one of them were offered to him or her first. This selective practice resulted in some dissatisfaction among 'non-specialist' members and was fairly quickly abandoned, books being announced in the main list only. Though the value of the books has been for the most part modest, the free offers have in my experience been quickly disposed of, and sale offers, providing the price was reasonable, have also gone to other members quite easily. The list of wanted books has been less successful perhaps, but a number of books have been offered to me by other members in the past, usually at modest prices, so it would seem that the wants list is to some extent effective.

Apart from publications – the journal, the members' pamphlets, *Private Press Books*, and the *Exchange List* – there were a number of more or less ambitious schemes started in the earlier years which were eventually abandoned. A library was formed, and fed by gifts from members and by exchange with other journals. An accessions list was issued periodically, but very few members borrowed any books (which had to be done by post) so the collection was sold through the *Exchange List* and the proceeds taken into PLA funds. The collection of dust-jackets which I had taken over from Malcolm Pinhorn had never been referred to by any of the members, and it seemed better to offer it to the St Bride Printing Library where it could be more easily studied by interested students. The Foreign Classics Committee, whose purpose was to suggest to possible publishers titles of classics that ought to be translated, had lapsed by the time Philip Ward moved to Libya in 1964.

Other early schemes survived however. The Specialist Committee, formed to answer members' queries, still operates, but more informally now, the Secretary calling on any of the experts in the Association for help as needed, with James Thirsk responding to more formal queries in the *Newsletter*. The Society of Private Printers flourished, though slowly, over some twenty-five years, with a total of six Exchanges by 1985. The fifth Exchange, *An Infant's Library*, in a wooden box with sliding front, sells for about £1,300 today.

Meetings and visits have been organized since the early days, but have for the most part been held in London. When the Association was relatively small it was difficult to arrange more than the annual lecture at the A.G.M., but in the seventies and eighties three or four meetings were held each year, together with occasional visits. Twenty or thirty members usually attended, but a smaller attendance in recent times has led to a reduction in the number of such meetings. Apart from talks, a series of 'bring your own book' discussion meetings were held, at which members talked about a particular book in their collection. Visits to other members' libraries were sometimes successful, those to Harold James and John Power particularly so. Visits to institutional libraries included the Pepys Library in Cambridge, the Sterling Library in London, and the Bodleian in Oxford.

The first book sale was held in October 1967, organized by Basil Savage, who managed the sales for many years. On arrival at the sale members sign a register and take a number, which they then use to mark slips of paper inserted in the books they wish to sell, and also to mark other people's books that they wish to buy. An amusingly complex lottery is held to distribute the books fairly between would-be purchasers: those books for which there is only one purchaser are distributed first, and the remainder are then taken at random and allotted to the lowest number on the slip, unless that number has already had a book for which more than one purchaser had asked, in which case the book goes to the next lowest number. Where all the numbers have had one book then the lowest takes it. Recorded on a sheet of paper, the lottery is suprisingly easy to operate. An auction of unwanted books takes place at the end.

The *Members' Handbook*, listing members' addresses and collecting interests, and the PLA Constitution, Exchange Scheme Regulations, and Officers, was printed for the first time for 1958–59, having previously been issued in duplicated form. Roderick Cave and Peter Reid edited 1960–61; Peter Reid 1962; Juliet Standing 1965, which was printed, at cost, by John Mountford at his Merrythought Press – a gesture we much appreciated. The issues since then, largely prepared by Frank Broomhead, have all been typewritten, nowadays on the computer, and printed by offset lithography.

Antony Wilson resigned as Secretary in 1964, and Bob Forster took his place, serving for ten years until 1973. Besides his work as Secretary, however, Bob served the Association, with the active help of his wife Eileen, in the capacity of distributor of our books to members and non-members wanting to buy from our increasing stocks. This was a task he took on for a trial period of three months, but which he continued until his death in 1997, and for which it is difficult to express adequate thanks. As the Association grew, it became necessary to appoint a Membership Secretary, the first of whom was Mrs Juliet Standing, who served from 1964 to 1965. She was followed by R. T. Standing (not a relation), 1965–66, and Group Capt. R. D. (Roly) Pratt, Rtd, 1966–69. This is another time-consuming job, rewarding only for the contact it gives with other members, and the enormous value of the work to the Association.

Our annual subscription was held at £1. 1s. until the end of

1967, but in August 1966 it became obvious that an increase would be necessary. I suggested raising the figure to £3.3s., based on the proposition that we should probably lose a large number of members anyway, and that we might as well strike high, and expect to double our income from this source, despite resignations. With this extra money we should be able to double the size of the journal, and issue clothbound members' books in future. There was a good deal of uncertainty about the wisdom of so large an increase, so we decided to circulate members to see what their reaction might be, and not to make any increase until the end of 1967. We were surprised and pleased to find that most members were willing to continue at three guineas, so a series of leaflets was issued during 1967 announcing the increase, and a final leaflet in 1968, sent out with the first of the enlarged journals, warning that no more numbers could be sent to those who had not paid their new subscription. Our final membership for 1968 was about 410, against about 550 for 1967, so in fact we more than doubled our receipts.

During these seven years, 1961–67, we established the Association, publishing a series of useful pamphlets as well as the journal, and laid the basis for the achievements of the next twelve years. The aims of the Association were also changed somewhat during this period. The emphasis had originally been towards amateur librarianship applied to private book collections, but though some of the essays in the journal had been usefully instructive, and *Simplified Cataloguing Rules* a well considered text, it seemed plain that what was really called for was a society catering for the general interests of book collectors, whether those studying literature or history or magic or book illustration or fine printing or whatever. Not an easy sort of society to please, we have found, though the fact that our membership grew from 410 in 1968 to some 1250 in 1980 must mean that we have not been entirely unsuccessful in the attempt. (Over the succeeding years, though, memberships fell back, by 2006 to about 600, as older members have died, and institutional libraries have withdrawn as their funding has fallen away.)

3

PUBLISHING
1968–1981

David Chambers

OUR SUBSCRIPTION having been increased at the end of 1967 to
£3.3s., we had to make sure that the enlarged journal and the
clothbound members' volumes would satisfy the large proportion
of our membership who had stayed with us. Cave and Wakeman
continued as editors of the journal for 1968, but then resigned,
and I then approached John Cotton, who had for some years been
producing a literary quarterly, *Priapus*, and suggested he might
also take on *The Private Library*. This he did, serving as editor
for ten years. I acted as assistant, helping to find essays, editing
parts of some issues and all of others, and reporting progress
to the Council. This was a long period of late night telephone
calls, for John lived in Berkhamsted and we met only occasionally. The Council was very sorry when he resigned as editor in
1979; since then I have worked in his place. Paul W. Nash became
joint editor in 1994, and with his strenuous help the journal has
been restored to regular quarterly production.

The first of our enlarged issues, Spring 1968, was a little late,
but had a quality which we have sought to maintain ever since.
The principal pieces in each issue have been a dozen or more pages
long, with as many suitable illustrations as we can find – sometimes none at all, of course, but sometimes in considerable profu-
sion. Entire issues have still been devoted to single subjects: in the
years up to 1981, for instance, to Edward Ardizzone; the Officina
Bodoni (now only available as part of the complete series); James
Guthrie; *The Boy's Own Paper*; and the Livre d'Artiste. Among
the shorter essays of importance have been Rigby Graham on
'Wuthering Heights and the Illustrator' and on 'German Expres-
sionist Woodcuts'; Iain Bain on 'Bewick MSS'; Anthony Reid on
'Ralph Chubb'; W. J. Strachan on 'Modern French Bestiaries';
Douglas Cleverdon on his 'Fifty Years'; Robin de Beaumont on

'Jessie M. King'; a series by Claude Prance; many essays on individual private presses, and on English bookplates; and indeed so many more that a short list of this sort can hardly do more than show their variety. We were very fortunate to have the whole of the first and the second series indexed by Joyce Post, which made their contents much easier to use. The third series was indexed by Bert Leith and the fourth by Thorsten Sjölin.

Suitable essays were not always easily found, and this difficulty, together with a lack of funds as inflation raised the cost of printing, eventually led to publication dates slipping a year or so behind. Clowes printed the journal for most of the second series, using Fournier type; in 1979 they went over to offset, and since it seemed that this produced a much thinner impression we moved to W. S. Maney, in Leeds, who were still printing letterpress. The text however had then to be set in Baskerville.

As well as increasing the size of the journal, our series of members' pamphlets was turned into a series of books, at first always issued annually, and then, with more expensive books, biennially.

The first of these, for 1968, was Anthony Reid's account of John Buckland Wright's book illustrations, printed letterpress by Mackay's, with offset reproductions of drawings and copper-engravings printed at the Stellar Press. There was some question at the printers over these plates, for Buckland Wright's eye for female beauty was sometimes, as he had put it, 'unrestrained', but our printer assured his men that we were a highly respectable society of book-collectors, and no more was said. The wood-engravings in the text printed rather darkly, with the loss of some white lines, but overall the book seemed an excellent beginning to our new series.

The next book was *John Pitts, Ballad Printer of Seven Dials*, 1969, also printed by Mackay's, and again designed by Iain Bain. We were able to sell 500 copies to Singing Tree Press, for distribution to non-members in the USA, and I remember anxiously awaiting their cheque, which we were much in need of, and our relief at its eventual receipt.

Iain and I had both been thinking of writing notes on the old-established bookshops that were closing down, or moving to new premises in London, and we suggested that it was time to issue a book of photographs to record some of them before they

Opposite: Specimen page from *John Buckland Wright*, 1968

JOHN BUCKLAND WRIGHT

BOOK-ILLUSTRATOR

JOHN BUCKLAND WRIGHT was born in Dunedin, New Zealand, at Bishop's Court, on 3rd December 1897. He was the third of four children. When he was still only five years old his father died as the result of an accident, and about three years later the Wright family (as they were then known) left the country. John first attended a preparatory school in Switzerland, where he acquired an early facility in French. Soon afterwards he moved to England and was educated at Clifton and Rugby. His mother, meanwhile, had remarried, and the boy was brought up by grandparents. Schooldays passed uneventfully and a series of bird studies, drawn at Rugby, were the only hint of latent artistic talent.

At the outbreak of war in 1914 he was seventeen years old and volunteered for active service, but the British Army authority found that he spoke with a severe stammer and promptly rejected him. In 1916, however, he managed to join a Scottish ambulance unit attached to the French Army and was responsible for collecting wounded and taking them to front-line dressing stations or to the rear.

The British authorities had considered the stammer a liability for sound reasons. One of these was that he might be unable to give a password. Strangely enough, this contingency actually arose on an occasion in France when, with two companions, he was returning to camp. John alone knew the password, but was unable to reply when an Algerian sentry challenged them. He stood there speechless, trying desperately to get the word out. The sentry had already raised his rifle and was about to fire went out of business. In the end there were two books, published in 1971 and 1977, with photographs by Richard Brown of nineteen shops. They took much longer to produce than we had intended, for the work proved to be substantial and had to be squeezed into the photographer's otherwise full life. Stan Brett wrote the notes, and we were very glad to be able to persuade Percy Muir to write an introductory essay for the first volume.

Then Anthony Reid suggested we might ask Mark Severin to work with us in the production of a book on contemporary book-plates, and so we spent several weekends in Dorset working on the content and layout of *Engraved Bookplates*, which was published in 1972 as the members' book for 1971. Mark wrote the text, which Anthony then worked over, revising the English where necessary, and spending an enormous amount of time on the index of artists' names and addresses which concludes the volume. My problem was to get in the 500 specimens that Mark was most anxious to include. In the end I made the book a quarto, and so got a great many more plates on the page, with smaller ones down the outer margins of the text. This was photoset by BAS, but made up into pages and printed by Mackay's – a combination I found very tiresome, for any faults were always the other printer's. In the end, however, the book came out very well indeed, the wood-engravings particularly sharp, and the copper-engravings only occasionally fading away. There was a special edition of seventy copies, quarter bound, with twelve plates tipped in, fifty copies of which were to be sold for £15; the buckram was uneven though, and ill-glued to the boards, so we reduced the price to £10: copies now sell for many times more.

For 1972 we issued a reprint of Faxon's *Literary Annuals and Gift Books*, the text printed on one side of the page only, with the facing page for notes. Eleanore Jamieson and Iain Bain contributed supplementary essays on the bindings and illustrations, and we added twenty-six illustrations, showing examples of these. A relatively cheap production, being printed for the most part by offset litho, but a most useful work nevertheless, the original of which appeared in an edition of only 150 copies in 1912.

Raymond Lister, I think it was, remarked in a letter in about 1971 that a friend of his, Brian North Lee, had an essay on Rex Whistler's bookplates that might interest us. It turned out that this was in fact being considered by a publisher at that time, but these negotiations falling through, we took it on and eventually published it in 1973. There were drawings as well as engraved bookplates to reproduce, for which we used half-tone, or in some cases where the engraving was sharp enough, line over a half-tone base. Brian had also been given copies of Christabel and Henry McLaren's bookplate, and we tipped these into 350 special copies, issued in slipcases. This was not a members' book, but was published at £10 for the specials, or £5 for the ordinary copies, or at £7.50 and £3.75 respectively to members.

Several years later, in 1976, we issued the next of Brian's books on bookplates, *Early Printed Booklabels*. This had not been going to be a members' book either, but when the copy arrived, and its costs became apparent, we decided to issue it for 1973 and 1974. A learned work, the proof-reading was a long and difficult job. The book cost £6,000 to print, a large amount, but has taken its place as a standard and original work on the subject.

In 1966 we had asked Ruari McLean for a book on some aspect of Victorian book design, and he had suggested that we might like to publish the result of his researches into the life and work of Joseph Cundall. Over the years I wrote or spoke to him – how is Cundall getting on? – and at last in 1974 he wrote to say it was ready. Ruari designed the book himself, and made a thin volume, the same format as *Engraved Bookplates*, with four coloured plates and a great many other black and white illustrations, which we published in 1976.

One of our most substantial volumes was Dorothy Harrop's *A History of the Gregynog Press*, which we published in 1980, for 1978 and 1979. I had listened to, and recorded, a talk by Dora Herbert Jones, one-time secretary to the Press, at a Printing Historical Society meeting at Gregynog in about 1972. She died in 1974, and I sought permission to print the talk, asking Dorothy Harrop to enquire of Dora's son whether this would be in order. They thought not, for Dora's voice and character would be missing, and the piece would lose some of its interest in consequence. But in one of her letters Dorothy remarked that she had herself written a complete history of the press, and was not finding it easy to find a publisher for so substantial a book. 'Could I see it?' was, of course, a prompt reaction, and five years or so later, after much work checking details in the text, entries in the bibliography, pursuing photographs of those who worked at the press, and so on, and then seeing the book slowly through the press, the book was published. Miss Sarah Herbert Jones, Dora's granddaughter, spent a day with a photographer and myself letting us work on the family collection of special copies of the books, a kindness which we much appreciated. Before this I had spent four or five months, and written a series of letters concerning the copyright in the engravings to the books. The blocks had been given to the National Library of Wales, whose librarian had himself, over many years, been writing an account of the press. In his view the Library held the copyright, and we would not therefore be able to illustrate our book. In the end he was not able to show that copyright had been given as well as the blocks, and we were able to get on. We decided to have Sangorski and Sutcliffe bind 100 of the copies in full or quarter morocco, and I had intended having these printed on mould-made paper, and should also have liked to tip in proofs of some of the blocks held at the National Library. Using mould-made paper would have cost another £1,600, however, and on reflection it seemed that the Basingwerk Parchment used for the ordinaries would take the line-block reproductions in better style; and the wood-blocks were untouchable at that time. The full bound copies came out very well nevertheless, a plain brown morocco, lettered in gold down the spine and with the Blair Hughes-Stanton device that we had used in blind on the ordinary copies blocked in gold on the front.

In preparation in 1981 were three more members' books: a bibliographical account of the children's books published by James Lumsden of Glasgow, an account of Joan Hassall's wood-engravings, and another on the books illustrated by Blair Hughes-Stanton – who died in June 1981, before he could see the book.

Sydney Roscoe produced the first draft of the *Lumsden*, to which he had devoted his attention after his bibliography of John Newbery had been published by the Five Owls Press. He was very ill for much of this time, and working from a nursing home in Hastings, though still surrounded by books as he had been when he lived near us in South Harrow. Before he was able to bring the text to completion he died, but he had fortunately been able to persuade his old friend Max Brimmell to finish the work. Max

A MODEST COLLECTION

ordered the entries, and added a number of books to the list, and I spent a great deal of time reading the text and raising queries, which it took most of another year to sort out. Printed by Clark Constable in Edinburgh, the text was set on a photosetter of some sort, and the proofs arrived with the number of words, line by line, printed at the left, and printer's errors to the right.

Apart from the members' books, we also published a number for sale, to members usually at half the price we charged to non-members. *The Bookplate Designs of Rex Whistler* was one such; others have been the annual *Private Press Books*, Holtzapffel's *Printing Apparatus for the Use of Amateurs*, 1971, John Carter's *Taste and Technique in Book Collecting*, 1970, 1972 and 1977, and *Cock-a-Hoop*, 1976, the fourth volume of the bibliography of the Golden Cockerel Press. The Holtzapffel was relatively cheap to produce, consisting of an offset reproduction of the third edition of 1846, with a prefatory essay and notes by James Mosley and myself. The Parlour Press it described, a simple but effective wooden machine, had been used to print substantial books in the mid-nineteenth century, and we spent much time searching for such copies in the Bodleian, the India Office, and elsewhere. I had one of the presses (two or three others have since turned up elsewhere) and made drawings of it to accompany photographs by Richard Brown.

John Carter's *Taste and Technique* came to us after we had tried to get permission to reprint one of the volumes from the 'Bibliographia' series. Carter was unable to help with these, but Cambridge had just remaindered the last few copies of their second impression of *Taste and Technique*, and so he offered us this instead. We added the talk he had given to the Bibliographical Society in 1969, on book collecting over the previous forty years, with various corrections to the text, and sold 3,500 copies in three separate impressions: a most important text, essential reading for any serious collector, and a book we were very pleased to have been allowed to re-publish.

Cock-a-Hoop came out of our work on Buckland Wright. Sandford's bibliography of the books had long been written for publication by the press, but the new owner, Thomas Yoseloff, only published a few books after taking it over, and the bibliography fell to one side. It was agreed the press would publish the book in America and we should do so elsewhere. I wrote a detailed list of the prospectuses, working from my own and various friends' collections, and designed the book exactly in the style of the three preceding volumes. We printed 300 specials, on mould-made paper, bound by Sangorski and Sutcliffe in quarter morocco, and split the whole edition one-sixth for America the remainder for ourselves. Unfortunately Sangorski lost ninety-one of our specials, so that the book is actually much rarer than first appears.

Our publications have always absorbed a large proportion of the Association's funds, and such an expenditure seems proper, since many of our members have little other direct contact with us apart from the *Newsletter* and *Exchange List*. On the other hand these last have continued to play a most significant part in our affairs despite their relatively low cost. The *Newsletter* was edited by Frank Broomhead, who took over as Honorary Secretary in 1973 and includes up-to-date details of meetings, book fairs, exhibitions, titles of new and remaindered books of interest to collectors, members' enquiries, as well as annual reminders of subscriptions being due. It is usually issued with the journal, so as to save postage, but this has meant that it has sometimes been delayed so that some of the meetings or exhibitions announced have already taken place – this difficulty aside, the *Newsletter* and the *Exchange List* have served to create a living society rather than merely a specialist book club or a readership of the journal. The dispatch of the quarterly mailing by air freight to America, that was started in the late seventies, and then to Australasia, has helped to draw the international membership closer together.

Meetings in this period fell into something of a regular pattern, with some twenty or thirty members and friends in attendance – usually a talk in early October, the book-sale in November, and two more talks in the Spring – in February, and in April at the A.G.M. We usually met at the headquarters of the Library Association, whose kindness in providing rooms for these meetings and those of our Council over many years was very much appreciated. Book collecting being such a wide subject it has been easy enough to vary the subject of the talks, and yet concentrate on the collector's approach to whatever is being discussed. Our Presidents have contributed a series of talks at A.G.M.s, and with the Bookplate Society we have listened to many of our finest engravers describing their work. Other subjects have included Wilfred Hodgson on book auctions, Anthony Rota on modern trends in book collecting, Arthur Johnson on bookbinding, Robert Akers on book restoration, Brian Alderson and, some years later, Peter Stockham on children's books, and so on, over a broad range of interests.

Visits to Peter and Margaret Eaton's house, Lilies, near Aylesbury, were started in the Autumn of 1971, and continued each year until his death in 1993, with picnic lunches in the grounds, the afternoon hidden deep within the many rooms of books, and a handsome tea supplied by Mrs Eaton and her family. Some thirty or forty members were usually there, but in the thirty or so rooms the only evidence of this small invasion was the rustling of books being taken from the shelves and occasional meetings of friends passing from one room to another. The Council also went one year to Hay on Wye, to consider the extent of Richard Booth's shops, and to see whether a general visit by the Association should be arranged. We had an amusing weekend, but did not think the overall quality of the books or hotels would justify the long journey most members would face getting to Hay.

Other visits included the library of the Wellcome Institute, in 1979, repeated in 1981, when an extraordinarily fine range of books on non-medical as well as medical themes was shown; Sangorski and Sutcliffe, also on two occasions due to members' interest; to Bath to see George Bayntun's bindery, and the bookbinding museum, as well as the ABA Fair; and Blackwell's at Fyfield, and the bookshops in nearby Oxford.

Our publication of *Engraved Bookplates* led to the formation of the Bookplate Society in 1972. The ExLibris Society, active at the beginning of the century, had wound up in 1909, but had left the Bookplate Exchange Club in existence, whose members exchanged bookplates every month or so by means of a circular packet of plates. Most of the sixteen members active in 1970 joined the PLA, forming the Bookplate Society as an associate body, membership of which would only be allowed (as was already the case with the Society of Private Printers) to PLA members. A small additional subscription was levied, and a duplicated *Newsletter* issued quarterly. As membership grew there were moves to allow separate membership outside the PLA, and though the question was argued for some time, the members of the Society narrowly voted for an independent existence, and our formal relationship finally ended at the end of 1982.

Substantial exhibitions of bookplates had been mounted: on contemporary plates in 1972, when *Engraved Bookplates* was published; on plates by book illustrators in 1974; on bookplate designers 1925–75 in 1976; and a historical exhibition, at the Victoria & Albert Museum, in 1979, to coincide with a very successful international weekend congress. Three exhibitions were organised for the nineteenth International Congress held in Oxford in 1982.

Supporting all our activities have been the Membership Secretaries and the Treasurer, the value of whose work has been fundamental to the growth of the Association.

The gathering in of subscriptions, refunding overpayments, pursuing underpayments, recording changes of address, compiling the membership list – these are time consuming and often dull enough activities, but also quite essential. During the seventies Peter Hall and Anthony Pincott served as Membership Secretaries, until John Allison took over in 1978, continuing to manage our affairs ever since. American membership was at first handled by Harold Berliner. Bill Klutts replaced him in 1977, and like John is still working actively on our behalf. Institutional Library membership has been looked after by James Wilson, then Frances Guthrie, Richard Goulden, and, most recently, Richard Faircliff.

The management of our funds, gathered in from members and from the sale of publications, has been the task of the Council as a whole, with more or less strict guidance from the Hon. Treasurer. In the 1980s a true balance was always in the red if the cost of the year's publications was included in the year's expenses, but we were usually somewhat behind with publications and the cash flow carried us forward safely enough. It had been intended to issue a free book to members each year, but some of these volumes grew into very substantial affairs, and we had perforce to issue them for two years instead of one. Book sales grew in line with the size and expense of the books; the stock, valued at pro rata of cost, and after reductions for slow moving volumes, more than amply covered the annual cash deficit, though the actual funds would have taken a long time to raise. A series of Treasurers have looked

A MODEST COLLECTION

after this aspect of our affairs, Basil Savage from 1969, Stan Brett from 1972, and from 1978 to mid 1981 Anthony Pincott; the latter brought much needed expertise into the payment of VAT and of Corporation Tax on sales of books etc. to non-members, and to stock relief to be set against the last.

Apart from the officers, of course, much was done, still is done, by others in the Association who have worked to carry its affairs to successful conclusion, some, but not all, serving on the Council: people like Helen Hardy who despatched the journal to private members for many years, and Trevor Hickman who sent it to institutions. Guy Powell, our Hon. Treasurer 1964–67, has also to be thanked for his practical legal advice on all aspects of our affairs since those early days.

4

CONTINUATION
1982–2006

Stan Brett

By the end of the first quarter-century of the Association's existence its shape and character were firmly established, and the second term seemed set fair to provide more of the same, with room for enlargement and improvements where possible. The first term ended with an upbeat report by David Chambers, Chairman of Council (*The Private Library*, Summer 1981, reprinted here in the previous pages). Frank Broomhead was the Hon. Secretary and this partnership was to last until Frank's retirement in 2001. The rest of the team were Anthony Pincott as Hon. Treasurer, John Allison in charge of membership with Frances Guthrie assisting with institutional members and Bill Klutts the American membership. The Hon. Secretary edited the *Newsletter* and Walter Broome the *Exchange List*, while Bob and Eileen Forster dealt with packing and posting the orders for books and the journal.

Ideally a society needs a mixture of continuity and new intake among its office-holders with a proportion promoted from the ranks. Anthony Pincott as Hon. Treasurer had introduced an element of professionalism to the office the benefits of which outlasted his term of office, which ended in 1981. Norman Waddleton, who succeeded him had to resign almost as soon as he began, and was followed by John Paton, who retired in 1988. Bert Leith stepped in and served us well until 1991, when he had to resign, and we then obtained the informed services of Derek White, whose retirement in 2000 occasioned a warm appreciation by the Council for his work for the Association. His successor was Dr Dean Sewell who is the present incumbent of this key office. Each change was an interruption to the organisation, but by a combination of circumstances the gaps were short and each time we benefited from a fresh mind and new ideas brought to the office.

There were, of course, other changes among the honorary

officers. Walter Broome had acted as Editor of the *Exchange List* for many years, until his death in 1988. Peter Bond agreed to serve as his successor, a duty which he performed punctiliously until ill-health compelled his resignation in 1991, when Richard Goulden proffered his services, which were also employed in managing the institutional membership. He resigned both these offices in 2004 and was warmly thanked for his services in a little ceremony at the following A.G.M. We are grateful to Richard Faircliff for managing Institutional Membership, and to Jim Maslen for editing the *Exchange List* since then.

The succession of Presidents is more regular, as they are invited to accept a tenure of usually three years. Thus Dr Glyn Tegai Hughes gave his retiring address on 'The Re-establishment of the Gregynog Press' in 1982, and was followed by Professor William B. Todd; John Russell Taylor took office in 1986, and was followed by Peter Eaton in 1989. Iain Bain was President from 1992 to 1995, and Robin de Beaumont from 1995 to 1998, to be followed by Barry Bloomfield, and in turn by Colin Franklin, 2001–2004. Our present President is Ms Lynn Brindley, Chief Executive of The British Library. It is appropriate to record our sincere appreciation of the services of our Presidents at this stage of our Association's history, relatively light though their duties may be, for we know that the time and energy required are quarried from crowded diaries and finely-tuned timetables. Frank Broomhead, our secretary from 1973 to 2001, was elected Honorary Vice-President on his retirement that year.

The affairs of the Association are managed by the Council, comprising the Honorary Officers, elected members who serve a three-year period and co-opted members selected for their perceived usefulness to the Association. It was logical to invite Bill Klutts to be a member, and associate membership of the Council is automatically extended to those on the recently established Editorial Board. The Association is of necessity very much London-based, and the elected members of Council must be within easy reach of Central London, for otherwise travelling and other expenses need to be recoverable from PLA funds. Time is probably as much a deterrent to would-be Council members as cost, and the consequent limits on membership must be accepted for the time being. This has been less a problem in the recruitment of the officers, and at present our Treasurer is in Scotland, our Membership Secretary is in the West country, James Thirsk, the Notes and Queries Editor in the *Newsletter* lives in Kent, and the *Exchange List* Editor lives in Hull.

A comparatively recent development is the establishment of Hon. Membership Secretaries in Canada and Australasia, presently Alan J. Horne and Cyril Wyatt respectively. They have already proved themselves of great value, and have an important role in the future of the Association. Another problem not peculiar to, but frequently met with in London is that of accommodation for meetings and small functions such as our own. Until the eighties we enjoyed the hospitality of the Library Association in Ridgemount Street. In addition to its convenience and economy, there was an appropriateness in the relation between the two Associations which we esteemed, and which was formally confirmed when we registered our wish to be 'In liaison with the Library Association' (now renamed the Chartered Institute of Library and Information Professionals). In the eighties there were unavoidable interruptions in the availability of the accommodation and by 1997 we had found an alternative location in the Durning-Lawrence Library, Senate House, University of London. We appreciate very much the graciousness of our surroundings, and the facilities available to us there.

The administration of the Association follows predictable lines – Membership, Finance, Publications and such matters as do not clearly fall under these headings. The areas listed are not mutually exclusive, of course, but have their own officers, and recognisable boundaries. The register of members demands constant attention, showing considerable coming and going, problems of subscription, changes of address, and periodical publication of the list in the *Members' Handbook*. We are immensely grateful to John Allison for his sustained work in this department over so many years and included in our gratitude are those who assisted him from time to time. Membership is at the core of many of the Council's concerns, with plans for expanding it, and, year by year maintaining it as our *raison d'être*. The level of subscriptions, book and journal production and effective communicating are always considered with the membership in mind. The *Newsletter* is the regular and official means of telling members what is being done, what has been done, and what is being considered for the future. The progress of publications, changes and reminders of subscriptions, changes in membership, changes in officers, forthcoming events and financial reports have always been circulated in the *Newsletter* and often supplemented by items of news from outside the Association. The membership has hovered around 600, with approximately a quarter of it in North America, for a long time and attempts to increase it have not been spectacularly successful. Does this represent what our activities can be expected to attract today?

Does it therefore reflect the place that book-collecting occupies in the current charts of interests? Is this a stable position, or declining, or expanding? These questions are posed against a background of great cultural change in the world. The membership suffered some losses when in 1982 the growing feeling among some members of the Bookplate Society that it would benefit from separating itself from the PLA led to that step being taken. The connection between the two societies had been mutually beneficial and we did our best to sustain it, so that good relations survived the break. Subscriptions moved in roughly four or five-year intervals from £12.50 to £16 in 1989 and to £25 in 1994, and book prices have been set with as much thought as the subscriptions. The relatively comfortable position of the last year or two owes much of its realising to good housekeeping, much to economies in the design and setting of our books, and some to marketing and production-sharing. Sadly, Bob Forster died in 1997 and arrangements had to be made to manage the storing and packing and mailing of our books. Storage has been a matter of much concern for years, given the increasing stocks to be dealt with, and the high and increasing costs of commercial provision. Accommodation provided by the Chairman has saved the Association many hundreds of pounds. Tony Cox of Claude Cox Books of Ipswich undertook Bob Forster's duties but circumstances are compelling us to reconsider the whole problem of storing and mailing in the very near future. This can only be done at some cost.

For five years the Chairman, Secretary, and Treasurer, with the invaluable advice of Guy Powell, worked to win charitable status for the Association. Success crowned their efforts and since 1996 we have had considerable benefits from that award. In the course of negotiations we had to amend the Constitution and re-define our aims and purposes, and that called for some beneficial thinking – and one of the consequences of achieving our objective was the establishing of a trustee system involving the members of Council as a whole.

The rest of Council business revolves round the Hon. Secretary's agenda of Council meetings, members' meetings (two a year), visits to places of interest and special occasions. The last have included Birthday celebrations – thirtieth, fortieth, and fiftieth – the first in the form of a party and exhibition in Bertram Rota's bookshop which some eighty attended, and the second a dinner at the Travellers' Club arranged by Guy Powell. For our fiftieth anniversary we held a dinner at the Oxford and Cambridge Club, and an exhibition of all our books, including much preliminary matter, at the St Bride Library.

Attendances at meetings are understandably modest, but a commendably high standard of talks has been provided by a variety of speakers only equalled by the variety of topics they have presented. Their audience has ultimately been the readership of *The Private Library* for their talks have often been made into excellent articles, making use of the illustrations they have introduced in their lectures. Merely to illustrate their diversity one may mention, randomly, the Hours of Etienne Chevalier, Gilbert White, Tauchnitz, Sherlock Holmes, pricing manuscripts, and books on surgery.

The arrangement of visits to places of interest has been a long-established practice, and has been maintained in the face of declining attendances. Seeking reasons for this points to fewer people appearing able to make daytime visits, and tastes and interests changing. Over the years visits were made to the libraries of many different institutions, a bindery, an auction house, and places of literary interest or bibliographical association. Those who have attended have usually attested to the value and pleasure they have derived from the visit, and our hosts have always been most obliging. Popular demand, an old slogan designed to keep alive what would have died, has kept the Members Book Sale an annual event, and likely to continue as a light-hearted occasion; it provides members with an opportunity to meet each other, and chat, get rid of some books – and acquire some more in exchange.

There can be no doubt that the Association is in good shape and in good hands and well-prepared for the next fifty years. It has its own web-site, setting out its aims and activities, details of its organisation and officers, its impressive list of publications and addresses for joining. The indexes to the first four series of *The Private Library*, as well as pdfs of the first series, now out of print, are also included, for which we have to thank Richard and Brenda Healey. (www.plabooks.org.)

The book world in the past decades had its share of turbulence from a large wave of change. Some will remember waiting for the postman's early delivery of an anticipated catalogue, that was consumed with the cereal, carried with the coffee to the telephone, and marked up with glee or glum before being shelved for future reference. Little more than the postman survives from that world of book-collecting, and late in the morning at that. The first disturbance of the pattern was the rise of the book fair, and we joined the queues at weekends for an early view of the stocks of a hundred booksellers from near and far. Today we have immediate access to the stocks of thousands of booksellers, worldwide, and the catalogues of most of the major libraries; efficient search-engines locate our wants, and mechanisms are in place to facilitate our ordering and paying for them – enter, again, the postman.

Methods will change, fashions change, but the PLA should survive as long as the Book, for it is the Book that is at the centre of the Association, not collecting.

5

PUBLISHING
1982–2006

David Chambers

THE PAST TWENTY-FIVE YEARS have, as Stan Brett has suggested, simply continued in much the same way as in the immediately preceding period. The content of the journal, the production of *Private Press Books*, and of the members' books have in general followed the style which we had established in 1967 when the subscription was increased to three guineas. Though the current subscription is £25, it is less, taking into account the general rise in the cost of living, than it was then. Over fifty years the effects of inflation have been very great, and one should refer to the chart on page 378 when considering relative figures during this time. Three guineas, our subscription in 1967, would be equivalent to about £38 in 2006.

The journal was for many years behindhand in publication, up to a year or so, indeed, but this was in part because our finances were often technically in the red, so there would not have been sufficient funds available to get up to date. Lack of suitable articles was also a problem. Our finances were in part restored to their present excellent state with the advent of computer setting and offset lithography, for we were able to prepare texts on the computer, send out proofs from its printer, correct on screen, and send completed files to the printer ready for press. There were many mistakes involved, of course, due to our completely amateur status so far as computers were concerned, but most were fortunately discovered in time.

Co-publishing with The British Library and, through it, Oak Knoll Press has also made a considerable difference to our financial position. Selling books to the general public was always difficult, for we had no really effective way of advertising our books, and large sales would, in any case, have involved more work than was possible for a society run on voluntary lines. We

co-published *John Pitts* with the Singing Tree Press, and management of our publications in this way has since proved most effective. For some time we sold 500 or 750 copies of books directly to
Oak Knoll, of New Castle, Delaware, sharing the costs exactly
pro rata. Michael Twyman's *Early Lithographed Books* was
shared with the Farrand Press in the same way. More recently we
have co-published with The British Library, which has sold part
of its side of the bargain to Oak Knoll – saving us the problems of
shipping abroad. The reduction in cost has been considerable, pro
rata of the charges for printing, although binding has still had to
be paid for at so much a copy. We have also been able to take
credit for part of the design costs. *Early Printed Booklabels* cost
£6,000 in 1976, whereas the much more substantial volume of
Millais engravings, *Beyond Decoration*, cost a little over half this
in 2005. Postage, of course, has risen sharply over this period,
much more than keeping pace with inflation.

Paul W. Nash joined me as editor of the journal in 1994, and
there has been assistance from other sources through the years.
We have recently had much help from an Editorial Board, Caroline
Archer, Rob Banham, David Butcher and Shelley Gruendler, who
have read proofs, written reviews and offered suggestions for
future articles. Most importantly, for some long time our proofs
have been read by John Byrne, expert in all things literary, good
at spelling (which I am not), and with a marvellous ability to
notice inconsistencies several pages apart. We have used a number
of different printers – after William Clowes to whom we had
moved in 1970, W. S. Maney of Leeds, and when they were sold,
the St Edmundsbury Press, Bury St. Edmunds. Derek Brown at
Maney's gave much good advice, but when he left the firm we
turned to our own computers, at first printing camera-ready copy,
then moving on to sending computer files, with a printout to show
exactly what we intended. Moreover, since we have turned round
our financial position it has been possible to add extra pages of
colour, printed by Ling's of Dorchester.

The content of the journal has always been something of a
difficult question, with such a membership whose particular interests are often so different. Wide-ranging essays on members'
libraries and collecting interests, illustration, fine/interesting
printing of all periods, and bookbinding have been our principal

subjects, and we have sought out authors wherever we could find them, from lectures at our own and other societies' meetings, from specialist members, from, in fact, anyone who sounded as if they might be tapped for an essay, long or short. One recent essay sprang from an American catalogue on perfume, whose dealer said that though he would not be able to write further, a customer in France would be glad to; the essay was written in excellent English, and the colour plates came across the Atlantic as computer files. Many members collect private press books, and essays on particular presses, as well as a regular series of notes on recent press books have catered for this particular enthusiasm. A good deal has always had to be written by the editors, in the early days sometimes under various noms de plume, and the content of the journal has to some extent followed their particular interests. In this way, three long essays on architectural books by Paul Nash helped us to get the journal up to date, as well as introducing a new field to many members. One might attempt some long account of what else has appeared over the past twenty-five years, but reference to the indexes now included in our web site must serve instead.

The annual checklist *Private Press Books* has continued through something over forty years, started in 1959 by Tom Rae and Roderick Cave, and now in Paul Nash's competent hands, with 2002 and 2003 in proof. It has been a very long, and often very tedious haul, with many people gathering the data, though often much more slowly than we would have liked. We decided at the beginning to limit ourselves to books and pamphlets of four, then seven, pages or more, printed on letterpress machines, with books printed by lithography only to be included where the printer actually had a lithographic press at home. Small presses were excluded, that is, books printed from typewriting, and later on computers. We felt that these were not 'private presses', however interesting their productions; and even more consequentially, so far as I was concerned, the amount of material would have been far too extensive for us to attempt to include it.

Tom Rae printed the first two issues, 1959 and 1960, and we then moved to Bill Hummerstone's Stellar Press. John Ryder designed the 1961 volume, and saw it through the press, and designed title-pages and covers of subsequent issues up to 1970, after which the task was taken over by the general editors of the time. Following an enthusiastic reception of our prospectus for the initial volume, the size of the run was increased from 750 to 1,500 and then 2,000 – in fact all printed at once, but described in the imprint as three separate impressions. More than half were later dust-binned, and future editions were limited to about 1,200, reducing to 500, with sales currently in the region of only 300. For the first three years Roderick collected details from the New World, Tom everything else.

In 1963 I took over from Tom, working with Roderick, and seeing to sales and despatch as I had since the beginning. The binders cut a quarter inch too much from 1963, leaving me apoplectic with rage, a rage that has still not completely evaporated. Peter Hoy joined us in 1964, preparing a list of essays and books on private presses that had appeared during the year, and he continued to do this until his death in July 1993. Anthony Baker joined us in 1969, taking on presses outside Britain and America. Cumulative indexes have appeared every ten years since 1970 (which Ed Chapman produced). In that year Lewis A. Prior contributed a short essay on 'Printing Machines used by Private Presses, 1962–9'. Kim Taylor designed the cover and title-page for 1971. Dwight Agner took over America from Roderick in 1975. Geoffrey Farmer (for Australasia) and Prue Chennells (for the rest of the world) replaced Anthony Baker in 1977.

Up to 1971 we had always managed to publish the checklist by the end of the succeeding year, but 1972 did not appear until January 1974, 1973 in September 1975, 1974 in February 1977, and the delays gradually extended so that 1980 was not issued until 1986. In that year, to my enormous relief, Philip Kerrigan took over from me as general editor as well as responsibility for English presses. Now started a determined attempt to get up to date again, with two combined volumes issued covering 1981–1984 and 1985–1986, followed by separate issues for succeeding years until Philip retired from the fray with 1990, which appeared in 1992. Over the period of his editorship there were only two changes in the batting order, J. Hill Hamon, and then Arthur Goldsmith handling American presses, Eric Swanick those from Canada.

PPB 1991, published in early 1993, was edited by Claire and David Bolton, and was the last to be contributed to by Peter Hoy, who had collected details of English presses as well as providing 'The Literature of Private Printing'. He had worked on the checklist for twenty-eight years. David Butcher replaced Prue Chennells, who had worked with us for fourteen years.

A very long delay ensued, with two general editors, Ken Mackenzie and Anthony Ward unable to complete the work, in the first case because of theft of the computer records, so that I feared the checklist had come to an end. Eventually, and again to my great relief, a new editor appeared, Paul Nash who said (despite warnings of the amount of work involved) that he would like to continue it. I edited 1992–93, using material collected by old and new friends, and Paul did 1994–98, with Margaret Lock collecting details from Canada, and Arthur Goldsmith from the States – his fifteenth and final year of involvement. 1999, 2000, and 2001 appeared in 2004, edited by Paul, helped by Asa Peavy for the States, and Margaret Lock for Canada. 2002 and 2003 are expected early in 2007, with 2004 and 2005 later in the year.

Private Press Books has been an enormous undertaking, particularly when considered as an amateur affair, with no payment to any of its editors apart from their personal expenses. There have been over 8,000 entries, the details prepared from the sight of the books themselves wherever possible, though too often simply from detailed questionnaires compiled by the presses – easier to make entries from, but rather too often inaccurate in some details. It does not include, generally speaking, books in languages other than English, but still includes some work from Holland, where much is printed in English as well as Dutch. The data included overall is nevertheless of considerable bibliographical value, for much of it is not to be found in the national catalogues of the various countries concerned.

We have attempted to make sure that our members' books have been as particularly useful as has been the checklist of private press books – avoiding generalities and concentrating on specific subjects which could be dealt with in their totality. The work of individual book illustrators, private presses and binders seem ideal subjects for such books, though we have also included two more general works by Anthony Rota.

James Lumsden & Son of Glasgow: their Juvenile Books and Chapbooks was published at the end of 1981, with double-page spreads from the books, which it was just possible to fit onto its pages between the bibliographical details. Justin G. Schiller Ltd took copies from us for the American market.

My wife and I had become friends with Joan Hassall after she had given the PLA a talk about her work one evening, which we had printed in *The Private Library*, Winter 1974. She cut a bookplate for our elder daughter, Clare, in 1977, the last she completed, actually cutting the block twice, having difficulty with the lettering. I was able to persuade her that we might produce a much larger work as a members' volume, to be printed by Mackay's, the illustrations reproduced from the best available proofs. Joan was able to provide a great many, but some were slightly defective in the inking, which she had often done holding the block in one hand with the roller in the other, rather than using a press. These I had to reprint myself, as well as those from blocks for the Jane Austen series, borrowed from the Folio Society. Great care was needed for Joan noted every detail, including the slight differences in size between original prints and the photocopies I was using for the layouts. Very fortunately I was warned that I needed to check the sizes of the reproductions prepared by the Curwen Press, since a third proved to be out of true by about 3% – their camera having been wrongly set up – and she would have been furious had we not discovered the fault in time. Joan wrote a long introduction, and George Mackley wrote on her 'Engraving Technique', which he afterwards said he found a most difficult task, though the essay itself is faultless. The illustrations had to be placed with great care, their various sizes making display on the pages quite complicated. For the endpapers I printed long strips from one of Joan's border engravings, moving a series of slips across the platen for the next impression, then mounting them alongside each other, at an angle, from which offset plates were made. We also produced 110 copies of a special version, with eight engravings that I printed from the wood, with a copy of *The Plain Facts*, by a 'Plain but Amiable Cat', inserted in the back, and bound in quarter black morocco. Sold to members at £110 a copy, we only had the cost of the binding to pay for, so there was £8,000 or so profit to be deducted from the total.

Frank Broomhead's *The Zaehnsdorfs (1842–1947)* followed in 1986. This was much easier to design, the text interspersed with full-page portraits of the Zaehnsdorfs and of their bindings. A hundred specials were bound in full leather by Zaehnsdorf's, at their expense (and profit).

Michael Twyman had been writing a book on *Early Litho-graphed Books* which I had been asking him to let us have, and had been able to provide him with copies of all the Middle Hill books that Sir Thomas Phillipps had had printed in this way. When the text was complete we arranged with the Farrand Press that we should share production costs with them, Book Press Ltd in Virginia taking copies for North America, so reducing the amount we each had to bear for our copies. Michael designed the book, in the Reading style, with wide margins for notes and small illustrations to the left of the text on both verso and recto pages, but I asked that its height should match that of our quarto volumes, so that it would stand evenly on the shelf. The book was handsomely printed at the Westerham Press, supervised by Michael. Entered in the second Premio Internazionale Felice Feliciano it was judged one of the three finalists. Roger Farrand had fifty copies bound in quarter calf, for sale to subscribers. The text proved to be of outstanding merit, a standard work covering all aspects of lithographic printing apart from music, which was to form a later volume that we thought too narrow for general issue to members, despite the importance of the research involved.

Gogmagog: Morris Cox & the Gogmagog Press was published in 1991. Colin Franklin, Alan Tucker and I had for many years been friends of Morris: Colin had published his first book of poems, Alan had been selling the books from his shop in Stroud, and I had written a piece about Gogmagog in its early days and been recording the books for *Private Press Books*. Our text was taken from our varied approaches to Cox's work: I wrote about the printing, and prepared the bibliography, to which Colin added a commentary, Alan wrote on the poetry and prose, and from Morris Cox we had a selection from his poetry and a long series of letters to Corrie Guyt, a collector in South Africa. The colour plates came out well, nicely displaying Cox's extravagance of style. The binding, black vertical stripes on a bright orange cloth, failed at the first attempt, the black often smudging. Most copies had to be rebound, the binding cut away so as to leave the original free endleaf in place, with a second one as the new boards were added.

In the end the effect seemed to be worthy of the books we were describing. There were sixty-nine special copies, bound in quarter black leather, with gold striped black buckram boards. Fifty-nine had nine mounted specimens at the end, seven had twenty, and the three authors' copies had a separate volume with seventeen more. There was considerable competition for those available for sale, and we had to be very firm in their allocation.

Blair Hughes-Stanton was one of the most important wood-engravers of the twentieth century, and a book about his work had long seemed something we should attempt. An essay by Paul Collet led to a consideration of the difficulties of reproduction of the engravings, whose fine lines had proved very difficult to manage using line-blocks printed letterpress in *The Gregynog Press*. Ian Mortimer knew Hughes-Stanton, and introduced me to him, and to his daughter Penelope who had been working on her father's work. She allowed me to take a large portfolio of proofs up to our printers W. S. Maney, in Leeds, and they successfully scanned and lithographed the reproductions for us, showing all the fine white lines as well as the contrasting blacks of the engravings – though they found it necessary to reprint some sheets in the process.

The book was designed to fit the largest of the images, full size, which established the text area, but the smaller engravings needed to be very carefully placed on the page. In the end they were placed with their 'golden section' (1:1.618) centres level with those of the full-page engravings, 38% down from their topmost points. Pairs of engravings were given an even space between them, and the centre taken of the two combined. This involved a lot of arithmetical calculations, but a pocket calculator eased the strain, and the resulting pages lay well against each other. Entered in the third Premio Internazionale Felice Feliciano the book was placed within the top fifteen. For the 112 special copies in quarter morocco Ian Mortimer printed eight blocks that I had bought many years earlier from Christopher Sandford, engraved for his *Primeval Gods*, 1934.

For *The Book Illustrations of Orlando Jewitt*, by Frank Broomhead, published in 1996, the reproduction of the wood-engravings was again one of our most serious problems, in this case because so many were only available in the original books, often bound with precarious rubber. In the end Frank and I took the books and such loose prints as were available down to a scanning shop in South London for the purpose. The prints were scanned on a revolving plastic cylinder nine inches or so in diameter, and the books were (probably most fortunately) taken to another building to be scanned. Most fortunately, I thought, because there seemed every chance that when out of sight the books would not receive such careful handling as we would have wished – though in fact little damage seemed to have been done when they were returned to us. Frank's text was the result of many years of collecting, with a series of biographical chapters followed by a detailed bibliography, which we shortened in extent, though not in detail, by listing the different editions of each book below the first to have appeared.

Apart from the Text, 1998, was an account of the physical aspects of the book, drawn from Anthony Rota's lectures in America. Anthony and I spent a lot of time working over the details of the chapters, and we were very kindly loaned some books from Jarndyce's for scanning by a firm near the shop. Oak Knoll handled the American market. The dust-jacket, an exercise in ephemeral typography, should have been on a more substantial paper to withstand the rigours of a bookshop, but, of course, most copies will have been sold by post.

Two or three of our books were by this time in various stages of progress, but when Anthony told me he was having difficulties with his publishers over his memoirs I suggested we might take these on as well. He wanted to insert short passages between the chapters, which seemed likely to break up the flow of the main text, but we overcame this by printing them in italic that could, if one wished, be easily skipped over. In fact they were entertaining enough to serve simply as snippets as one finished one chapter and moved to the next. There was, again, much joint editorial work involved, but the resulting text is now much referred to by historians of the trade, as well as by book collectors at large. Oak Knoll again took copies for America – and this time the paper used for the dust-jacket was much more robust, the design following that of its predecessor.

Brian Alderson has spent many years researching Edward Ardizzone's book illustrations, and his preliminary account was published in the Spring 1972 issue of *The Private Library*, using his 3 × 5 index cards for printer's copy. Over ten years or so we sold 500 copies of this issue of the journal, which served as a working guide for collectors. When Ardizzone died in 1979 we said we should like to publish a complete account of his work, and after long delays Brian finally produced a masterly text – to which he nevertheless made considerable additions in proof. I started to lay out the book, but when Paul Nash said he would like to take it on, was glad to pass it to him. His detailed bibliographical expertise served us well in organising that side of the book, and the many illustrations will have made up for the solid matter inevitable with a bibliography such as this.

The printing went well, but the binding was disastrous, many copies being damaged in a faulty binding machine, and others bound upside down. We did not realise what had happened until I needed fifty copies for the Ardizzone family, which were to be provided in lieu of royalties – and found that out of 160 copies stacked in the hall, only 35 were satisfactory. A partial reprint took six months to complete, but after a few copies had been dispatched we discovered that eight pages of index had been printed twice. The binders said they could extract these two pairs of leaves, and were able to do so successfully, though fifty copies were lost in their first attempt. The main issue of the book was in July 2003, but the final copies were not available till July 2004. The British Library, and through them Oak Knoll, shared the expenses with us, nicely reducing our final cost.

Beyond Decoration, The Illustrations of John Everett Millais was offered by Paul Goldman when I asked him whether he would write about the wood-engraver William Harvey. The text of the Millais had already been accepted by David Way, of The British Library, who said they would gladly share production costs with us. I offered to design it, but we had to wait twelve months before the scans of the wood-engravings and etchings could be made from the copies in the Library. These proved to be darker in tone than the originals, and not quite true to scale – a new scanner has since been put in place which gives very much better results. Meanwhile I decided to rescan from Paul's own copies, which took something like an hour for each, sometimes longer, but which resulted in much sharper images. There were, in the end, twenty-six CDs needed, with fresh copies constantly required as revisions to text or plates were made.

The preliminary text was relatively short, in three chapters, with a checklist of the engravings and etchings, each entry including a quotation from the story or poem it illustrated. On reflection we moved the quotations to their respective places underneath the engravings, which resulted in a very narrow format, with one or two images to a page, and the text underneath or opposite. I had originally intended the outer margins to be thirty millimetres wide, but at the last moment, when everything had been delivered to the printers and we had retreated to the Yorkshire moors to relax, it turned out that the paper was seven millimetres too narrow. The cost of buying a fresh supply was too great to contemplate, so I slightly reduced a few engravings in size, turned a couple on their sides, and the format became that much narrower, though perhaps more effective overall.

The principal engravings on the dust-jacket had been scanned, as were all the others taken from Paul's books, at 1200 dpi. Unfortunately the files were lost sight of in preparing the plates for printing, and duplicate files were added above them, so that two images were visible, very slightly overlapping. When reprinted, with only a single set of images, the final result was excellent, though a further reprint proved necessary due to some fading of the green background.

The printing of the body of the book, by the St Edmundsbury Press, was excellent, the varying darks and lights of the engravings managed to excellent effect, and Woolnough's, the binders, managed the trimming to perfection – essential since there was nothing at all to spare at the fore-edges. Again we shared the costs with The British Library and through them Oak Knoll, so that the final cost of production was a good deal less than the postal charges.

This present volume, *A Modest Collection*, took us longer to prepare for press than had been expected, for more than eighty members contributed essays, and much time had to be spent over corrections, and obtaining photographs and suitable images to fill any remaining spaces. It also proved difficult to get all the essays together in the first place, for our secretary suddenly fell ill, and following a listing in the *Newsletter* of those whom we knew had contributed, a further dozen essays came in – and a couple of new ones at the same time. In proof, now, the results look promising, and though such delays, as have often been involved in the production of our books and the journal, have always troubled us, it has seemed preferable to avoid rushing authors or printers in order to match some particular deadline.

The savings we have made by setting the texts ourselves and co-publishing rather than attempting to sell copies to non-members ourselves have been very considerable, and a careful analysis of our accounts shows that we have something like ten thousand pounds in hand now, compared to the deficit of nine thousand pounds at the end of our first twenty-five years. Obviously the money will not lie in reserve for too long, for we have a long list of books in hand, some almost ready to go to the printer, some only part way to completion. Already allowed for in our accounts is the collection of photographs of English country bookshops, that should be issued during 2007, though intended for publication some years ago. Also nearly ready is *John Sharpe, Reprint Publisher and Bookseller, 1777–1860*, by Iain Bain, a slim volume, compared to the Ardizzone and Millais, but as full of interest. In 2007 we shall also publish John Arnold's history and bibliography of the Fanfrolico Press. In preparation are my own account of the private presses of the eighteenth and nineteenth centuries, with checklists of their productions; Frances Guthrie's account of the Pear Tree Press; and Paul Nash on *Guido Morris and the Latin Press*, and *British Cottage and Villa Books 1775–1850*. Whether these will be issued on an annual or biennial basis will depend on our financial state at the time. Our membership has dropped to something over 600, all growing steadily older. So though this note can end in as upbeat a style as was that made twenty-five years ago, our need for the coming years must be to persuade younger people to join us, as members of the Association and where possible as members of our Council.

6

PUBLICATIONS
a descriptive checklist
Paul W. Nash

THE FOLLOWING BOOKS and pamphlets were published by the Private Libraries Association, either alone or in conjunction with other publishers and societies. The books are arranged chronologically. Dimensions are of the leaves. Original published prices are given, with the discounted price for PLA members (when different) in brackets.

1 SIMPLIFIED CATALOGUING RULES FOR GENERAL USE IN PRIVATE LIBRARIES: AUTHOR AND TITLE ENTRIES [by Philip Ward and Roderick Cave]. 253 × 203 mm. viii, 22 pp. Duplicated by Philip Ward in an edition of 250 copies. Stapled into pale blue card covers, printed letterpress by David Chambers at the Cuckoo Hill Press. 5s. 1959.
This, the first 'book' published by the Association, was a modest pamphlet distributed to interested members in January 1959 at the price of five shillings. A second impression was printed and issued in September of the same year, offered at 7s. 6d. to members and 10s. to non-members. A third impression was produced, and, eventually, photocopies when that was exhausted.

2 TWELVE BY EIGHT: A PAPER READ BEFORE THE DOUBLE CROWN CLUB by John Mason . . . 210 × 150–155 mm. [8] pp. Printed by the John Roberts Press. Sewn and loosely inserted into paper covers. 2s. 6d. 1959.
Seventy-five copies were printed on one of John Mason's papers, the remainder of the edition being on mould-made paper. The special copies were signed and numbered by Mason, and some of these were issued in a card folder with 'The twelve by eight Paper Mill' blocked in gold on the front. The text is printed from the same setting of type used to print Mason's paper in The Private Library, *January 1959 (1st series, vol. 2, no. 3).*

Opposite: Cover, *Twelve by Eight*, 1959

TWELVE BY EIGHT

a paper read before
the Double Crown Club

BY JOHN MASON

and now reprinted
for members of
The Private Libraries
Association

1959

3 CONCERNING BOOKPLATES: ESSAYS by Philip Beddingham. 216 × 139 mm. 14, [2] pp. Printed by the John Roberts Press. Stapled into brown paper covers printed in black. 5s. (2s.). 1960.
A gathering of four short essays that had been published in The Private Library.

4 EARL GREY'S PAPERS: AN INTRODUCTORY SURVEY by Ronald P. Doig. 212 × 137 mm. 3–14 pp. Printed by H. Sharp & Sons in an edition of 500 copies. Stapled into pale grey paper covers printed in black. 2s. 6d. 1961.
This was David Chambers' first piece of commercial book design, for which he wood-engraved the small crest used on the cover as the only decorative feature.

5 CONCERNING BOOKLABELS by Philip Beddingham, Will Carter and Reynolds Stone. 216 × 140 mm. 16 pp. Printed by the Stellar Press. Stapled into pale grey paper covers printed in black. 5s. (3s. 6d.). 1963.
Designed by David Chambers. Original essays, printed in a style to match Concerning Bookplates *(item 3). The main text is by Beddingham, with notes by Carter (on his technique of making booklabels) and Stone (on the designing of wood-engraved booklabels).*

6 THE DEVELOPMENT OF CERTAIN STYLES OF BOOKBINDING by Howard M. Nixon. 215 × 140 mm. [16] pp. Printed by the Lavenham Press in an edition of 700 (or perhaps 800) copies. Stapled into pale blue card covers printed in black. 5s. (3s. 6d.). 1963.
Designed by David Chambers. The text is a lecture which Nixon gave to the PLA in 1962.

7 FRIENDSHIP'S OFFERING: AN ESSAY ON THE ANNUALS AND GIFT BOOKS OF THE 19TH CENTURY by Anne Renier. 216 × 138 mm. 23, [1] pp. Printed by Unwin Brothers. Sewn into lilac card covers printed in black. 9s. 6d. (5s.). 1964.
Designed by Iain Bain.

8 ROMANTIC BOOK ILLUSTRATION IN ENGLAND 1943–1955 by Rigby Graham. 215 × 140 mm. 34, [2] pp. Printed by W. & J.

A MODEST COLLECTION

Opposite: Cover, *Romantic Book Illustration in England 1943–1955,* 1965, drawing by Rigby Graham

Romantic
Book Illustration
in England
1943-1955

Mackay Ltd in an edition of 1,000 copies. Sewn into pale blue-green paper wrappers printed in black. 9s. 6d. (5s.). 1965.
The bulk of the text is a 'Handlist' of books with romantic illustrations published between 1943 and 1955.

9 THOMAS FROGNALL DIBDIN: BIBLIOGRAPHER & BIBLIO-MANIAC EXTRAORDINARY, 1776–1847 by E. J. O'Dwyer. 215 × 138 mm. [2], 45, [1] pp. Printed by W. & J. Mackay Ltd in an edition of 1,400 copies. Bound in pale grey paper-covered boards printed in black. Matching dust-jacket. £1. 10s. (15s.). 1967.
Designed by Iain Bain; the first hard-bound volume published by the Association. Includes a checklist of Dibdin's bibliographical publications.

10 A CHECK-LIST OF THE BOOK ILLUSTRATIONS OF JOHN BUCKLAND WRIGHT, TOGETHER WITH A PERSONAL MEMOIR by Anthony Reid. 247 × 155 mm. 94, [2] pp + XVI leaves of plates. Printed by W. & J. Mackay Ltd, the plates by the Stellar Press, in an edition of 1,400 copies. Bound in full blue cloth blocked in gold. Glassine dust-jacket. £4. 10s. (£2. 10s.). 1968.
Designed by Iain Bain. The plates reproduce intaglio prints and drawings by Buckland Wright.

11 JOHN PITTS: BALLAD PRINTER OF SEVEN DIALS, LONDON, 1765–1844: WITH A SHORT ACCOUNT OF HIS PREDECESSORS IN THE BALLAD & CHAPBOOK TRADE by Leslie Shepard. 248 × 155 mm. 160 pp + [3] leaves of plates. Printed by W. & J. Mackay Ltd in an edition of 1,600 copies. Bound in full red cloth blocked in black and gold. Glassine dust-jacket. £4. 10s. (£2. 10s) 1969 [i.e. 1970].
Designed by Iain Bain.

12 TASTE & TECHNIQUE IN BOOK COLLECTING by John Carter . . . with an epilogue. Third impression, revised. 216 × 138 mm. xiv, 242 pp. Printed by the Stellar Press in an edition of 1,000 copies. Bound in full green cloth blocked on the spine in red and gold. Pale green dust-jacket printed in black and blue (designed by Michael Harvey). £2. 10s. (£1. 10s.). 1970.
Designed by Iain Bain. Earlier impressions were published by Cambridge University Press from 1948. A fourth impression was published by the PLA in 1972 (1,020 copies) and a fifth, with further corrections and notes, in 1977 (1,500 copies).

Opposite: Title-page, *John Pitts*, 1969

JOHN PITTS

Ballad Printer
of Seven Dials, London

1765–1844

*with a short account of his predecessors
in the Ballad & Chapbook Trade*

BY

LESLIE SHEPARD

LONDON
PRIVATE LIBRARIES
ASSOCIATION

13 CHARLES HOLTZAPFFEL'S PRINTING APPARATUS FOR THE USE OF AMATEURS: REPRINTED FROM THE THIRD GREATLY ENLARGED EDITION OF 1846 and edited by James Mosley and David Chambers. 220 × 136 mm. xxxvi, [2], iv, [1], 6–79, [1], xliii–xlviii pp + 4 pages of plates. Printed by the Gresham Press (Unwin Brothers Ltd) in an edition of 1,000 copies. Bound in full dark green cloth titled in gold. £2.00 (£1.50). 1971.
Designed by David Chambers. The main text is a facsimile of Holtzapffel's printing manual, with a lengthy introduction by Mosley and Chambers discussing amateur printing in general and Holtzapffel's contribution in particular.

14 THE LONDON BOOKSHOP: BEING PART ONE OF A PICTORIAL RECORD OF THE ANTIQUARIAN BOOK TRADE: PORTRAITS & PREMISES by Richard Brown and Stanley Brett, with a prefatory reminiscence by Percy Muir. 180 × 246 mm. 95, [1] pp. Printed by W. & J. Mackay Ltd in an edition of 1,500 copies. Bound in full grey cloth titled in gold on red cover- and spine-panels. £3.00 (£2.00). 1971.
Designed by Iain Bain. Describes and depicts the following: James Bain Ltd, Andrew Block, Louis W. Bondy, Stanley Crowe, H. M. Fletcher, Harold Mortlake and Co., Bernard Quaritch Ltd, Bertram Rota, Charles J. Sawyer, Stanley Smith, and Suckling and Co. The second part was published in 1977 (item 23).

15 ENGRAVED BOOKPLATES: EUROPEAN EX LIBRIS 1950–70 by Mark Severin and Anthony Reid. Edited by David Chambers. 273 × 183 mm. 176 pp. Printed by W. & J. Mackay Ltd in an edition of 2,000 copies. Bound in full dark green cloth blocked on the spine in red and gold. £6.00 (£4.00). 1972.
Designed by David Chambers. With 500 wood-engraved and intaglio bookplates. There were 70 special copies, each with a dozen original bookplates, bound in quarter morocco, price £10.00.

16 CATALOGUE OF THE BOOKPLATE EXHIBITION AT THE NATIONAL BOOK LEAGUE, SEPTEMBER 1972 [by Brian North Lee *et al.*]. 251 × 203 mm. [30] leaves. Duplicated. Stapled into orange card covers printed in red. 10 pence (at the exhibition). 1972.
Published jointly by the Bookplate Society and PLA. The

exhibition grew out of research for Mark Severin's Engraved Bookplates *(item 15) and copies of the catalogue were available at the
National Book League, and later from the Association.*

17 LITERARY ANNUALS AND GIFT BOOKS: A BIBLIOGRAPHY
1823–1903 by Frederick W. Faxon, reprinted with supplementary essays by Eleanore Jamieson and Iain Bain. 217 × 135 mm.
25, xix pp, 140 leaves + 24 plates. Printed by the Gresham Press
(Unwin Brothers) in an edition of 1,750 copies. Bound in full red
cloth blocked on the spine in black and gold. £6.00 (£3.00). 1973.
*Designed by Iain Bain. A facsimile reprint of a work first pub-
lished in an edition of 150 copies by the Boston Book Company in
1912.*

18 THE BOOKPLATE DESIGNS OF REX WHISTLER by Brian North
Lee. 248 × 154 mm. 39, [8] pp + 41 leaves of plates. Printed by
W. & J. Mackay Ltd in an edition of 1,000 copies. Bound in full
grey cloth blocked on the spine in black and gold. £7.50 (£3.75).
1973 [i.e. 1974].
*Designed by David Chambers. Of the edition of 1,000 copies,
650 have a printed frontispiece while the remainder, in a cloth-
covered slipcase, have an original intaglio bookplate pasted-in
instead and were sold at £10.00 (£5.00). Published by the PLA for
the Bookplate Society.*

19 COCK-A-HOOP: A SEQUEL TO CHANTICLEER, PERTELOTE,
AND COCKALORUM: BEING A BIBLIOGRAPHY OF THE GOLDEN
COCKEREL PRESS SEPTEMBER 1949–DECEMBER 1961 ... WITH
A LIST OF PROSPECTUSES 1920–62 by David Chambers and
Christopher Sandford. 247 × 150 mm. 126 pp. Printed by W. & J.
Mackay Ltd in an edition of 2,526 copies. Bound in full blue cloth
blocked in white. £12.50 (£10.00). [1976].
*Designed by David Chambers. There was also a special edition of
300 copies bound in quarter morocco and sold at £35.00 (£30.00);
only 209 copies were issued, due to the loss of the first gathering
by Sangorski & Sutcliffe. The text is lavishly illustrated with wood-
engravings and facsimile pages from Golden Cockerel books.
Published by the PLA for the Golden Cockerel Press, which took
421 ordinary copies and 49 specials.*

398. Miss *Elizabeth Gregor*, | Of *Trewarthennick*. | Printed at TRURO *Nov.* 3. 1743.

Label within a wide floral border, comprising four separate pieces of engraved decoration. There is also a row of ornaments placed horizontally between the second and third lines of the inscription. There was a copy of this label in the Marshall Collection (M. 402), and Ellis of Bond Street offered a copy, or copies, for sale in his catalogues of 1908 and 1909. (V. 1760) 120 × 147 mm.

399. *John Hepburn*, | SURGEON, | IN | *Stamford, Lincolnshire*, | 1743.
Label within a decorative border. It was listed by Hamilton, and also on p. 111 of Volume 11 of *The Ex Libris Journal*. (R) 48 × 49 mm.

1744

400. Henry Arundel, Oxford, Sep. 4, 1744.*
There was a copy of this large printed label in the Marshall Collection (M. 23), but it appears to be elsewhere unrecorded, and further details are wanting.

20 JOSEPH CUNDALL: A VICTORIAN PUBLISHER: NOTES ON HIS LIFE AND A CHECK-LIST OF HIS BOOKS by Ruari McLean. 273 × 180 mm. vii, [1], 96 pp. Printed by T. & A. Constable Ltd in an edition of 2,052 copies. Bound in full red cloth titled in gold. Cream dust-jacket printed in red and black. £8.00 (£4.00). 1976.
Designed by the author. Lavishly illustrated, in colour and monochrome; pages 47–91 bear a bibliography of Cundall's books. Twelve copies were quarter bound in black cloth, lettered in gold, with patterned paper boards.

21 EARLY PRINTED BOOK LABELS: A CATALOGUE OF DATED PERSONAL LABELS AND GIFT LABELS PRINTED IN BRITAIN TO THE YEAR 1760 by Brian North Lee. 249 × 155 mm. xxii, 185, [1] pp. Printed by W. & J. Mackay Ltd in an edition of 2,000 copies. Bound in full dark red cloth blocked in gold. £12.50 (£10.00). 1976.
Designed by David Chambers. Published in conjunction with the Bookplate Society.

22 CATALOGUE OF THE BOOKPLATE SOCIETY'S THIRD BIENNIAL EXHIBITION: BOOKPLATE DESIGNERS 1925–1975, HELD AT THE NATIONAL BOOK LEAGUE ... SATURDAY 16TH TO THURSDAY 28TH OCTOBER 1976 [by Philip Beddingham *et al.*]. 254 × 200 mm. 52 pp + [4] pages of plates. Duplicated by Ken Davey, the plates and cover printed by the Monument Press. Stapled into pale blue card covers printed in black. 65 pence. 1976.
Published jointly by the Bookplate Society and PLA.

23 THE LONDON BOOKSHOP: BEING PART TWO OF A PICTORIAL RECORD OF THE ANTIQUARIAN BOOK TRADE: PORTRAITS & PREMISES. 182 × 245 mm. 75, [5] pp. Printed by W. & J. Mackay Ltd in an edition of 2,000 copies. Bound in full grey cloth titled in gold on red cover- and spine-panels. £10.00 (£5.00). 1977.
Designed by David Chambers. Brief descriptions and monochrome photographs, continuing the pattern set in volume I (item 14). The subjects are: Francis Edwards Ltd, Frank Hollings, E. Joseph, Maggs Brothers Ltd, Marks and Co., Henry Sotheran Ltd, Harold T. Storey and Thomas Thorp.

Opposite: Specimen page from *Early Printed Book Labels*, 1976

24 A HISTORY OF THE GREGYNOG PRESS by Dorothy A. Harrop. 271 × 182 mm. xv, [1], 266, [2] pp + [16] pages of plates. Printed by T. and A. Constable Ltd in an edition of 2,600 copies. Bound in full brown cloth blocked in gold and blind. £20.00 (£10.00). 1980. *Designed by David Chambers. 500 copies in sheets were lost, and some bound copies found to be damaged, when Constable (which had been storing them) closed down. 100 copies were signed by the author, of which it was possible to issue seventy-one: twenty-one in buckram at £45.00 (£22.50); twenty in quarter morocco at £100.00 (£75.00); and thirty in full morocco at £160.00 (£120.00).*

25 JAMES LUMSDEN & SON OF GLASGOW: THEIR JUVENILE BOOKS AND CHAPBOOKS by Sydney Roscoe and R. A. Brimmell. 248 × 156 mm. xv, [1], 134 pp. Printed by Clark Constable Ltd in an edition of 2,000 copies. Bound in full dark blue cloth blocked and titled in gold on black panels. £14.00 (£7.00). 1981. *Designed by David Chambers. Published in collaboration with Justin G. Schiller of New York.*

26 JOAN HASSALL: ENGRAVINGS & DRAWINGS by David Chambers, with an introductory memoir by Joan Hassall and an appreciation of her technique by George Mackley. 247 × 153 mm. lxii, [2], 160 pp. Printed by W. S. Maney & Son Ltd in an edition of 2,610 copies. Bound in full black cloth blocked in gold. £24.00 (£12.00). 1985. *Designed by the author. Includes reproductions of more than 470 wood-engravings. 110 copies were available with seven additional wood-engravings printed from the wood by David Chambers, bound in quarter morocco, with a copy of Hassall's* The Plain Facts *in a pocket at the back, in a slipcase, at £100.00 (£75.00).*

27 THE ENGRAVED BOOKPLATES OF ERIC GILL, 1908–1940 compiled by Christopher Skelton, with an introduction by Michael Renton and an afterword by Albert Sperisen. 211 × 150 mm. 79, [5] pp. Printed by the September Press in an edition of 1,000 copies. Bound in full red cloth titled in gold. Pale grey dust-jacket printed in red and black. £18.00 (£10.00). 1986. *Designed by Christopher Skelton. Of the 1,000 copies printed,*

400 were available to PLA members, 200 to Skelton, and the remainder were published in America by the Book Club of California.

28 THE ZAEHNSDORFS (1842–1947): CRAFT BOOKBINDERS by Frank Broomhead. 247 × 155 mm. 109, [1] pp. Printed by W. S. Maney & Son Ltd in an edition of 2,350 copies. Bound in full red cloth titled in gold on a black spine-panel. £20.00 (£10.00). 1986. *Designed by David Chambers. One hundred copies were available from Zaehnsdorf's, bound in morocco, with two coloured illustrations, at £289.00 (£220.00).*

29 EARLY LITHOGRAPHED BOOKS: A STUDY OF THE DESIGN AND PRODUCTION OF IMPROPER BOOKS IN THE AGE OF THE HAND PRESS, WITH A CATALOGUE by Michael Twyman. 250 × 188 mm. 374, [2] pp. Printed by the Westerham Press Ltd in an edition of 2,900 copies. Bound in full pale brown cloth blocked in gold. £68.50 (£25.00). 1990.
Designed by the author. The first book to be printed in Britain by waterless lithography. Published in conjunction with the Farrand Press of London, which took 1,550 copies. The text is illustrated with numerous reproductions of lithographs. This book was short-listed for the Premio Felice Feliciano in 1991. Fifty copies were available from Farrand in quarter calf, with vellum tips and marbled paper boards, at £150.00.

30 THE WOOD-ENGRAVINGS OF BLAIR HUGHES-STANTON by Penelope Hughes-Stanton. 300 × 195 mm. xii, 183, [1] pp. Printed by W. S. Maney & Son Ltd in an edition of 1,862 copies. Bound in full black cloth titled in gold. £45.00 (£22.50). 1991.
Designed by David Chambers. Includes reproductions of some 140 wood-engravings, plus a number of photographs. 112 copies were specially-bound in quarter morocco and were accompanied by eight wood-engravings from Primeval Gods, *printed by Ian Mortimer, at £150.00 (£100.00).*

31 GOGMAGOG: MORRIS COX AND THE GOGMAGOG PRESS by David Chambers, Colin Franklin and Alan Tucker. 272 × 180 mm. 184 pp. Printed by W. S. Maney & Son Ltd in an edition of 1,715

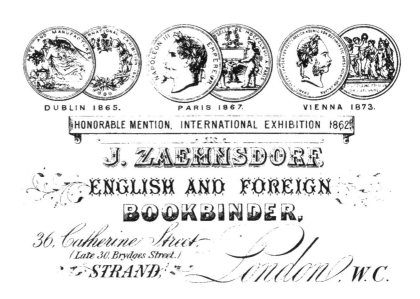

Zaehnsdorf Business Card, 1873

apace, particularly in the larger binderies, in order to meet the increased demand for books from the new middle class. Although machines were to be beneficial in the long-term, their immediate effect was to result in disputes between the employers and the men being displaced by the machines. The larger binderies, who could better afford the capital outlay on new machines, then had the consequent advantage of reduced costs, and could, therefore, capture a larger share of the available work, to the detriment of the smaller binders. The first rolling machine, to replace hand beating to obtain a solid book, had been introduced as early as 1827 and it was in widespread use by 1830. A blocking press, for titling, to replace hand methods, followed in 1832. These developments were only the beginnings, and by the 1850s the basic mechanical process had been introduced — a folding machine, for folding the sheets as received from the printer; a cutting machine, for book edges; a backing machine, which gives the book the ridges or shoulders where the boards fit; and a sewing machine. The steam engine was now a reliable source of

18

copies. Bound in full orange cloth blocked in black. £45.00 (£22.50). 1991.
Designed by David Chambers. The text includes sixteen pages of full colour plates. Sixty-nine special copies were bound in quarter black morocco with black buckram boards, blocked in gold. Of these, fifty-nine had nine mounted specimens at the end, at £150.00 (£100.00), seven had twenty specimens, sold to members at £160.00, and the three authors' copies had a separate volume with seventeen more specimens included.

32 THE BOOK ILLUSTRATIONS OF ORLANDO JEWITT by Frank Broomhead. 271 × 179 mm. xvi, 256 pp. Printed by W. S. Maney & Son Ltd in an edition of 1,250 copies. Bound in full black cloth blocked in gold on the spine. £45.00 (£22.50). 1995.
Designed by David Chambers. This book was selected for the British Book Design and Production Exhibition in 1996.

33 APART FROM THE TEXT by Anthony Rota. 216 × 140 mm. 253, [3] pp. Printed by the St Edmundsbury Press in an edition of 2,200 copies. Bound in full grey cloth blocked on the spine in red and gold. Pale grey dust-jacket printed in black. £24.00 (£12.00). 1998 [i.e. 1999].
Designed by David Chambers. Published in conjunction with Oak Knoll Press. One hundred and fifty copies had an additional portrait frontispiece and were signed by the author. Of these a hundred were specially bound in quarter morocco by the Green Street Bindery, price £75.00 (£50.00); the remainder are as yet still in sheets.

34 BOOKS IN THE BLOOD: MEMOIRS OF A FOURTH GENERA-TION BOOKSELLER by Anthony Rota. 218 × 142 mm. 313, [7] pp. Printed by the St Edmundsbury Press in an edition of 1,700 copies. Bound in full grey cloth blocked on the spine in red and gold. Red dust-jacket printed in black. £24.00 (£12.00). 2002.
Designed by David Chambers. Published in conjunction with Oak Knoll Press. Uniform with item 33.

35 EDWARD ARDIZZONE: A BIBLIOGRAPHICAL COMMENTARY by Brian Alderson. 249 × 155 mm. [ii], 309, [1] pp + 4 colour plates.

Opposite: Specimen page from *The Zaehnsdorfs (1842–1947)*, 1986

Printed by Butler & Tanner Limited in an edition of 1,700 copies. Bound in full dark red cloth blocked in gold. £45.00 (£22.50). 2003. *Designed by Paul W. Nash. Published in conjunction with The British Library and Oak Knoll Press, which together took 700 copies of the first impression; these copies were issued in a pale pink dust-jacket printed in red and black. Due to a fault in the binding, many copies had to be scrapped and a second impression of 350 copies was made in 2004.*

36 BEYOND DECORATION: THE ILLUSTRATIONS OF JOHN EVERETT MILLAIS by Paul Goldman. 296 × 172 mm. 337, [1] pp. Printed by the St Edmundsbury Press in an edition of 1,878 copies. Bound in full green cloth titled in gold. White dust-jacket printed in green and black. £35.00 (£20.00). 2005.
Designed by David Chambers. Published in conjunction with The British Library and Oak Knoll Press, which together took 1,018 copies. The book includes reproductions of more than 300 of Millais' book and magazine illustrations.

A MODEST COLLECTION

Opposite: Specimen page from *Edward Ardizzone*, 2003

appears to be a creamy cartridge but with the wire side markedly yellower than the felt side, the colour of alternate page openings thus changes in a slightly disconcerting manner. § Yellow cloth boards, the front with the image from the d.j. blocked in blue, the spine lettered in blue and red. D.j. cream, with a large pink wash front panel within a quadruple black ruled frame, typographic lettering on front and spine in black and blue, and with a central line-block from a drawing by E.A. not among the illustrations in the book.

REPRINTED: November 1946.

'"I'm tired of books," said Jack,' from *Peacock Pie* (1946 item 15)

1953 REPRINT IN LARGER FORMAT: crown 4° in eights. 248 × 180 mm. Same pagination and illus. on antique wove paper. Green paper boards, decorations and titling in 2 colours, line-block on rear cover as that on p. 46. D.j. as binding, but ads. on rear. An exact reprint (apparently stereotyped) of the first ed., with partially reset imprint. The paper retains – but consistently – the warm creaminess of the earlier printing. Reprinted 1955 and 1962.

APPENDIX A

THE PRIVATE LIBRARY
special issues and reprints

A1 H. G. DIXEY PRESS by Peter C. G. Isaac. 215 × 138 mm. [8] pp. Printed by John Roberts Press. Stapled. 1965.
Reprinted for the author from the issue for April 1965 (first series, vol. 6, no. 2).

A2 THE TYPOGRAPHICAL SOCIETY OF NEWCASTLE UPON TYNE by L. A. Leake. 216 × 142 mm. [2], 86–98, [1] pp + 4 plates. Printed by John Roberts Press. Stapled. 1968.
Reprinted for the author from the issue for Autumn 1968 (second series, vol. 1, no. 3).

A3 A CHECKLIST OF THE MANUSCRIPTS OF THOMAS BEWICK . . . WITH ADDENDA by Iain Bain. 216 × 140 mm. 46, [2] pp. Printed by William Clowes & Sons Ltd in an edition of 100 copies. Sewn and glued into white card covers, with a grey-green jacket hand-printed in black and brown by the author. 1970.
Reprinted for the author from the issues for Summer and Autumn 1970 (second series, vol. 3, nos 2 and 3). Iain Bain prepared his own jacket (bearing the title given above) and added some manuscript addenda to page 46.

A4 RALPH CHUBB, THE UNKNOWN, A CHECKLIST AND EXTEN-SIVELY EXPURGATED BIOGRAPHY by Anthony Reid. 216 × 140 mm. [2], 141–156, 193–213, [1] pp + 12 plates. Printed by William Clowes & Sons Ltd in an edition of 200 copies. Sewn and glued into grey card covers printed in black. 1970.
Reprinted for the author from the issues for Autumn and Winter 1970 (second series, vol. 3, nos 3 and 4).

A5 EDWARD ARDIZZONE: A PRELIMINARY HAND-LIST OF HIS ILLUSTRATED BOOKS 1929–1970 by Brian Alderson. 215 × 137 mm. [2], 64 pp. Printed by William Clowes & Sons Ltd in an edition of 500 copies. Sewn and glued into pale grey card covers printed in black. £1.50 (75p). 1972.
A run-on of the issue for Spring 1972 (second series, vol. 5, no. 1), with a new title-leaf and illustration pasted in.

A6 CHARLES HAMILTON, GREYFRIARS AND MYSELF: PRESIDENTIAL ADDRESS TO THE PRIVATE LIBRARIES ASSOCIATION by Raymond Lister 9 April 1974. 277 × 184 mm. [2], 47–68 pp. Stapled. 1975.
Reprinted, in enlarged format, for the author from the issue for Summer 1974 (second series, vol. 7, no. 2).

A7 FIFTY YEARS, by Douglas Cleverdon. 216 × 137 mm. 51–83, [1] pp + 4 plates. Printed by William Clowes & Sons Ltd. Sewn and glued into grey card covers printed in black. 1978.
Reprinted for the author from the issue for Summer 1977 (second series, vol. 10, no. 2).

A8 THE BOOKPLATES OF VALENTIN LE CAMPION, by W. E. Butler. 216 × 137 mm. [2], 51–67, [1] pp. Printed by W. S. Maney & Son Ltd. Sewn into grey card covers printed in black. 1981.
A run-on of the issue for Summer 1981 (third series, vol. 4, no. 2), with an added title-leaf.

A9 MINIATURE LIBRARIES FOR THE YOUNG, by Brian Alderson [plus 'An Infant's Library' by David Chambers]. 216 × 137 mm. 48 pp. Printed by W. S. Maney & Son Ltd in an edition of 100 copies. Sewn and glued into red card covers printed in black, with a white paper cover-label. £5.00 (£4.00). 1983.
A run-on of the issue for Spring 1983 (third series, vol. 6, no. 1), including the original editorial and reviews.

A10 JONATHAN STEPHENSON & THE ROCKET PRESS by John R. Smith. 216 × 143 mm. 97–116 pp. Printed by W. S. Maney & Son Ltd. Stapled into blue paper covers and inserted into grey paper wrappers, with a white paper cover-label. 1985.
A run-on from the issue for Autumn 1985 (third series, vol. 8,

no. 3). There were also fifty copies, signed by the author, 216 ×
138 mm, [2], 97–116, [1] pp, bound in natural canvas-covered
boards, with a white paper cover-label.

A11 PETER FLEMING, SA PLACE DANS LA LITERATURE ANGLAISE,
par Comte Henri Hacquart de Turtotz, summarised and set
down by John Collins. 212 × 136 mm. [2], 3–26 pp. Printed by
W. S. Maney & Son Ltd in an edition of 13 copies. Grey buckram-
covered boards, lettered in white on the spine. 1998.
A run-on from the issue for Spring 1997 (fourth series, vol. 10,
no. 1), with an added title-leaf.

APPENDIX B

PRIVATE PRESS BOOKS
1959–2001

Each volume measures 221–222 × 138–140 mm.

B1 PRIVATE PRESS BOOKS 1959 edited by Roderick Cave and Thomas Rae. [2], v, [1], 34, [6] pp. Printed by Thomas Rae at the Signet Press in an edition of 2,000 copies. Stapled into white card covers printed in black and blue. 7s. 6d. (5s.). 1960.
Three separate impressions are recorded on the verso of the title-leaf, but in fact all 2,000 copies were printed at the same time. This proved to be much too large a print-run, and some thousand or more copies were subsequently pulped.

B2 PRIVATE PRESS BOOKS 1960 edited by Roderick Cave & Thomas Rae. [2], iv, [1], 43, [15] pp. Printed by Thomas Rae at the Signet Press in an edition of 1,250 copies. Stapled into white card covers printed in black and red. 10s. 6d. (7s. 6d.). 1961.

B3 PRIVATE PRESS BOOKS 1961 edited by Roderick Cave, Thomas Rae & David Chambers. [2], v, [1], 37, [15] pp. Printed by the Stellar Press in an edition of 1,250 copies. Stapled into yellow card covers printed in black and red. 10s. 6d. (7s. 6d.). 1962.
This was the first volume to include reproductions of pages and illustrations from some of the books described.

B4 PRIVATE PRESS BOOKS 1962 edited by Roderick Cave, Thomas Rae & David Chambers. [2], iv, [2], 53, [15] pp. Printed by the Stellar Press in an edition of 1,250 copies. Stapled into pale brown card covers printed in black and blue. 10s. 6d. (7s. 6d.). 1963.

B5 PRIVATE PRESS BOOKS 1963 edited by Roderick Cave & David Chambers. [8], iii, [1], 59, [13] pp. Printed by the Stellar Press in an edition of 1,100 copies. Sewn and glued into pink card covers printed in black and red. 15s. (10s. 6d.). 1964.

B6 PRIVATE PRESS BOOKS 1964 edited by Roderick Cave, David Chambers & Peter Hoy. [6], 65, [13] pp. Printed by the Stellar Press in an edition of 1,100 copies. Sewn and glued into orange-red card covers printed in black and green. 15s. (10s. 6d.). 1965.

B7 PRIVATE PRESS BOOKS 1965 edited by Roderick Cave, David Chambers & Peter Hoy. [6], 64, [14] pp. Printed by the Stellar Press in an edition of 1,100 copies. Sewn and glued into yellow card covers printed in black and grey. £1. 1s. (15s.). 1966.

B8 PRIVATE PRESS BOOKS 1966 edited by Roderick Cave, David Chambers & Peter Hoy. [6], 61, [13] pp. Printed by the Stellar Press in an edition of 1,100 copies. Sewn and glued into white card covers printed in black and red. £1. 1s. (15s.). 1967.

B9 PRIVATE PRESS BOOKS 1967 edited by Roderick Cave, David Chambers & Peter Hoy. [6], 71, [11] pp. Printed by the Stellar Press in an edition of 1,150 copies. Sewn and glued into pale pink card covers printed in black and red. £1. 5s. (£1). 1968.

B10 PRIVATE PRESS BOOKS 1968 edited by Roderick Cave, David Chambers & Peter Hoy. [6], 81, [9] pp. Printed by the Stellar Press in an edition of 1,150 copies. Sewn and glued into green card covers printed in blue. £1. 5s. (£1). 1969.

B11 PRIVATE PRESS BOOKS 1969 edited by Roderick Cave, David Chambers, Peter Hoy & Anthony Baker. [6], 83, [7] pp. Printed by the Stellar Press in an edition of 1,200 copies. Sewn and glued into white card covers printed in black and red. £1. 5s. (£1). 1970.

B12 PRIVATE PRESS BOOKS 1970 by Roderick Cave, David Chambers, Peter Hoy, Anthony Baker, Edward Chapman & Lewis Prior, edited by David Chambers. [2], xii, [2], 125, [7] pp. Printed by the Stellar Press in an edition of 1,300 copies. Sewn and glued into pale lilac card covers printed in purple. £2.25 (£1.50). 1971.
Includes a summary of the contents of the foregoing volumes. The cover-lettering, designed by Michael Harvey, was repeated, mutatis mutandis, for the 1980, 1990 and 2000 volumes.

B13 PRIVATE PRESS BOOKS 1971 by Roderick Cave, David Chambers, Peter Hoy and Anthony Baker, edited by David Chambers. [6], 91, [7] pp. Printed by the Stellar Press in an edition of 1,200 copies. Sewn and glued into pale brown card covers printed in black and red. £1.50 (£1.00). 1972.

B14 PRIVATE PRESS BOOKS 1972 by Roderick Cave, David Chambers, Peter Hoy and Anthony Baker, edited by David Chambers. [6], 82, [8] pp. Printed by the Stellar Press in an edition of 1,200 copies. Sewn and glued into pale yellow card covers printed in black and grey. £2.25 (£1.50). 1974.
With this volume the annual programme of publication began to slip. Various troubles afflicted the bibliography over the following years and publication has yet to be brought up to date (although this is achievable in the near future).

B15 PRIVATE PRESS BOOKS 1973 by Roderick Cave, David Chambers, Peter Hoy and Anthony Baker, edited by David Chambers. 75, [3] pp. Printed by the Stellar Press in an edition of 1,200 copies. Sewn and glued into pale blue card covers printed in black. £2.50 (£1.50). 1975.

B16 PRIVATE PRESS BOOKS 1974 by Roderick Cave, David Chambers, Peter Hoy and Anthony Baker, edited by David Chambers. 78, [2] pp. Printed by W. & J. Mackay Ltd in an edition of 1,200 copies. Sewn and glued into yellow-brown card covers printed in black. £3.00 (£1.50). 1977.

B17 PRIVATE PRESS BOOKS 1975 by David Chambers, Peter Hoy, Anthony Baker and Dwight Agner, edited by David Chambers. 110, [2] pp. Printed by W. & J. Mackay Ltd in an edition of 1,200 copies. Sewn and glued into pale grey card covers printed in black. £4.00 (£2.00). 1978.

B18 PRIVATE PRESS BOOKS 1976 by David Chambers, Peter Hoy Anthony Baker and Dwight Agner, edited by David Chambers. 117, [3] pp. Printed by W. & J. Mackay Ltd in an edition of 1,200 copies. Sewn and glued into orange-red card covers printed in black. £4.00 (£2.00). 1979.

B19 PRIVATE PRESS BOOKS 1977 by David Chambers, Peter Hoy, Dwight Agner, Geoffrey Farmer and Prue Chennells, edited by David Chambers. 116, [4] pp. Printed by W. S. Maney & Son Ltd in an edition of 1,200 copies. Sewn and glued into blue card covers printed in black. £6.00 (£4.00). 1980.

B20 PRIVATE PRESS BOOKS 1978 by David Chambers, Peter Hoy, Dwight Agner, Geoffrey Farmer and Prue Chennells, edited by David Chambers. 118, [2] pp. Printed by W. S. Maney & Son Ltd in an edition of 1,200 copies. Sewn and glued into yellow-brown card covers printed in black. £8.00 (£5.00). 1982.

B21 PRIVATE PRESS BOOKS 1979 by David Chambers, Peter Hoy, Dwight Agner, Geoffrey Farmer and Prue Chennells, edited by David Chambers and Kenneth Langford. 110, [4] pp. Printed by W. S. Maney & Son Ltd in an edition of 1,200 copies. Sewn and glued into green card covers printed in black. £10.00 (£6.00). 1984.

B22 PRIVATE PRESS BOOKS 1980 by David Chambers, Peter Hoy, James Birchfield, Geoffrey Farmer and Prue Chennells, edited by Philip Kerrigan. 144 pp. Printed by W. S. Maney & Son Ltd in an edition of 1,150 copies. Sewn and glued into brown card covers printed in dark brown. £12.00 (£7.00). 1986.
Includes a summary of the contents of the volumes for 1971–1980.

B23 PRIVATE PRESS BOOKS 1981–1984 by Peter Hoy, Prue Chennells, [Philip Kerrigan], J. Hill Hamon and Eric Swanick, edited by Philip Kerrigan. 235, [1] pp. Printed by W. S. Maney & Son Ltd in an edition of 1,000 copies. Sewn and glued into cream card covers printed in black or black and brown. £21.00 (£12.50). 1987.
This was the first multiple volume, of which several were issued over subsequent years in an attempt to catch up lost ground. The bibliographical structure of the entries was also somewhat simplified, in an attempt to make the gathering of information easier.

B24 PRIVATE PRESS BOOKS 1985–1986 by Peter Hoy, Prue Chennells, Philip Kerrigan, Eric Swanick and Arthur Goldsmith,

edited by Philip Kerrigan. 115, [1] pp + [1] folded colour plate. Printed by W. S. Maney & Son Ltd in an edition of 1,000 copies. Sewn and glued into pale brown card covers printed in black. £12.00 (£7.00). 1988.
The colour plate reproduces one of J. G. Lubbock's etchings from From the Snows to the Seas.

B25 PRIVATE PRESS BOOKS 1987 by Peter Hoy, Prue Chennells, Philip Kerrigan, Eric Swanick and Arthur Goldsmith, edited by Philip Kerrigan. 83, [1] pp. Printed by W. S. Maney & Son Ltd in an edition of 1,000 copies. Sewn and glued into orange card covers printed in black. £12.00 (£7.00). 1989.

B26 PRIVATE PRESS BOOKS 1988 by Peter Hoy, Prue Chennells, Philip Kerrigan, Eric Swanick and Arthur Goldsmith, edited by Philip Kerrigan. 99, [1] pp. Printed by W. S. Maney & Son Ltd in an edition of 1,000 copies. Sewn and glued into green card covers printed in black. £15.00 (£10.00). 1990.

B27 PRIVATE PRESS BOOKS 1989 by Peter Hoy, Prue Chennells, Philip Kerrigan, Eric Swanick and Arthur Goldsmith, edited by Philip Kerrigan. 72 pp. Printed by W. S. Maney & Son Ltd in an edition of 800 copies. Sewn and glued into pale blue card covers printed in black. £15.00 (£10.00). 1991.

B28 PRIVATE PRESS BOOKS 1990 by Peter Hoy, Prue Chennells, Philip Kerrigan, Eric Swanick and Arthur Goldsmith, edited by Philip Kerrigan. 101, [3] pp. Printed by W. S. Maney & Son Ltd in an edition of 600 copies. Sewn and glued into pink card covers printed in red. £20.00 (£13.50). 1992.
Includes a summary of the contents of the volumes for 1981–1990.

B29 PRIVATE PRESS BOOKS 1991 by Peter Hoy, Eric Swanick, Arthur Goldsmith, David Butcher, Claire Bolton and David Bolton, edited by Claire and David Bolton. 78, [2] pp. Printed by W. S. Maney & Son Ltd in an edition of 600 copies. Sewn and glued into pale grey card covers printed in dark brown. £20.00 (£10.00). 1993.

B30 PRIVATE PRESS BOOKS 1992–1993 by David Chambers, Eric Swanick, Arthur Goldsmith, David Butcher, Trevor Weston, Ken Mackenzie, John Pitt, Anthony Ward, Paul W. Nash and Margaret Lock, edited by David Chambers. 128 pp. Printed by the Bath Press in an edition of 600 copies. Sewn and glued into orange card covers printed in black. £10.00 (£5.00). 2002.
There were severe delays in publishing this volume, and that for 1994–1998 (the two appeared together), due to various disasters including the theft of a computer and the death of Peter Hoy.

B31 PRIVATE PRESS BOOKS 1994–1998 by Paul W. Nash, Margaret Lock and Arthur Goldsmith. 205, [3] pp. Printed by the Bath Press in an edition of 600 copies. Sewn and glued into pale green card covers printed in black. £20.00 (£10.00). 2002.
The Bath Press made a number of errors in printing this volume, resulting in the misplacing of several illustrations and of the lettering on the cover.

B32 PRIVATE PRESS BOOKS 1999 by Paul W. Nash, Margaret Lock and Asa Peavy. 96 pp. Printed by Henry Ling Ltd in an edition of 500 copies. Sewn and glued into green card covers printed in black. £10.00 (£5.00). 2004.
This and the two subsequent volumes were published together in 2004.

B33 PRIVATE PRESS BOOKS 2000 by Paul W. Nash, Margaret Lock and Asa Peavy. 95, [1] pp. Printed by Henry Ling Ltd in an edition of 500 copies. Sewn and glued into pale blue card covers printed in dark blue. £10.00 (£5.00). 2004.
Includes a summary of the contents of the volumes for 1991–2000.

B34 PRIVATE PRESS BOOKS 2001 by Paul W. Nash, Margaret Lock and Asa Peavy. 63, [1] pp. Printed by Henry Ling Ltd in an edition of 500 copies. Sewn and glued into blue card covers printed in black. £10.00 (£5.00). 2004.

Opposite: Specimen page from *Private Press Books 1992–1993*, 2002

I. M. IMPRIMIT

IAN MORTIMER, 219A VICTORIA PARK ROAD,
LONDON E9 7HD, ENGLAND.

Ornamented types, with an introduction by James Mosley. 25 ornamented alphabets by L. J. Pouchée.

45 pp. 20⅞ × 15⅛, introductory text in cloth boards and slipcase, + 52 sheets, 21 × 15, in a solander box. Text set in 11, 12 and 14 point Scotch Roman. 210 copies printed in black on Zerkall mould-made paper on Albion and Columbian presses (illustrations) and a Stephenson Blake proofing press (introduction). Bound by The Fine Bindery in black buckram, with paper labels printed in black. 200 copies for sale, price £1650.00, since increased to £1950.00. 1993.

Winner of the Premio Felice Feliciano, 1995. 92–3.151

Initial from ORNAMENTED TYPES (I. M. Imprimit)

INANNA PRESS

MAUREEN CUMMINS, 432 E 13TH STREET, APT 20,
NEW YORK, NEW YORK 10009, U.S.A.

Song of songs. With 11 double-page hand-coloured wood-block prints, decorative dedication, colophon, and title-pages, by Maureen Cummins.

29pp. 9 × 11. Text set in 14 point Kennerley bold. 25 copies printed on Lana laid paper, on a Vandercook SP20 press. Bound accordion-style in cloth, price $400.00. 1990. 92–3.152

APPENDIX C

SOCIETY OF
PRIVATE PRINTERS

David Chambers

The PLA Society of Private Printers was started in 1960 and there have so far been five Exchanges and a small Bibliographical & Typographical Appetizer for 1963. *For the first two Exchanges members sent their pieces of printing to others in the group. For subsequent Exchanges the pamphlets were sent to Pinner and boxed sets were distributed when the final contributions had been received.*

C1 FIRST EXCHANGE. 22 pamphlets. Exchanged between members. 1960–1964.
Bibliography or typography. Adagio, Allenholme, Battle, Between Hours, Cave, Cog, Cuckoo Hill, Garamond, Gogmagog, Grove, Herity, Juniper, Karuba, Keepsake, Laverock, Merrythought, Pandora, Pardoe, Piccolo, Power, Signet and Squires Presses.

C2 BIBLIOGRAPHICAL & TYPOGRAPHICAL APPETIZER FOR 1963. Eight leaflets. 164 × 95 mm. Green card folder with label on spine. 1963.
Typographic themes. Allenholme, Cuckoo Hill, Garamond, Laverock (pamphlet and title-leaf), Merrythought, Pardoe, and Stilt Presses. Intended to have been ready (but in fact too late) for a dinner in London for members of the Society.

C3 SECOND EXCHANGE. 24 pamphlets. Exchanged between members. 1965–1969.
New or unhackneyed verse. Adagio, Battle, Black Knight, Crabgrass, Cuckoo Hill, Elefante, Garamond, Gazebo, Gogmagog, Grian-aig, Invicta, Keepsake, Magpie, Martlet, Merrythought, Nightowl, Pandora, Pardoe, Piccolo, Plough, Tabard, Taurus, and Yellow Kid (two pamphlets) Presses.

C4 THIRD EXCHANGE. 27 folders/pamphlets. 127 × 89 mm. In a blue card chemise and pale grey paper covered box. 50 copies. £15.00. 1974–1976.
'*A Display of Presses*'. *Pressmarks and photographs from Adagio, Biscuit City, Black Knight, Bookhaven, Cog, Crabgrass, Cracked Bell, Cuckoo Hill (plus title/contents folder), Eilertson, Gogmagog, Happy Dragons, I. M. Imprimit, Invicta, Keepsake, Kit-Cat, Laverock, Narbulla, Plain Wrapper, Plough, Proverbial, Pump, Quarto, Quoin, Rosemary, Scarlet Ibis, and Taurus Presses. Issued October 1977.*

C5 FOURTH EXCHANGE. 31 pamphlets. 115 × 64 mm. In a wooden box with sliding front with wood-engraving by Pam Reuter. 70 copies. £80.00. 1975–1980.
An 'Infant's Library'. Biscuit City, In de Bonnefant, Brandywine, Cherub, Crabgrass, Cracked Bell, Cuckoo Hill (plus introductory pamphlet), Gogmagog, Golden Key, Happy Dragons, Invicta, Keepsake, Laverock, Narbulla, Pardoe, Perdix, Perhaps, Plough, P'Nye, Priapus, Proverbial, Pump, Quarto, Scarlet Ibis, Septentrio, Slow Camel, Stilt, Stockham, All'Insegna della Tarasca, and Typographeum Presses. Brian Alderson contributed an essay on Infants' Libraries, which was included in the introductory pamphlet. A detailed note appeared in The Private Library, *Spring 1983 (third series, vol. 6, no. 1).*

C6 FIFTH EXCHANGE. 28 pamphlets + title/contents leaf. 164 × 101 mm. In a brown cloth-covered chemise and slipcase, with yellow paper label printed in brown on the front. 125 copies. £50.00. 1982–1986.
'*Chap-books*'. *Adagio, Alembic, Boetharson, Brandywine, Bullnettle, Cadenza, Cobtree, Contre Coup, Cracked Bell, Cuckoo Hill (plus title/contents leaf), Feathered Serpent, Golden Key, Keepsake, Old Stile, Perdix, Perhaps, Plough, P'Nye, Proverbial, Pump, Recalcitrant, Rocket, Scarlet Ibis, Septentrio, Sesame, Set and Forget, Studio d'Arte Tipographica, and Typographeum Presses.*

MEMBERS'
COLLECTIONS

Lynne Brindley

Chief Executive, The British Library,
Hon. President, Private Libraries Association

The British Library is the national library of the United Kingdom and, as such, it exists to support anyone with a need to use its research collections. With our close involvement in the UK library network and our deep commitment to serve the nation as a whole, it may seem surprising to write about the British Library in the context of the Private Libraries Association. But this is not a real contradiction.

Lynne Brindley

As the national library we are here for everyone. Anyone needing to use our collections can do so, and it is perhaps the services we provide through our reading rooms that people first think of in connection with the British Library. However, our flagship St Pancras building is one of the great public spaces of London, with its free exhibitions, public events and literary talks in our conference centre, educational activities for schools, and much else all aimed at introducing a wide public to the collections which we hold on behalf of the nation and the world. We also reach a wide audience on the web, nationally and internationally, where millions have taken up the opportunities that we offer. For instance, you can consult full digital facsimiles of some of our treasures, Caxton's two editions of *The Canterbury Tales,* or our collection of the pre-Civil War quarto editions of Shakespeare's plays. Or you can leaf through selected pages of the Sherbourne Missal.

Our core users are of course researchers (understood in the widest sense of the word), and they too are served both on site and through our website.

The British Library's provisions for researchers have been much enhanced in recent years through our constantly developing position in the network of library provision for UK based researchers. The number of activities is large and I will mention here only a few. We work closely with the Consortium of University and Research Libraries in the British Isles (CURL), and our catalogue is now also available through COPAC, a union catalogue which provides free access to the merged online catalogues of CURL members. The Arts and Humanities Research Council, AHRC, has funded, through a cooperation with Warwick University, the digitisation and web site devoted to over 200 of our collection of Renaissance festival books. On a much larger scale, the Joint Information Systems Committee (JISC) has funded the digitisation of two million pages of nineteenth-century newspapers and 4,000 hours of recorded sound.

However, under the surface, behind our integrated catalogue, one finds an astonishing complexity, variety, and depth. This is one of the reasons why, even with its reputation as one of the world's great national libraries, the British Library continues to surprise our users (and sometimes even ourselves), with the richness of its collections. An important reason why our collections have this depth is that – in addition to the research collections that we and our predecessors have collected, and in addition to the material which we receive as a result of the legal deposit legislation – the British Library is also a collection of collections. The most important ones are listed and briefly described on our website. Some are very extensive, some very small, but all add to our ability to document the complexity of the world around us. All are, in their very different ways, also social documents in their own right. They tell us about the interests, fashions, intellectual movements, and political or religious attitudes through the 250 years or so in which the oldest of our component institutions has existed, namely the British Museum Library.

The foundation of the Library's collection began with a great private library, that of Sir Hans Sloane, which was bought for the nation from his executors in 1753. Sloane, a physician, collected – naturally – medical and botanical books (botany still being part of medicine), and science books more generally. However, his collection was in the eighteenth-century encyclopaedic mould, and is really universal in its aim. The Museum did not keep his books separate; as other collections were acquired they were added to his, and Sloane's printed books have to some extent become dispersed amongst other collections acquired later. Many volumes were sold during the Museum's sales of duplicate books during the late eighteenth and early nineteenth centuries; others were rebound and no longer bear any marks of ownership. But, in conjunction with his own manuscript catalogue, a variety of identifying marks can be used to determine a Sloane provenance, including manuscript annotations, paper labels, and the use of a special British Museum library-stamp. We estimate that some 30,000 printed volumes, formerly in the library of Sir Hans Sloane, are in the British Library today. As a piece of long-term research, one of my colleagues, Alison Walker, is compiling a database of books which can be shown to have been part of Sloane's magnificent private library.

The Reverend Clayton Mordaunt Cracherode (1730–1799) was as characteristic of the eighteenth-century as Sloane, but of a completely different nature. While Sloane's library was vast and universal – the creation of a successful physician – Cracherode's was the select bibliophile collection of a man who lived in great comfort from the income of a sinecure. A sinecure suited him, for he was not enterprising by nature; his longest journey was from Oxford to London. His collection is a fine example of the taste of the wealthy private collector of the last decades of the eighteenth century. The authors were chiefly the classical authors, and the editions were the earliest editions and Aldines, and notably most often in copies with fine bindings, wide clean margins or printed on vellum, in copies which resonate with the names of great collectors of the preceding centuries.

Cracherode bequeathed to the British Museum his collection

of some 4,500 volumes of these fine books, which he had partly chosen to buy because they were not represented in the Museum's Library. This was the first major donation that can be said to represent the bibliophile approach to collecting that was so prevalent among aristocrats and the very rich bourgeoisie during the period of bibliomania. Our greatest eighteenth-century collection, that of George III, was much more of a tool for the improvement of the King's enlightened monarchy than the creation of the tasteful connoisseur. He had a practical aim, to enable his nation to make economic, social and moral progress.

Although George III was a monarch, the King's Library qualifies as a private library, for it was created at his own initiative and it was all financed from the privy purse. He began collecting when he was still Prince of Wales, and the collection of course grew faster when he became king. In the 1770s he spent over £2,000 a year on books. To put that sum of money into perspective: in the same years the Bodleian Library in Oxford had an annual book buying budget of ten pounds. When George III died in 1820 his collection contained 65,000 volumes and 19,000 unbound pamphlets. No other individual, whether private or royal, had collected such a large library. In 1823 it was offered to the nation by George IV, whose ambitions were less intellectual, on the condition that it was 'kept entire and separate in a repository to be appropriated exclusively for that purpose'. This is a promise which we have kept and this private library is now at the core of our public institution. The books are housed in the King's Tower, the visual centre point of our building in St Pancras – a stunning sight for the first-time visitor as well as for the seasoned user who perhaps knows well what is behind the glass walls of the tower. For like all our formerly private collections, this is very much part of our working library; the books from the King's Library are in heavy demand in our rare books reading room. George would have been pleased to know that his library still serves to achieve his enlightenment ambitions.

A striking contrast to the collection of George III is the highly specialised private library which was created by Henry Evanion (1832?–1905), the conjuror and ventriloquist. It contains some 5,000 pamphlets, handbills, posters, trade cards and miscellaneous printed matter relating to theatres, fairs, etc. dating from around 1800 to 1895. The collection is also fascinating because it represents a wide variety of reproduction methods, much of the material being printed in colour, using the growing number of techniques which were available during the nineteenth century. It was acquired in 1895 and we must be very grateful to our predecessors who had the foresight to acquire the collection. This sort of printing was ephemeral from the point of view of its producers but not from the point of view of the scholar. Evanion's collection of ephemera is an invaluable source for the study of popular culture, of the theatre, and of entertainment in Victorian Britain, especially London. The collection is now catalogued, digitised and (since this summer) available on the British Library's website. Printing which emanates from beyond the mainstream publishing world is difficult for an established institution to collect itself – here we are utterly dependent on private collectors and their generosity. This is no less true today than it was a hundred years ago.

I began by mentioning the vast private library of Hans Sloane, the beginning of the Library. Let me end with a private library which we have more recently received. We have, under the shelfmark Bloomfield 1–297, a collection of over 300 printed books relating to the poet Robert Bloomfield (1766–1823), including many early editions of his works. The collection was formed by Barry Bloomfield, a collateral descendent of Robert, and it was donated by Valerie Bloomfield, Barry's wife, in 2002, whom I had the pleasure of meeting briefly after the event which marked the completion of the cataloguing of the collection. I knew Barry well so this was a very special donation for me as well as for the British Library. To the wider rare books world, Barry Bloomfield is perhaps best known as the editor of *A Directory of Rare Books and Special Collections*. But as most readers of this volume will know, he was a professional librarian; he retired in 1990 as Director of Collection Development at the British Library and held numerous honorary positions, not least President of the Private Libraries Association. It is a great pleasure for me that the British Library and the Private Libraries Association can continue this close relationship, bridging with ease the apparent divide between private and public collections.

With thanks to Kristian Jensen
for his substantial contribution to this article.

Brian Alderson
(Photograph Geneviève Larose)

Brian Alderson

Riffling through the Strata

How I envy those strong-willed persons whose self-denying ordinances permit them to collect books only within carefully-drawn limits – pre-1611 Bibles, say, or the works of H. E. Bates.[1] The depth of such collections notably offers the opportunity for profound insights into texts and the nature of their transmission.

In this household, I am afraid, things are very differently ordered (or rather disordered). There are indeed present a large number of books but they do not form a collection so much as a series of bibliographic strata which have suffered various seismic shifts and now exist in barely analysable confusion. They owe their origins to no inherited weakness or baneful influence but seem to have come into being through some natural quirk. Thus, a childhood passion for model railways bred a desire to own books on the subject and I still remember the joy with which – in the teeth of wartime constraints – I collected Basset-Lowke's *Model Railway Handbook* from W. H. Smith's in Palmers Green. But I had no funds to expand on so small a beginning and had to rely mainly on works borrowed from the public library.

By school-leaving time, cricket had taken over as a more promising subject for collecting (and still exists as such in an offhand way) but I was put off by all the ghost-writing that went on and anyway was soon fixated upon less boyish matters: twentieth century poetry, and – separately – the history of printing, which was somehow conjoined to a discovery of the publishing activities of William Pickering. (That began – I can date it precisely – on 31 October 1950 when I bought his edition of the translation of the *Novum Organum* [Keynes, starred, p. 51] for a shilling off a market stall.)

Books within those categories remain with me and occasionally there is some augmentation: Pound's *Personae* of 1909 not long ago and the Pickering *Hunting Songs and Ballads* (1846) bought defiantly on the day when fox-hunting was banned in Scotland. As you will remark though, this is already heterogeneous collecting and it became more so by what turned out to be a rather obsessive pursuit of children's books and (as frequently yoked together by the trade) illustrated books and reference works on their production and publication. This emerged almost accidentally through professional work as lecturer, translator, reviewer and editor and it was stimulated by the realisation of how neglected – and how demanding – is the bibliographic study of children's books.

That topic will not bear enlargement here, but my belief that children's books owe their being, and most of their character, to publishers rather than to their named creators handily justifies the collecting of secondary as well as primary sources. The trouble is, though, that two-and-a-half-centuries-worth of books pose problems of selection for the acquisitive student (exacerbated by a side-interest in German and American children's books) for one can find an excuse for buying almost anything. As a result heterogeneity is redoubled, although I have tried to impose certain purposes on 'the collection' by concentrating on areas within the subject that shed light on publishing practices: treatment of the work of individual illustrators, the chronological study of particular works (one day *The Private Library* will be offered a barmy survey of the illustrated editions of *The Water Babies*), folktales and the vagaries of their transmission to children, and the output of specific publishers.

Nevertheless, I am frequently seduced away from these defined projects by meeting treasures unknown to history that renew my sense of wonderment at our ramifying ignorance of the subject. What more satisfying than to bring in to the uncoordinated muddle such things as Thomas Bodkin's nowhere-noticed *Guide to Caper* (1929) illustrated by Denis Eden (his drawings advertised for sale on the penultimate leaf) – a drily comic account of the land of the Ursors – or the recently-acquired *Beauties of Shakespeare* whose sixteen all-engraved leaves of (pretty dreadful) limericks precede Edward Lear by about twenty years?

Richmond, North Riding of Yorkshire

1. Selection of those two examples is inspired by articles in *The Private Library* by Naseeb Shaheem (Summer 2003) and Richard Holroyd (Spring 2005).

BRIAN ALDERSON

John Allison

There always seemed to have been books around. As a small child I can remember a glass fronted bookcase, made by my father, with books in it – to be looked at but not handled.

Then there were the libraries, both at school and public, to explore.

Even when working in the middle of Africa in the early fifties, I managed to find a book club which would send me books although they sometimes took a very long time to arrive.

It was whilst I was at Art College in the mid fifties that I became seriously interested in collecting. The college had a wonderful library and I became fascinated with books illustrated with wood-engravings. I also became interested in bookbinding, but more about that later.

I joined the Readers Union, for apart from the usual monthly offerings they also issued some rather splendid 'specials' such as 'The National Gallery'. The Folio Society, which for a few years I belonged to, also produced very good editions as indeed they still do.

Visiting second-hand book shops is a wonderful experience. On family holidays around the country there always seemed to be a bookshop – often tucked away in the back streets – to provide added enjoyment and occasionally a 'good find'. Many happy hours have been spent with my very good friend, the late David Gould, visiting bookshops and book fairs.

In the early seventies and now working in London, as a form of relaxation, I took up bookbinding again on an evening course at the London College and stayed doing bookbinding for the next twenty odd years or so. There I met Frank Broomhead doing the same thing and we became friends. It was he who introduced me to the Private Libraries Association and thus opened up new fields to explore. I was shortly afterwards elected to the Council of the PLA and became its Hon. Membership Secretary in 1978, a job I am still doing.

My collecting interests are very catholic and fairly modest. I spent a good few years collecting the complete run of the Satur-

John Allison

day Books. These annual books, edited at first by Leonard Russell and later by John Hadfield, were beautifully designed and produced and one can always pull a volume off the shelves and find it full of interest on all sorts of subjects and topics.

Being interested in book production I managed to collect the complete set of the 'Dent Memorial Lectures'. The books in this delightful little series were extremely well printed and bound.

As a Yorkshire man I do have quite a collection of books on Yorkshire, with some oddities such as 'Yorksher Puddin', the dialect writings of John Hartley, 1876. One of the most interesting collections in my Yorkshire section are the books illustrated by Marie Hartley. These books produced in collaboration with, firstly Ella Pontefract and later with Joan Ingilby are wonderfully evocative of rural Yorkshire from the 1930s.

Books illustrated with wood-engravings are one of my passions especially those with wood-engravings by Robert Gibbings, who is my favourite wood-engraver as well as a superb writer. He ran the Golden Cockerel Press in what I consider its finest period. But I just collect what interests me.

Being a bookbinder – I took up bookbinding full time when I managed to arrange early retirement, and did the full time course at the London College of Printing – I have quite a collection of books on this ancient, fascinating and satisfying craft.

Do I have a favourite book? Well not really, I have lots of 'favourite' books, but one which I treasure is *Bookbinding and the Care of Books* by Douglas Cockerell, published by John Hogg in 1901. It is still in print you may say?, 'ah', but my copy is inscribed by Douglas Cockerell to his brother Sydney Cockerell, one time secretary to William Morris, and dated Nov 1st 1901, which makes it rather special.

The trouble with collecting books is that they take up space, lots of it, but I can't imagine life without books.

Dudbridge, Stroud, Glos.

Iain Bain

Diverse paths to Bewick and beyond . . .

Although there may be eleven to twelve thousand books about the house, only a tenth of them have been assembled with any firm intent to build a coherent 'collection' by theme or subject. For the most part they occupy one large space known to us as 'the book room' – library being too formal a word for such a haphazard accumulation of sixty years. Systematic and spacious arrangement is hardly possible and although a certain order prevails the calm serenity conveyed in the photographs in books such as Alan Powers's *Living with Books* seems unreal. Where in these are the piles on the floor, where are the books flagged with markers, the projecting quartos creating extra perching space for new acquisitions or for pictures, the signs of constant activity and use?

The home of my youth was the main influence and I was lucky enough to have access to books of every sort, ancient and modern. A family bible printed by Baskerville, an Aldine Cicero, and John Johnson's *Typographia* of 1824 were probably strong influences in my later involvement in printing and typography. Likewise a number of small elegantly produced editions of the eighteenth-century poets published by John Sharpe of Piccadilly and an 1821 set of Greig's *County Excursions* were eventually to provoke an enthusiasm for the printers and publishers of the Regency. The greater part of Sharpe's output has a space to itself, a number in the elegant morocco dress of his later neighbour, the binder Charles Lewis, and most printed by Charles Whittingham the elder, founder of the Chiswick Press. It was the availability and reasonable prices of early nineteenth-century books in the fifties and sixties in the shops of Marks & Co., George Suckling, Stanley Crowe, and H. M. Fletcher in London, and Sanders of Oxford, and Heap of Wells, that encouraged their acquisition. Once aware of the archive of the Chiswick Press my knowledge of production and costs was greatly enriched and the search for printing plates and original illustrations led to the wider enthusiasms already described in *The Private Library* (Summer 1998). Alas the heady days of forty years ago have long gone and although there are still gaps to fill, new acquisitions are rare indeed.

Iain Bain

Thomas Bewick the Newcastle wood-engraver is another subject on which I have concentrated, but then never to the extent of
acquiring every known edition of a title. Original drawings, wood
blocks, copper plates, manuscripts and memorabilia have added
greater interest than an obsession with variants. Bewick's friendship with the Shropshire naturalist John Dovaston has led to the
acquisition of a number of Dovaston's manuscripts and scrap
books, first among them being his Tour Journal of 1825 which
describes his journeys in Scotland and his visit to Bewick in
Newcastle. Books on the history and topography of Newcastle
and Northumberland provide background to Bewick's life and
times, and I cherish particularly the folio commonplace book of
John Bell, the Newcastle bookseller and land surveyor (1783–
1864).

For the rest I have much nineteenth-century biography; art history; printing and publishing history; typography; engraving – Papillon in particular; early printing manuals – Luckombe, Hansard, Bosse, Berthiaud; track and field athletics; folk music of Scotland and Northumberland; poetry; and photography. Collected letters of Samuel Johnson, Burns, Garrick, Wordsworth, Tom Moore, Byron, Smollett, Clare, Stevenson, Fitzgerald, Charles and Mary Lamb, Blake, Turner, William Morris and many others delight my interest in their lives and times and provide stimulus for my labours on the correspondence of Bewick.

Scotland and its history occupies several long runs of shelving: here the remarkable works of Hugh Miller, the Cromarty stone mason and geologist, are much prized. (Cromarty was the home of my father and several generations of his seafaring forbears). Books on the history of highland piping and collections of early pipe music feed an active interest in the instrument and here Patrick McDonald's rare account and collection of Highland music of 1784 holds pride of place. This particular copy had been given to Bewick when he visited Edinburgh in 1823. Another fine collection, the dance music of the great Scottish fiddler Neil Gow, came to me on a visit to America; by happy coincidence its front board label shows that it once belonged to an Edinburgh forbear of my mother.

Missed opportunities and books sold continue to haunt me. Although I have important odd volumes, how did I manage to fail on a complete run of Sir John Sinclair's wonderful *Statistical Account of Scotland* (1791–99)? and what possessed me to part with the *Nonesuch Century*, Macklin's massive seven-volume Bible in blue morocco – printed by Bensley, a grangerised copy of Dibdin's *Bibliomania* and Shepherd's *Metropolitan Improvements* complete, in wrappers? A modest group of early nineteenth-century watercolours has stimulated an interest in the drawing manuals of the period, and although those of David Cox (1814), Francis Nicholson (1823), J. D. Harding (1850) and a few others, have come to hand, what opportunities there were in the fifties – foolishly ignored. Less myopic at times, I made good stores of prints from Turner's *Liber Studiorum*, Daniell's *A Voyage Round Great Britain* and Constable's *English Landscape Scenery*, though the memory of a complete set of the latter, in wrappers and touched by the artist, still haunts me. Etchings of Samual Palmer and William Strang, and drawings by that remarkable draughtsman Charles Keene rank among my special treasures.

Topographical guides, road books and maps have always intrigued me, and the Marquis of Stafford's copy of Paterson's *British Itinerary* (1785) is an unhappy reminder of his family's fearful part in the Highland clearances. Of more recent times, a full set of the Ordnance Survey's one-inch maps of Scotland (1945) on cloth, dissected, was a particularly happy find.

Long rows of periodicals are an uneasy reminder of Time's Wingèd Chariot, but complete runs of *The Private Library*, *The Book Collector*, *Matrix*, forty years' worth of *The Library*, and thirty of *Piping Times*, so greatly continue to surprise with their usefulness that weeding out cannot be contemplated. A rolling press with many copper and steel plates and a small folio Albion letterpress with attendant type and equipment take up a good deal of room, but their departure to make space would be beyond reason.

What of the future? As the shades lengthen, the dilemma faced by all of us who cherish books weighs heavily – to disperse or keep together by bequest? But for the moment 'Why look upon futurity, darkening present joy?'

Hertfordshire

'I am glad you are alive & well enough to scold . . .'
Part of a letter to Bewick from his printer Edward Walker in 1826,
written on the back of a proofed engraving

Bob Bartlett

Selborne and Other Places

I became a member of the Association more than forty years ago after responding to an advertisement in *The Observer* inviting applications from those who collected, studied or produced books, and also those who derived pleasure and satisfaction from simply owning and handling books. I definitely fell into the latter category, for although I had acquired a number of books on topics which interested me, purposeful collecting came later.

I had been collecting county maps for some time and this led me to books on topography which included maps. When this in turn led to local histories, I came by chance across Francis Brett Young's *Portrait of a Village* and Joan Hassall's wood-engravings. I started collecting other books with Hassall illustrations and was delighted when David Chambers proposed to produce a bibliography of her work as one of the Association's publications. He called for additions and amendments to a tentative listing in the *Newsletter* and I was able to provide one or two minor suggestions. It remains a major disappointment to me that I missed the meeting when Joan talked to the Association about her work.

My other main collecting interest has been Gilbert White's *The Natural History and Antiquities of Selborne* and this again started by chance. I had read the book and visited Selborne and decided I wanted an illustrated copy. Two booksellers' catalogues turned up in the same post and both included illustrated copies of *Selborne* in different editions. Which one to choose? Assuming that one or the other would already be sold, I ordered both – and both subsequently arrived. Unable to decide which to keep, I kept both and so started off my collection which now includes examples of most of the numerous editions published (but not all of the variant printings).

Some years ago, one of the Association's meetings was addressed by Ian Lyle who had produced a checklist of *Selborne* editions. He had most of these in his collection but mentioned that he had not been able to get hold of a decent copy of the Nonesuch edition of 1938 with illustrations by Eric Ravilious, said to be the most desirable and most sought after edition. I could sympathise

Bob Bartlett

since I was also lacking this item but a short time later I came across it in a bookseller's catalogue, not in the 'Natural History' section where *Selborne* is usually found but among the 'Illustrated Books'. This catalogue arrived one day when I was not feeling well and I did not look at it until the following morning, a Sunday, when still feeling slightly fragile, I browsed through it in a rather half-hearted way. When I found the *Selborne* listed, any residual weakness dropped away and I was on the phone expecting at best to get an answering machine. The cure was completed when a human voice answered and said it was still available. I have since seen it at bookfairs on two occasions, satisfyingly at prices somewhat higher than I paid.

Over the years, I have collected in other areas such as travel in Britain, from Leyland's *Itinerary* through to Cobbett's *Rural Rides* and beyond, taking in Defoe's *Tours thro' the Whole of Great Britain* and Byng's *Torrington Diaries* (all, I must add, in early twentieth century editions, but with a bonus in the case of Cobbett, edited by G. D. H. and M. Cole, in the form of having 'Numerous Vignettes by John Nash'). I have copies of all the books by J. J. Hissey on his tours around England from 1884 up to 1917, and on one occasion appealed for information on this author through the 'Bibliographical Questions and Answers' section of the PLA Newsletter'. I had one reply so this is clearly a subject of minority interest (but I was pleased to have seen a complete collection of the books, sumptuously bound, in the library of one of our stately homes).

I have also collected books on the history of chemistry, my professional subject up to about thirty years ago, and on Samuel Johnson, an (earlier) fellow citizen of my home town, Lichfield, but only in a fairly casual way. Indeed, most of my collecting has been casual, perhaps 'slightly disconnected' would be a better description; the definition of a dilettante as 'one who studies without seriousness' certainly applies in my case. In other words, my book collecting has been fun, and still is, but has been slowing down in recent years and is going into reverse gear as I have started to dispose of some of my collection – my wife would say 'not before time' as our small house has been in danger of being overwhelmed. But it is going to be a wrench; books which at first appear to be disposable become increasingly attractive when taken from the shelf. It is going to take an effort not to put them back again. All members have benefited from the Association's publications; those living in the London area have been fortunate in being able to attend the meetings when a variety of speakers have addressed us on aspects of 'the book' which I, at any rate, have found interesting, informative and entertaining. Some of us will remember with great pleasure our once annual visits to 'Lilies',

BOB BARTLETT

the country home / bookshop of the late Peter Eaton, and especially the delicious teas provided by Mrs Eaton. I have never taken part in running the Association but I shall be forever grateful for those more active and enthusiastic members who by their keenness and dedication have kept it going for the past fifty years. Long may they continue the good work!

East Molesey, Surrey

'The Common Swallow' wood-engraving from
The Natural History and Antiquities of Selborne,
Bohn's Illustrated Library, 1854

J. S. F. Botha

Collecting – East and West

During sixty years and more as a dedicated lover of books and book history, my collecting interests covered various fields. It probably started with my youthful exposure to the annual nineteenth century Almanacs and Directories of the Cape of Good Hope. Among the books I grew up with, several odd volumes had come down in the family from earlier generations. The bald recital of facts, events and personalities of earlier times chronicled so precisely in these volumes was a constant source of fascination to me. My endeavours to add to the few volumes I had appropriated from the family shelves led me to ransack the attics of friends and relatives who seemed glad to find a home for unwanted books. My ambition was to collect all of the hundred annuals published in the nineteenth century. Alas, I was fooled by my small early success. I soon discovered that these were prized items in the bibliophilic field. Others, older and wiser than I, had been around before me and sources had dried up. Over the years I managed to fill only a few gaps. Nevertheless, there they stand on my shelves today, seventy years later – gaps and all – a gentle reminder of youthful enthusiasm, yet often used for reference and a jog to failing memory.

My itinerant life in the diplomatic service took me to other shores and other interests. Eight years in Tokyo exposed me to traditional Japanese bookbinding and to the delight of the traditional Japanese woodblock print, *Ukiyoe*. My collecting interest focussed on the eighteenth and nineteenth century illustrated Japanese storybooks – *kusasoshi*. Popular subjects were Japanese legends, historical romances, *The Tales of Genji* and poetry. Outwardly, these books of some 200 pages may look like undistinguished, somewhat drab paperbacks but, once opened, they reveal a wonderland of text and illustration intermixed. They were printed entirely from hand-carved woodblocks, the text in graceful cursive characters – referred to by some Japanese as '*grass writing*'. In addition to the illustrations in black on the textual pages, ten or more original polychrome *Ukiyoe* in six or seven colours are bound in as extra illustrations. Well-known artists of the period like Toyokuni Utagawa (1769–1825) and Kunisada (1786–1864) are among those whose names appear in the storybooks I bought in the excellent bookshops in the Kanda district of Tokyo.

Frikkie Botha

These storybooks were made quite unlike what we in the west are accustomed to. In woodblock printing, the sheet of paper with the manuscript text and illustrations is pasted face down on a block of wood. The paper is then oiled so that the text and illustrations can be clearly seen by the craftsman carver. The finished carved block is then inked and a sheet of paper laid on it and pressed with a thick pad. Since the paper is thin and absorbent, it is printed only on one side. The sheet is then folded to form two pages with a hollow unprinted area inside. A stack of these 'doubled' pages are then bound in what is known as a 'pouch' binding. The cut end is stitched and forms the spine while the folded edges become the fore-edge of the book. Bound Japanese style, the spine lies to the right and the fore-edge to the left.

During the sixteen years I spent in the United States between 1949 and 1975, I focussed on collecting books with significant South African content published in the USA. Traditionally American interest in South Africa has been sporadic and short-lived, a tendency reflected in the paucity of American imprints on this field, probably not more than 400 titles in the nineteenth century. These include many books reprinted from British imprints and applied especially to early exploration and missionary accounts, which found eager publishers in New York, Philadelphia and Boston such as Harpers, Dutton and Lippincott. Early American missionaries Lewis Grout, Josiah Tyler and William Taylor are among the few whose books on South Africa were first published in the USA. For the rest, and until the end of the century, South Africa featured mainly in the accounts of American travellers who touched on these shores. Prominent examples are *Narrative of Commodore Perry's Expedition of an American Squadron to the China Seas and Japan* (New York, 1856); and *Voyage of the United States Frigate, Potomac* by J. N. Reynolds (Harper, New York, 1835).

The discovery of diamonds and gold and the Anglo-Boer War late in the nineteenth century attracted many Americans to South Africa. Their participation in the mining activities, the Jameson Raid and the Anglo-Boer War produced a relative avalanche of books published widely all over the United States. Other prominent American visitors published their experiences in South Africa: Mark Twain in *Following the Equator* (Hartford, 1897) and the intrepid seafarer, Captain Joshua Slocum, in *Sailing Around the World Alone* (New York, 1899).

Olive Schreiner, the South African author of *The Story of an African Farm,* had by the 1890s already established a name for herself in the United States. Her books were widely published by various American publishers well into the twentieth century and her *Woman and Labour* (New York, Frederick A. Stokes, 1911) was listed as a Best Seller in the United States, making her the first South African ever to achieve that distinction.

The largest book and the smallest books relating to South Africa deserve special mention. The largest, an oblong folio, is *The War in South Africa: A Narrative of the Anglo-Boer War from the Beginning of Hostilities to the Fall of Pretoria* by

Captain Arthur T. Mahan, the American naval historian, author of *The Influence of Sea Power on History*. First published in 1900 by Collier, New York, it appeared in three editions, each new edition augmented with additional text as the war progressed. All were quite sumptuous volumes, profusely illustrated with many photographs, maps and illustrations. Eighteen full-page colour plates were specially commissioned paintings by well-known artists. One of them is by Frederic Remington the American artist, famous for his paintings and sculptures of the American West. He painted a very dramatic action scene from an impression he got from a photograph!

Unlike Mahan and Remington, both of whom had already achieved fame when their works were published, the author of the smallest book was only to achieve fame fifty years after the appearance of his own book. The reason for this is that the author, Alan Welsh Dulles, was only eight years old when he wrote *The Boer War: A History* (Washington, D.C., 1902). Forty years later Alan Dulles was to achieve international prominence for his activities in the OAS in World War II and as head of the American Central Intelligence Agency.

The booklet arose from his constant youthful exposure to the intellectual discussion of international affairs among prominent American public figures, many of whom were close relatives. His grandfather John Watson Foster (1836–1917) had been Secretary of State; another relation Robert Lansing (1864–1928) and his own older brother, John Foster Dulles (1888–1959) were to become Secretaries of State. The events unfolding in South Africa made up a large part of what he heard discussed at home. While the views of the older generation tended to be either strictly neutral or pro-British, the young master Dulles had pro-Boer sympathies. He sought to convey these in the 31 pages of his small booklet. His parents were impressed with his efforts and had the booklet published and sold in aid of Boer charities. The booklet was reprinted five times in 1902 and again since then. The latest is a facsimile reprint in 2002 by Alice Gertrud and Hans Rudolf Bosch-Gwalter of Zurich, Switzerland, and is dedicated to the author of this article in whose library they were first introduced to the booklet. In a conversation I had with Dulles in 1952, he was quite modest – even apologetic – about his naïve youthful venture.

Because of their interesting American provenance, I mention two association copies published elsewhere: *The Letters of Lady Anne Barnard from the Cape of Good Hope (1795–1801)* inscribed in ink on the half-title 'W T Watts-Dunton from A C Swinburne, May 10th, 1901', with the *ex libris* of Jerome Kern in gilt on green morocco pasted inside the upper cover; and *The Journal of a Visit to South Africa in 1815 & 1816* by C. I. Latrobe who inscribed it 'To Benj. Henry Latrobe by the author'. Benjamin Henry Latrobe, brother of the author, was the Architect of the Capitol in Washington at the time.

The North American collection helped me to compile a bibliography on the subject, published in 1977. Among the other rewards, indeed pleasures, of collecting these and other books, are the valued friendships formed with book-dealers in many countries.

Constantia, Cape Town

'Pentaceros Capensis, native of Cap [*sic*] of Good Hope',
copper-engraving from *The Naturalist's Library, Ichthyology,*
edited by William Jardine, *c.* 1840

J. S. F. BOTHA

Stan Brett

My first job was that of an assistant in a public library, and something of the philosophy and atmosphere of those years have remained in my mind, in particular the pleasure and satisfaction felt by bringing the book to the person who needs or wants it for what it is and what it can do. I was in the Army throughout the War, did a lot of instructing in which books had no place, and still have the Palgrave I carried in my pack (Oxford World's Classic with *Omar Khayyam* in it).

On demobilisation I returned to my library, and had the job of finding homes for hundreds of books which had been donated to help the war effort, but which the librarian couldn't bear to send for pulp without examination, for which he had no time. A stint at Library School led to a number of jobs, and eventually to teaching future librarians the elements of historical bibliography.

It was all about the Book and communicating something of the fascination of setting a text and printing it, or collating an eighteenth century duodecimo, or exploring the mechanism of a cancel. At some time Gilbert White's *Natural History of Selborne* seemed an ideal book to collect to illustrate publishing and printing practices since its publication in 1789, and whose bicentenary might be commemorated with a scholarly bibliography.

Alas, such ambitions came to little and years ago the file of slips was dumped and the last addition to the collection acquired. It was Gertrude Hermes' *Selborne*, one of 240 copies, the sole memorial to Gregynog's planned two-volume edition to rival the Nonesuch set with the Ravilious engravings. I was right to collect *Selborne*, for none of my collections has given me more pleasure, or made more demands on my time and attention. I have always had Nonesuch Press books on my shelves which I like for their character and diversity. Of what remains on my shelves I should least like to lose *The Nonesuch Century* (the 1936 bibliography) and John Dreyfus' *History* (1981), and in a box, which signals my caring, is a book easily overlooked: *The Book of Ruth* (1923) a mint, slip-cased and unopened copy of the third book to be issued by the Press and described by Meynell as 'a toy book' the 'most

Stan Brett

sought after' and 'the Press's most fragile book'. There were 250 copies. A Vectensian by birth, I felt little curiosity about the Isle of Wight (Vectis to the Romans) until I saw it from a distance. It is of course a bit of England, but relishes its separateness, its picturesqueness, and the affection its visitors and sojourners, amongst whom are Celia Fiennes, John Wilkes, Thomas Pennant, Queen Victoria, Tennyson, Lewis Carroll and Edward Edwards (creator of the free library system) have lavished on it.

Many of the visitors recorded their tours, and initiated a wealth of illustrations to enhance them. A considerable collection of interesting steel and copper engravings, wood-engravings, aquatints, lithographs and photographs survive for the collector. My last acquisitions were one of George Brannon's scarcer volumes, and Charles Raye's *A Picturesque Tour through the Isle of Wight*, published 1825, in landscape format with twenty-four fine coloured aquatints. The Island's history, because of its location, was always centred on coastal defence, and several times chronicled invasion. In the Civil War it was a divided society as the events around Charles the First's attempts to survive show, and the history of these decades was effectively recorded in the journals of one, Sir John Oglander of Nunwell. These were edited and published as *The Oglander Memoirs* (1888) and *A Royalist's Notebook* (1936) and are essential volumes in any Island collection. Predictably the sea, ships, piers, wrecks, smugglers etc. figure in the Island literature, and the collector has to find a number of nautical charts to go with the many maps that have followed Speed if his collection is to be comprehensive. He should be grateful to Professor Raymond V. Turley for clearing the ground for him in this and other fields.

So, at the end of the day, what have I, by concious selection or happy accident, retained from my collecting days? On the oversize shelves Morison's *John Fell . . . and the Fell Types*, and his *German Incunabula in the B.M.*, Craig's *Irish Bookbindings*, Oldham's *Blind-stamped Bookbindings* and Maggs' two-part 1987 Catalogue. Alongside are a folio or two from Plantin, one of Baskerville and half a dozen Golden Cockerels including *The Chester Play of The Deluge* with David Jones' engravings. Below them are a small number of incunabula and in boxes to disguise as well as protect their contents there reside two of those most impracticable of bindings produced by Remnant in the 1860s to encase Noel Humphreys' *Coinage of the British Empire* and *The History of Writing* with its illuminated cousin Gray's *Elegy*. There are some sad, dull shelves with the residue of my teaching years, text-books, printing and binding manuals, histories of publishing houses and bookshops, an Adana, a paper mould, some partly sorted wooden type etc., and on the wall a leaf from Wynkyn de Worde's *Golden Legend* with Tate's Watermark, which I found in a volume of Lactantius I purchased fifty years ago. Lacking the focus and commitment of the real collector, I have acquired my heterogeneous collection casually and much by chance, and disposed of it or retained it by only a slightly more purposive impulse. On reflection I would qualify that by recognising my unremitting interest in books about books, else why did I persist in collecting *Matrix*, *The Book Collector*, *The Private Library* etc., and A. E. Newton, and Augustine Birrell or anyone who could and would write about their books and how they acquired them.

New Barnet, Herts

QUARR ABBEY, ISLE OF WIGHT.

Wood-engraving from *Island Scenery*, [1893]

116   STAN BRETT

Maurice Bridger

Thomas Bewick: the Beginning of a Collection

It was in the 1980s that my interest in Bewick started. At an antiques lecture, a bookdealer talked about wood-engraving, and referred to Bewick's *Birds*. Having an interest in natural history, I was amazed how the engraver could portray in black and white a likeness that could be instantly recognised. After reading his *Memoir* (1862) my collecting began.

A cornerstone of my collection is a royal edition of *British Birds* 1797–1804 bound by Bedford in full green morocco. The McGeorge copy sold at Sotheby's in July 1924 mounts as a frontispiece to the first volume the original watercolour drawing of a grey squirrel by Thomas Bewick which was engraved for *The History of Quadrupeds*. It is inscribed on the verso, 'from Miss Bewick May 1877', in the hand of John Handcock, one of Bewick's executers. My thanks go to Peter Miller and Anthony Fothergill, of Ken Spelman Books of York, from whom I bought the book, for the research which went into confirming the watercolour was by Bewick, and to Iain Bain who did the research for them

Also in the collection is a letter dated October 16, 1823, signed by Thomas Bewick to Messrs John and Arthur Arch, booksellers of Cornhill, London, responding to their request for details of his publications. In this letter he states that he has nothing left to offer except a few copies of the 1821 supplements to the *Birds*, and a few royal copies of the *Birds*, dated 1804. It is interesting to note that to match the first royal edition of *Water Birds* (1804) a royal edition of *Land Birds*, dated 1804 on the title-page, was published in 1814–1816 to make a set of royal copies dated 1804. It seems that Bewick had copies of the *Water Birds* left over and the *Land Birds* dated 1804 were published to make complete sets to sell. This edition can be identified by the description of the peregrine falcon on page 72. Copies of the edition were still on sale in 1823.

In a London saleroom I acquired a lot containing Bewick items in which were six late eighteenth century woodblocks of birds, i.e. coot, duck, flycatcher, parrot, ringed ouzel and woodcock. It was of interest that on the back of the block of the duck there was

Maurice Bridger

engraved a geometrical drawing of three triangles with a small square in the centre, the whole surrounded by a circle with four squares attached. Part of this was damaged, hence the other side was used to engrave the duck. The Bewick items came from the 'Bewick Ward Collection', More research is needed to see if the blocks came from the Bewick workshops.

Recently I purchased an imperial copy of Bewick's *Land Birds* uncut, 2nd edition dated 1797, in its original boards. Inside was a two pence receipt signed by Thomas Bewick for three pounds two shillings on account of Messrs Oliver and Boyd printers, Edinburgh, dated 1809. Hugo 258 records Oliver and Boyd publishing a book with a frontispiece by Bewick in 1810.

The search continues.

Leigh-on-Sea, Essex

Grey Squirrel, watercolour by Thomas Bewick
(enlarged to 133%)

MAURICE BRIDGER

Frank Broomhead

Frank Broomhead

Books about Books

As far back as I am able to remember I have enjoyed and been fascinated by books, beginning with prewar children's annuals – one book that I well remember from those early days is *The Modern Boy's Book of Railways*. The beginnings of a serious interest in book collecting began shortly after September 1939 when I started at Doncaster Grammar School. Here in an introductory talk our new biology master advocated the great benefit and pleasure to be derived from a personal library. Within a few days I had made my first purchase of a second-hand book, a finely illustrated Victorian volume dealing with natural history, priced at sixpence. A personal system of book classification followed, though there were at the time no more than a dozen books in my collection. An interest in architecture derived from its study in preference to art, which seemed one subject in which I could never excel; an enthusiasm for local history similarly stemmed from lectures by the history master who was writing a history of the school. On a number of visits to local churches on Sunday afternoon church parades with the Army Cadet Force (in which I played the cornet in the band) the incumbent told us something of the history of the church and its architecture, which proved the basis of an interesting sermon, and led to a growing interest in church architecture. One of these talks that I especially still remember gave a description of a number of heraldic shields on the walls of the church, relating to local families, and this resulted in an interest in heraldry. A love of poetry, too, started at school, with many poems learned by heart.

Bookbinding, using the most primitive equipment, was another early school subject, a hobby that I took further after we moved to London, when I took evening classes under H. A. de Coverley. Most book collectors, on being asked what are their collecting interests, will include in their list books about books or bibliography. It is a natural and common interest, and a little consideration will show that this is a desirable circumstance, if book collecting is to be more than mere acquisition and not much more than a young schoolboy's stamp collecting. Even before opening a book and considering the typeface which has been used, the illustrations, the layout of the page and the nature of the paper, there must be an awareness of the exterior of the book. It may have a simple wrapper, or be further protected by boards covered with either paper, cloth or leather, with varying degrees of decoration. Additionally and sadly, when through use, or frequently abuse, a book begins to disintegrate, it is possible to see the manner in which it is constructed. It is these distinctive features of a book, its typography, illustration, design and binding, which normally form the collector's classification, Books about Books – of which bookbinding is an important subcategory. Indeed it offers a wide and sufficient range of material to be a major collecting interest for many people. My own collection includes many of the standard works, including the classic bibliography by Wolfgang Mejer, *Bibliographie der Buchbinderei-Literatur* (Leipzig, 1925) which was updated by Herman Herbst, *Bibliographie der Buchbinderei-Literatur 1924-1932* (Leipzig, 1933). Though now outdated, Mejer-Herbst is a comprehensive listing of the literature of all aspects of bookbinding up to 1932.

Some of my early reading was to provide me with information for my growing interest in local history and especially architecture, and I cycled out to see many churches within reach of Doncaster. I have now all but one of the twenty books on the town. Matthew Bloxam's *Glossary of Architecture*, as well as the architectural books published by John Henry Parker, fostered another of my collecting enthusiasms, the engraved work of Orlando Jewitt, 1815–69, who contributed so many of the illustrations for these books. My interest was first aroused by noticing his work in volumes relating to the topography of South Yorkshire, my birthplace and the area where my interest in local history and architecture first developed. From my collection of his illustrated books I was eventually able to write an account of Jewitt's life and work, with a bibliographical account of his books and bookplates, which was published by the PLA in 1995.

Apart from Jewitt, I have found much pleasure in illustrated books generally, and was a member of the Folio Society from its earliest days. A most serious interest in books began in the early 1940s with the study, for School Certificate, of Siegfried Sassoon's *Memoirs of a Fox-Hunting Man*, with its early reference to a complete set of Surtees, whose adventures I was able to follow from copies in the public library, but it was not until Folio published its reprint that I was able to add the series to my own collection.

I can much share Sassoon's feelings: 'There was no doubt that I had a fondness for books – especially old ones. . . . I esteemed my books mostly for their outsides. I admired old leather bindings, and my fancy was tickled by the thought of firelight flickering on the dim gilt, autumn-coloured backs.' At the same time, though, it has to be their content that is of most consequence in my own collection.

Kenton, Middlesex

Ashmolean Museum.

Wood-engraving by Orlando Jewitt, 1835,
designed by W. A. Delamotte,
from Ingram's *Memorials of Oxford*, 1835–6

FRANK BROOMHEAD

123

Geoffrey Burkhardt

Geoffrey Burkhardt

Australiana

My collecting interests have two major emphases, Australian school centenary and jubilee history publications and Australian regional and local history publications. I have a modest library of approximately 5,000 books, focusing predominantly upon the above aspects of Australian social and educational history. Prior to my retirement I was senior lecturer in the history of education and curriculum at the University of Canberra for many years. What prompted my interest in the collection of Australian school histories was my desire to encourage my post-graduate students to pursue research projects in the domain of the history of Australian government and non-government primary and secondary schools. In 1970 I began to put together a private collection of published Australian school histories as examples of the large variety of historical treatments of this specialised category of Australian local / social historical research.

The Australian 'bush schools', being small isolated rural elementary schools, were dominant features of the scattered pastoral and bush communities across 'outback' Australia. The history of these schools especially, encapsulated the history of those isolated rural settlements, some of which were hundreds of miles from their nearest neighbours. This domain of educational history research, dating from the early 'Dame Schools' of Australia's convict days to the colonial Compulsory Education Acts of the 1870s and 1880s had been a comparatively neglected aspect of Australian professional education history research. These Acts generated across the Australian colonies a sustained era of government school establishment in the isolated pastoral, mining, forestry and farming communities. The majority of schools established following the 1870s Acts were one teacher schools. Primary schools, of course, had existed in the towns from the colonial settlement decades of the early nineteenth century. During the last fifty years, many of these schools have celebrated their centenaries or 150 year jubilees with a school history publication, often in very limited print runs of only 300–500 copies, catering specifically for their local clientele. Thus, many of these books and booklets are now scarce items keenly sought by collectors of Australiana.

I have accumulated a collection of over 1,000 of these school centenary and jubilee histories and related curriculum items. Some of these histories are large casebound dust-jacketed prestige publications of 300 or 400 pages, others are semi-ephemeral pamphlets of 20–30 pages in length. My interest in this collecting specialisation culminated in 1995 with my compilation of the first published bibliography of Australian School Centenary and Jubilee history publications, *Australian School Centenary and Jubilee Histories: A Select Bibliography*, Magpie Books, Angaston, South Australia, 1995.

The other large component of my private library consists mainly of regional and district histories of Australian towns, villages and localities. The majority of these books have been published during the last fifty years, as the study of Australian local and regional social history has gradually become an 'academically respectable' sphere of research in Australian University history departments. Very few books in this field could be classed as 'rare' or even 'scarce', yet they have become increasingly collectable because of the growth of interest in Australian regional and district history, inspired by national events such as the 1788–1988 Bi-centennial Celebrations and more recently the Centenary of the Federation of the Australian Colonies in 2001. Gradually Australians are becoming more aware of and sensitive to the uniqueness of their comparatively short colonial history and the extraordinary archaeological record of an aboriginal pre-history experience extending back over 50,000 years. These are some of the themes which generated a flowering of Australian regional and local history publication over recent decades, a field most worthy for an Australiana collector.

Canberra, Australia

GEOFFREY BURKHARDT

Richard Burleigh

The collection spreads over quite a wide range of subjects – archaeology, geology, natural history, the countryside, local history and topography, architecture, folklore, science, history, biography, literature, poetry, bibliography, and principal reference works – to list broadly, and in random order, the main themes covered. It comprises a mere 4,000 or so books, crammed from floor to ceiling into a smallish room in the quietude of a late Victorian cottage in West Dorset. Temperature and humidity are carefully controlled, dust is minimal, sunlight into the room is subdued, and the books are robustly and accessibly shelved, despite the restrictions of space. One or two earlier works are held (the first edition in full calf of Fuller's *Worthies of England* of 1662, for example) but the majority are nineteenth and twentieth century cloth-bound editions.

The passion for accumulating books can probably be traced to the mid-1930s, when, in childhood, the seeds were first sown (and there will be every excuse for a spending spree on books in the year 2006, to celebrate seventy years of the addiction). The collection as it stands today has mostly been put together from the late 1960s onwards. Some culling (with resultant consolidation) has taken place from time to time meanwhile, but nothing further is to be parted with. About 500 particular titles are still sought (and this takes no account of others that may materialize and prove irresistible). Quite how all these can be accommodated in the limited space available has yet to be worked out. Books that are in at least 'good' condition are preferred, but sometimes the earlier association(s) that a particular copy may happen to have is of more consequence and (apart from any careful cleaning that may be needed) theses are kept as found. Needless to say, systematic browsing in bookshops is a special pleasure and is nearly always rewarding.

Not every book in the collection has been read from cover to cover, but each has at least been carefully examined page by page. In some instances the presence alone of a particular book is the prime consideration (and almost invariably it will eventually be

Richard Burleigh

consulted). Indeed, modest in size though the collection indubitably is, access to a library proper is seldom called for, most queries being answerable directly from the shelves. Thus the books are used, the plethora of knowledge packed into the collection being almost beyond belief.

To be surrounded in every direction by shelves brimming with esteemed books that have such a benign and harmonious presence is incontrovertible proof of how fortunate one is to be blessed with the tendency towards bibliomania, that irresistible urge so aptly described of late as 'a gentle madness'.

Charmouth, Dorset

Grotesque at Puncknowle, Dorset,
wood-engraving by William Barnes, from
The Gentleman's Magazine, 1835, reproduced
from *William Barnes: The Dorset Engravings*, 1986.
Courtesy, Trustees of the Mansel-Pleydell Trust.

David Burnett

David Burnett

A Paper Cellar

The owl of Minerva, as Hegel aptly observed, begins to fly at dusk. It is not in the morning or even at the noon of life that we fully understand our purpose and achievement. We perceive with hindsight, by looking back, and only rarely by looking forward. What is true of individuals applies equally to societies: the creation by the British of a liberal empire of unequalled extent and power and the inception of modernity throughout the earth were not at first intended but secured, as Seeley wryly conceded, in a fit absence of mind.

Like many another collector, therefore, I have been surprised to discover that I am one and that there is in my later years a fairly substantial and varied collection with particular objectives and structure. Like Topsy it has 'just growed', but there are reasons for this growth and its present form.

In part, and no doubt *au fond*, I am a squirrel and not a grasshopper. This acquisitive and prudential instinct has been reinforced by a desire to preserve what is good and, in particular, to shore up time's ruins. There has, thus, been an innate propensity both to collect and to conserve, an instinct sharpened and informed by my professional career as an academic librarian responsible for our printed and manuscript heritage. In my own case this propensity has expressed itself primarily in the mental and not the physical sphere. In part, it has been realised in small and miscellaneous collections of family memorabilia and furniture as well as of paintings and sculpture. For the most part, however, it has reinforced my need to secure material which can serve my principal talents and interests in life – notably in writing poetry and criticism, in studying literature, art and history, and in enhancing my appreciation of contemporary fine press printing and wood-engraving. For the individual, as for society, collecting is often a valuable foundation for understanding. The support – it is hardly patronage – of contemporary writers and artists has been a further objective. What has been assembled is, as it were, a paper cellar, but it is the slowly ripened fruit of personal taste and sensibility and of a fundamental desire to make sense of the world imaginatively through both the arts and the past.

What is now explicit was, however, for many years implicit and not fully recognised. Like a coral reef it gathered itself and cohered unseen. Indeed, for long its growth and extent were hardly perceived beneath the tides and tempests of a more pressing life. The collections are, therefore, more miscellaneous and less consistent than if the purposes which have shaped them had been fully grasped and consciously articulated *ab initio*. In addition, one must allow for contingent factors independent of the individual such as market prices and availability. In collecting as in life we do not act wholly alone since circumstance as well as choice determines what is created. Nonetheless, in recent years it has been possible to advance the growth of the collections more consciously and effectively and, as with children, to cherish and foster their directions.

To a degree, it is a question of size. Just as the dark matter of the universe can coalesce, achieve critical mass and blaze into a galaxy of stars so too can a collection find its own proper shape and light. Increasingly, a positive feedback cycle develops in which the collection stimulates and enlightens the collector and in its turn is expanded so that each becomes both a means and an end to the other. For myself, however, as no doubt for others, there has been also for each collection a Damascene illumination, a crisis which precipitates awareness and which crystallises an understanding of the opportunities of a new road and its costs. This is, as it were, a rite of passage. None, indeed, can be truly a collector who is unwilling to sacrifice the self to the collection, to buy wisely as a collector but also foolishly as an individual. In collecting as in all fields, nonetheless, we should seek the golden mean and temper each fine excess with moderation. I am, therefore, a bibliophile but not a bibliomaniac.

The core of the collection is a complete archive of my publications in poetry and criticism as well as in professional and scholarly monographs and journals. This includes notes and foul papers as well as revised drafts both in manuscript and typescript, corrected proofs, printed texts, and relevant correspondence.

There is, further, a similar and complete archive of the Black Cygnet Press, a fine private press which I have established to further both my own work and that of others and to engage more

DAVID BURNETT

closely with letterpress printing and wood-engraving. This likewise contains texts in manuscript and typescript, corrected proofs,
printed texts, and relevant correspondence with printers, artists
and others. In particular, there is a very substantial correspondence with Alan Anderson of the Tragara Press, whose own
archive is housed at Dartmouth College in the United States.

In addition, there is a substantial and related correspondence
over several decades with many others on a wide range of issues
in life, literature, criticism and the arts and crafts. This complements and informs these two archives and also in part – in the
absence of a diary – documents my life. With some writers, such
as James Kirkup, whose books and papers are at Yale, there is an
extended and valuable correspondence.

In the field of printed books there is a substantial collection of
British and American contemporary fine press printing over the
past fifty years, a collection which has served to inspire and in-
form my own work in this field. This material is necessarily selective, but nonetheless representative of the nature and quality of
several dozen such presses. It also contains some material from
other countries and earlier periods. I am not a bibliographer *pur
sang*, however, and in this as in other fields, apart from my personal and press archives, I have not sought for absolute fullness
or perfection. What I collect I read and ponder as well as enjoy.
Copies are, nonetheless, normally in good or often mint condition, occasionally with fine bindings, and not infrequently enriched
by provenance or association. There is also a large collection of
keepsakes and ephemera as well as relevant prospecti. Many of
these items, moreover, are illustrated by engravings printed from
the wood. To be fully appreciated, these need to be studied in the
context of this medium which embodies both independent prints
and images created in response to particular texts. As such, this
printed material complements another very substantial personal
collection of over five hundred prints, primarily of British wood-
engraving during its renaissance in the later twentieth century.

There is also a very substantial, though not complete, collection of several hundred books, pamphlets and some journal publications by or relating to Walter de la Mare. This reflects my appreciation both of his poetry and prose and also of good book
design and production and illustration since much of his work was

finely published. This collection is further enriched by association copies and some autograph letters as well as by some very rare and unusual items.

Finally, there are several thousand commercially published books and pamphlets in various fields. The book as text rather than as artefact does, indeed, predominate in the library as a whole since this in my view is the primary purpose of the codex. Text matters rather than its vehicle and this is a working library, for reading and for reference. I am a bibliophile only in part. Individually these items are typically of little value, but collectively they are certainly more valuable since with critical mass the sum becomes more than its parts. Most notably, there is a substantial selection of English and American poetry over the centuries as well as of foreign poetry in English translation – the latter a resource which has also served my own work in translation from several languages. There are also quite substantial holdings of works in literary criticism, art and history, especially of the classical period. These as well as other miscellaneous publications serve my creative and intellectual interests and form, as it were, a surrogate memory for them. They also offer a mirror to my mind, not least my concern for the symbiosis and synergy of text and image.

A private library is, as it were, a paper cellar. Like a good cellar it is laid down for pleasure and for use (in my own case equally), even though some of the vintages may not be immediately consumed. Its rewards are, no doubt, less tangible and are of the mind, yet these can be enjoyed at will and never diminish. Each collection is, moreover, in part a form of conspicuous consumption since it suggests an index to the purse as well as to the mind and taste of its collector. At its best, however, each can serve as a witness to learning and to a subtle and widely ranging discrimination. As such, the best can also enrich not only an individual and a few chosen friends but also in the long term society.

Is there, however, a place today for the printed book and, as a corollary, for its collection both by individuals and society? A collection such as this may appear to some, particularly in modern libraries, a quixotry and an irrelevance, a whim, a private folly. Is there, indeed, a future and a place for books and manuscripts today?

The repeated reports of the death of the book are, however,

much exaggerated, even though its role in the dissemination and preservation of knowledge will necessarily be reduced and modified by electronic media. It is, in fact, an exceptionally compact, portable and accessible vehicle for both information and ideas. Texts can still be read twice as quickly in printed rather than in electronic form and passages in them are also easier both to access and to annotate. The book will, therefore, never be wholly displaced. Some caution, indeed, is desirable regarding the claims advanced for these new media. What precisely are the status and integrity of digital texts and images? Are they secure from endogenous and exogenous corruption? Are archival permanence and secure access on new platforms possible? These are questions which cannot be ignored. Until they are satisfactorily resolved it would be sensible to be cautious. Printed matter remains a bastion of our culture and heritage which we should not lightly abandon. Indeed, such collections are arguably more necessary in present circumstances than before. We need, therefore, in this, as in other fields, to sail against the wind and to challenge the prevailing received wisdom of the age.

Nonetheless, it must be conceded that the rapid and increasing migration of text to electronic forms and its ready availability throughout the earth in digital surrogates will undoubtedly challenge and erode the value of many historic and traditional collections. However, digitisation of many existing codical and manuscript texts will not take place. When it does, moreover, it will not be able satisfactorily to replicate certain features of printed books or manuscripts. The preponderance of digital texts will, therefore, paradoxically privilege and enhance both the manuscript and the exceptional book, not as text but for copy-specific features such as binding, provenance and annotation and for properties which are integral to it as a physical medium such as engravings printed from the wood. The digitisation of texts will, in short, enhance the value of the book as a cultural artefact, even though it will reduce its value as a vehicle for text. As a consequence, collections of books rich in such features and, *a fortiori*, manuscripts will not be displaced by but will on the contrary complement their electronic siblings or descendants. As a corollary, however, collections of standard texts without such distinguishing features will depreciate in importance and must in present circumstances obsolesce.

In the economy of collecting as in that of society at large there is a need for both the individual and the community. Neither should be paramount and the collections of each can and should enrich the other. As a librarian, I am particularly aware of this and as a collector I have been informed and inspired by resources held in common. The community can, moreover, be enriched in the long term not only by its own institutions in the fields of the arts and sciences but also by the energies, initiative, opportunities, varied taste and generosity of individuals. Indeed, to serve the public best we need first to serve ourselves, as Adam Smith observed. What I have assembled has been a source of pleasure and of understanding to me over fifty years. In the long term, however, it is better that it should fructify the public rather than myself. One should seek in collecting as in living not to own and command but on the contrary to serve and to give since, as Carnegie wisely and tellingly observed, to die rich is to die disgraced. What is private and what is public can be distinguished but should not be divorced.

Durham

Thomas Hardy, wood-engraving by Simon Brett,
from David Burnett, *Nine Poets*, Gwasg Gregynog, 1993

Paul van Capelleveen

Ricketts, Shannon & the Vale Press

It all started with a poster that I never saw. In about 1977 Ton Leenhouts, who later came to share the collection with me, bought a poster in a Verkerke shop in Amsterdam, which specialized in modern posters, most of which were published by this firm. 'Our' poster was of an imitation brown packing paper with a blown-up image from a Ricketts wood-engraving for *Hero and Leander* (1894) printed in gold and blue. It was one of a series concerned with Aubrey Beardsley and art nouveau. In London these posters were advertised by Gallery Five and presented as wall panels in the late sixties or early seventies.[1] For many years Ton's poster must have decorated his office at Netherlands Dance Theatre of The Hague where he was director of publicity and public relations, but when I met him it had vanished.

In November 1977 Ton started a collection of Ricketts's book designs as he obtained his first one, T. S. Moore's *Danaë*, which incidentally was the last publication of the Vale Press (followed later by a bibliography). Ton must have thought this book a nice acquisition for his collection of nineteenth and twentieth century illustrated works. Over the years he bought quite a few Vale Press books, mostly illustrated with wood-engravings by Ricketts. One of the earlier ones was *Daphnis and Chloe* (bought February 1978) with pencilled notes by T. S. Moore. Others were *Beyond the Threshold* (May 1978) and the two-volume Vale Press edition of Chatterton's *Rowley Poems* (July 1978). Subsequently Wilde's *A House of Pomegranates* (July 1978), Ricketts's *Recollections of Oscar Wilde* (August 1978) and a proof copy of Symonds's *In the Key of Blue and Other Prose Essays* (October 1978) were added to the collection.

One day Ton read a short notice in a Dutch newspaper about an exhibition in London. He rushed over to Orleans House Gallery at Twickenham and arrived just in time to see the show before it was taken down that same afternoon, the 20th of May 1979. This of course was the influential exhibition mounted by Stephen Calloway and Paul Delaney, which changed the appreciation of the work of Ricketts and Shannon. Correspondence with the authors of the exhibition (and of several books on Ricketts and Shannon) helped to direct Ton on his collector's path. When we met in 1983, my zest for completeness drove us into the field of variant bindings and ephemera. By then the Ricketts collection had been separated from the illustrated works in general. Especially our friendship with Paul Delaney and with dealers and other collectors has given us much pleasure over the years. The early collection grew with the help of dealers such as Robin Greer in London (a good friend ever since), Erasmus in Amsterdam (discontinued after the death of Mr Horodisch), Hatchard's, Warrack & Perkins (who offered a wealth of rare Ricketts materials until the untimely death of Geoffrey Perkins) and Blackwell's (from our friend Philip Brown). Later purchases were done at Eric Stevens and a large number of internet booksellers.

We love to share and publish our findings, and did so in England as well as in the Netherlands. The Dutch literary magazine *Maatstaf* published a portfolio of 36 illustrations alongside an article by Ton and myself in 1989.[2] In 1996 we mounted two exhibitions in The Hague to commemorate the founding of the Vale Press a hundred years before. Surprisingly there was no exhibition in London at the time. The Koninklijke Bibliotheek, the National Library of the Netherlands (my employer) had a small exhibition on Ricketts and his circle of friends including Oscar Wilde, Michael Field and W. B. Yeats.[3] Later that year the museum of the book of The Hague, Museum Meermanno, showed a complete collection of Vale Press books mainly based on our collection. On that occasion my checklist of books designed by Ricketts and Shannon appeared, listing circa 270 books and ephemera.[4]

Over the years we acquired a number of items of interest, such as autograph letters on book and magazine designs, early drawings and original sketches (for *The Parables* among others), which will help us in the writing of an iconography of Ricketts's graphic works, started in 1996. We collected variant bindings for Oscar Wilde's *A House of Pomegranates* (see my article in *The Private Library*, Summer 2005) and a great number of other books. File copies, dedication copies, American editions of books with cover designs by Ricketts, all of these have augmented our knowledge of Ricketts's style and technique and of the publisher's influence on the way his designs were adapted and reused. Ricketts's designs should always be studied in context.

As we now have a complete set of Vale Press books and many related books and publications, we can concentrate on ephemera and deluxe books. We have never collected Ricketts's theatrical designs nor Shannon's paintings: we leave that to our friends and other collectors. Nowadays it is difficult to find a complete set of Vale Press books in good condition, many copies offered for sale at this moment are browned, worn, or rebound, so we may be grateful that Ton's fascination for Ricketts began quite a while ago. Even an artist who has been the subject of an outstanding biography (Delaney) and a poor bibliography (Watry) gives the collector the opportunity to have new discoveries, for example, that the number of copies of *The Rowley Poems* in the special 'flame' binding is not three (as stated by Ricketts in a notice) but more. Some of these discoveries can be made at home, others around the corner, as when we saw a small book with chromo-lithographic illustrations, one of which was by Ricketts and, as yet, unrecorded. Fascinating though it is, this will have to wait for a future publication.

The Hague, The Netherlands

1. See a photograph in Stephen Calloway, *Aubrey Beardsley*. London: V&A Publication, 1998, p. 217.
2. Ton Leenhouts & Paul van Capelleveen, 'Portfolio/Charles Ricketts', in: *Maatstaf*, 37 (1989) 7 (juli), pp. 28–64.
3. *De Vrienden van Charles Ricketts*. Compiled by Paul van Capelleveen. The Hague, 1997.
4. *A New Checklist of Books designed by Charles Ricketts & Charles Shannon*. Compiled by Paul van Capelleveen. With an introduction by J. G. P. Delaney. The Hague: Museum van het Boek / Museum Meermanno-Westreenianum, 1996.

Sebastian Carter Collection

Sebastian Carter

The Book Arts

The collection was started by my father Will Carter and carried on by me. We have both devoted our lives to running a letterpress printing workshop, the Rampant Lions Press, and the collection reflects our interest in the book arts. The photograph shows the larger-format and grander books. On the second shelf and half the third is a selection of the most important books we have printed, often in the special edition format. The top shelf carries complete sets of three typographical journals, *The Fleuron*, both series of *Signature*, and *Matrix*. On other shelves not shown are complete runs of *The Imprint*, *Motif*, *Fine Print*, and *Bookways*. After the Rampant Lions books there is a selection of books by other presses and designers we have both admired. Highlights here are the Golden Cockerel Press *Four Gospels* (bought by Will) and *Twelfth Night* (by me), several Officina Bodoni titles including the Ovid *Amores* and Terence's *Andria* (the latter a present from Giovanni Mardersteig), and a number of books featuring the work of Adrian Frutiger, Eric Gill, Victor Hammer, Georg Trump, Adrian Wilson, and Hermann Zapf. There are a number of press bibliographies, of the Officina Bodoni, Nonesuch (as well as *The Nonesuch Century*), and Whittington Presses. I have made a point of collecting books illustrated by Edward McKnight Kauffer: three for the Nonesuch Press, *The Anatomy of Melancholy*, *Benito Cereno* and *Don Quixote*, and two Arnold Bennett stories featuring *pochoir* plates done at the Curwen Press for Cassell. The Kelmscott Press is represented by *The Nature of Gothic* and the Doves Press by its first book, *Agricola*. Among more recent press books I particularly treasure Miriam Macgregor's beautiful *pochoir* studies of New Castle, in Delaware, from the Whittington Press, and Claire van Vliet's magnificent edition of *King Lear*.

On other shelves there is a collection of smaller-format books, including a number of the delicious Typophile chap books, two of Jan Tschichold's chief publications, *Die neue Typographie* and *Typographische Gestaltung*, a collection of Rudolf Koch's books, and extensions of the subjects covered in the large-format shelves.

Cambridge

Roderick Cave

An inveterate book buyer, who has written quite a lot about rare books, and who was also a founder-member of PLA and heavily involved in the preparation of its *Simplified Cataloguing Rules*, ought to have formed an exemplary private library. And so mine is – but what it exemplifies is lack of discrimination. It is the result of being interested in too many different subjects, living in too many different homes, and alas, always having too little money to spend on my collection.

The range of collecting interests resulted from my career taking me to eighteen different homes in five different continents in the past fifty years, rather often in places without antiquarian bookshops and in which the climate was inimical to books. No use trying to collect gothic novels in the West Indies, pointless looking for the works of C. L. R. James in Nigeria, imprudent buying modern fine printing to be kept in Singapore. All were areas in which I collected at one time, and I have small residual collections of each to baffle my executors or the charity shops.

Some other collecting interests are no longer visible on my bookshelves, but can be discerned from boxes in my attic. Others survive only in my memories, because I have disposed of the books at one stage or another. An inherited collection of nineteenth century Mission Press imprints from India was given to SOAS (*St John's Gospel* in Tibetan was not really to my taste). Fairly comprehensive collections of Puffin Picture Books, the Grey Walls Press Crown Classics series, and of some other series have come and gone; so have smaller collections of the work of Morris Cox and Count Potocki de Montalk, and a very large proportion of my working library on printing and the book arts.

What remains is something like a beach after a storm, with all kinds of jetsam. A small collection on nature-printing, an early enthusiasm to which I have returned for a book now in progress. Some fine printing, too often in less than fine condition. A few miniature books. A modest working collection of books and pamphlets on Chinese prints and popular arts, of interest mostly because of the variety of imprints. The novels of Hugh Edwards.

Oddities – a Thai printed palm-leaf edition of the Buddhist scriptures, Burmese and Sumatran manuscripts and books of divination; books considered by the Golden Cockerel Press but not published by them; Vietnamese piracies of Graham Greene. . . . Some have come as gifts and their value is entirely sentimental; other such things interested me when I found them or because of work I was doing at some time in the past. They have not only filled my shelves but have made life more fun than it would otherwise have been. Such acquisitions, I have to confess, are very far from showing the taste and technique which John Carter recommended to book collectors. But I am not very penitent.

Somerby, Melton Mowbray, Leics.

'Woodsia Alpina', from *Nature-Printed British Ferns*, 1859
Printed by Henry Bradbury (leaves in green, roots in brown)

RODERICK CAVE 143

David Chambers

David Chambers

Early Private Printing

After *Peter Rabbit*, *The House at Pooh Corner*, an odd volume of *Chums* and so on, my book collecting really started on my tenth birthday with the Nelson Classics *Tom Sawyer*. *Sea Stories* in the same series followed at Christmas, but a Collins Classics *Three Musketeers*, that same day, spoilt the neatness of the row that was starting on the mantelpiece in Chichester, where we had been evacuated. Literary texts of all sorts, were bought at sixpence a go from Foyle's outside racks through later school days, using Seymour Smith's *English Library* as the basis for my wants list, marked off as the books were bought and again when read.

Starting with a non-marine syndicate at Lloyd's when I was sixteen, I found five bookshops in the city, visiting them in turn at lunch time, and going every evening at tea time to Hugh Jones and Cyril Nash, who had just opened their tiny shop a hundred yards from Lloyd's building. They led me into minor twentieth century private press books, and on one occasion into agreeing to take sixteen fine copies of books from the Eragny Press, priced at a guinea or two. As my salary slowly increased, so did the quality of the books, so that eventually the Eragny Press collection was completed, and added to it were many of the more important books from the Golden Cockerel, Nonesuch, Officina Bodoni, and Cranach Presses. From Anthony Reid came most of Ralph Chubb's lithographed volumes, and most importantly, from Morris Cox nearly all of his miraculous inventions. Working on the annual checklist of current private press books over twenty or thirty years added another dimension to this part of the collection, with large numbers of thinnish pamphlets and more elaborate octavos and quartos from the private printers working at the latter end of the twentieth century.

In 1970 I added an Holtzapffel Parlour Press to my collection, made for the use of Victorian amateur printers, and with James Mosley edited the third edition of its manual. A search in the British Library for books printed on such presses excited an enthusiasm for this earlier period of private printing, and purchases from Alan Thomas of books and ephemera printed by Thomas Phillipps at Middle Hill led to a complete change of direction – everything now had to have been printed before William Morris set up his press in Hammersmith. Five major presses form the backbone of the collection: Strawberry Hill, Hafod, Lee Priory, Middle Hill and Daniel. Often of greater interest, though, are the books printed by less wealthy people: clergymen, antiquaries, and domestic Victorians with time to spare and family magazines to print.

The account that I have been preparing of these printers and their work has added enormous interest to making the collection, with new presses still surfacing to extend the quest. Over many years now I have been able to add two books to the shelves each month, with occasional days of delirium such as a trip to Kraus's a few years ago when I came away with fifty-five items printed at Middle Hill, books and leaflets that I had long been searching for – and really given up. Earlier I had been able to buy from the Robinson Brothers a large collection of pamphlets and ephemera from Middle Hill, and some years later a great many proof sheets and overs from the Phillipps' Manuscript Catalogue. Hafod has never had the same following amongst collectors as Strawberry Hill, so coloured folios and quartos have come more easily than might be expected, given their great rarity. Books from Lee Priory have similarly come in without too much trouble including some on large or on India paper, with even *Lee,* limited to twelve copies and suppressed for two lines critical of Roman Catholics, eventually coming to hand.

Two books a month, though, can hardly satisfy, however rare they may be, and there are a great many others of less consequence that are easier to find and still of considerable interest. So we have cases devoted to book collecting, printing practice and history, Victorian technology, Victorian natural history, Bohn's Illustrated Library, nineteenth- and twentieth-century illustrated books, sets of Medieval Towns and the like, literature in general, and, of course, erotica. Seven rooms full of books so far, plus a good deal more in the loft, fortunately blessed with seven-inch beams and an easy sliding ladder.

Pinner, Middlesex

DAVID CHAMBERS

Denis Collins

Initially, I collected first editions of crime fiction (as this was my favourite leisure reading) but in time I became disillusioned with the shoddy production standards of most modern hardback books as well as the often extravagant prices that were asked for those books which had retained their dust-wrappers. If virtually all the cost of, say, a John Dickson Carr or Eric Ambler first edition related to the dust-wrapper, I began to wonder whether I was really a collector of printed wrappers rather than of books.

I knew that I wanted still to collect books but of what kind? An interest in nineteenth-century English watercolours led me to discover English colour plate books of the period 1790 to 1840. I came to realise fairly quickly that, for less than the price of a watercolour, I would be able to buy a book which might contain dozens of illustrations in aquatint or lithography that were near-perfect facsimiles of the artist's original watercolours. However, so vast was this field of collecting that I decided to become a 'high spot' collector (rather than a 'completist') buying, when I could afford to, only the finest books produced by the best book artists of the period.

The core of my collection is made up of works illustrated by Thomas Rowlandson. In my opinion, his seventy-four colour plates for *The English Dance of Death* surpass in quality the illustrations in any other English book. Also in the collection is William Daniell's *A Voyage Round Great Britain*, with its 308 hand-coloured aquatint plates probably the most important book on British topography, and Thomas Shotter Boys's *Picturesque Architecture in Paris, Ghent, Antwerp, Rouen etc.*, a milestone in the history of colour lithography.

Once I had conceived this enthusiasm for illustrated books I soon widened the scope of my collecting. By and large, I found the books of the high Victorian period not to my taste and I concentrated instead on the outstanding British and French illustrators of the 1890 to 1940 period including Beardsley, Dulac, Rackham, Harry Clarke, and Heath Robinson. I developed a particular regard for French illustrated books of the 'Art Deco' period between

Denis Collins

about 1910 and 1930. These books, which were beautifully printed, and usually hand-coloured by the pochoir process, reached a degree of perfection – above all in the work of George Barbier – which has never been surpassed. I have often wondered why British presses, both private and commercial, have mostly ignored such a simple but effective process as pochoir.

Martin Steenson, of Books & Things, gave me particular help in building up my collection of modern illustrated books. On innumerable occasions I have been gratified by his uncanny ability to find for me a rare and desirable item at a price that I can afford.

In general, I have found that (apart from Eragny) the private presses of the same period have limited appeal for me. Happily, the remarkable revival in the fine press movement since the 1970s has produced (among some dross) much work that is inventive, colourful and exciting. The most interesting artist to come out of this revival is Susan Allix, who, over three decades, has produced nearly forty artist's books of a brilliance and originality that is entirely their own. As well as collecting many of these, I have had the pleasure of commissioning from her 'designer bindings' of illustrated books in my collection. Starting modestly enough with a Folio Society edition of Lampedusa's *The Leopard*, she has to date executed ten of these, the most recent being of the two-volume Cresset Press edition of *Gulliver's Travels* with illustrations by Rex Whistler. Unlike some other binders, Susan enjoys discussing her ideas for a binding as they develop and it is a considerable pleasure to have some, albeit very small, input into the final result. It is certainly fascinating to watch a contemporary artist 'collaborating' (so to speak) with the author and illustrator of the book in order to produce what is, when completed, an unique object.

As for any deeper wellsprings of motivation that may underlie my collecting activities, I would comment only that, for me, owning rare and beautiful books just makes life more enjoyable than it would be otherwise. What more need one say?

Richmond, Surrey

DENIS COLLINS

Simon Cooke

Victorian Illustration

I began my collection in the late seventies, as an undergraduate reading English at Birmingham University. My first acquisition was a copy of Montgomery's *Poems*, published in 1860, with a gilt binding and illustrations by Birket Foster. This started me on what has turned into a life-long pursuit of illustrated gift books and periodicals of the 1850s and '60s. Over the past twenty five years I have built a large collection which includes the landmarks of the 'golden age' of Victorian illustration. My aim has always been to acquire copies in very good condition, with equal emphasis being placed on the wood-engravings and on the books' elaborate bindings. Among the most interesting are Millais's *Parables*, *The Music Master*, illustrated with Rossetti's famous design of 'The Maids of Elfinmere', and the Moxon *Tennyson*, as well as items such as *A Round of Days*, Wilmot's *Poets of the Nineteenth Century* and *Pictures of Society Grave and Gay*. I have also acquired substantial runs of the illustrated periodicals of the period, with special emphasis on *Once a Week*, *The Cornhill Magazine* and *Good Words*. These books form the core of a library which now numbers around five hundred items. My interests are not limited to the 1860s, however. To provide a context, I have assembled a collection which embodies developments before and after the golden period, starting with illustrations by Doyle, Cruikshank and Leech and finishing with Beardsley and Ricketts. Taken as a whole, the collection forms what I think is an important archive. If all other Victorian illustrated literature were to disappear from the earth, and my collection survived, it would be possible to reconstruct what the form of this sort of book was like, both in its externals and in its development of illustrative styles and techniques. Looking at these books, it is possible to characterize all of the main trends – from the scratchy burlesque of Cruikshank and Phiz to the intricate medievalism of Rossetti, the intense lyricism of Houghton and Millais, and the exotic art nouveau of Beardsley. I have written several articles on the collection, for example: 'George du Maurier's Illustrations for M. E. Braddon's *Eleanor's Victory* in *Once a Week*' (*Victorian*

Periodicals Review, 35:1, Spring 2002, pp. 89–106) and 'A Forgotten Collaboration of the 1860s: Charles Reade, Robert Barnes and the Illustrations for *Put Yourself in His Place*' (*Dickens Studies Annual*, 30, 2002, pp. 321–342). I have also written in *Studies in Illustration* on Samuel Lucas (the editor of *Once a Week*), Victorian frontispieces, and Richard Doyle. A full account of the 1860s element within the collection was published in *The Private Library*, Autumn 2003, pp. 118–138.

Coventry

'The Palace of Art'
Wood-engraving by Dalziel after a design by
Dante Gabriel Rossetti,
Alfred Tennyson, *Poems*, Moxon, 1857

Claude Cox

1920–2006

This is a short account of our library; at least as much an enthusiasm and preoccupation of my late wife Joan, as of myself. We have a joint bookplate. This is important; not only is a pleasure shared a pleasure doubled, but an enthusiasm for collecting can be addictive; it is solitary drinkers who become alcoholics.

Arnold Muirhead will be remembered by many members of the PLA as a somewhat scholarly bookseller who issued catalogues for thirty years after the war. Before the war he had been a schoolmaster at the Latymer School, London, where he taught Joan and me Latin. He was a bibliomane and member of an exclusive booklovers dining club, the Biblio Boys, which included Michael Sadleir, Percy Muir, John Carter and Simon Nowell Smith. Joan and I were often included in a small group of sixth-formers invited to dine at the flat in Arnos Grove and by the time we left school, to have an interesting collection of books was a natural ambition.

We had a common enthusiasm for poetry. Our first acquisitions of the moderns were signed copies of Vita Sackville West's *Orchard and Vineyard* and *Poems of East and West*. The highlight of that collection is a copy of the edition limited to a hundred of *The Heir* (1912), with a delightful inscription: 'My dear P. M. Overcome as I am at finding that someone has actually bought this edition, I feel that your request to "write your name in my book please" cannot be met by a mere signature, but calls for an inscription. As however, I am unable to think out a suitable inscription at a moment's notice, I have no other alternative than to write you this note to say so. Yours affectionately, Vita.' Stanley Baldwin was almost a neighbour of the Nicolsons at that time. Our collection of poets grew backwards rather than forward; the war poets, Eliot, the thirties poets (C. Day Lewis was my predecessor by several years as President of the Wadham JCR) and the romantics. Keats is everyone's first love but we have had to be content with only one of the three key first editions. I missed the essential 1820 volume in 1946 when Sexton catalogued it at £15 (and I still had some of my Navy gratuity). Arnold advised against it – 'It'll be a poor copy – it's a £20 book!' Many years

Joan and Claude Cox

later the beautiful Diana Cooper's copy came up at Sotheby's. I determined to have it even at £1,000. I did not get a bid in. Quaritch paid more that twice that on behalf of some rich bibliophile.

Keats's *Poems*, 1820, comes to mind whenever the question of condition is considered. Everyone likes fine copies but the magic of first editions is not in the eye, but in the mind, in the heart. When Trelawny found Shelley's body on the Italian shore, days after a sudden squall had capsized the boat he and Williams were sailing, there was 'the volume of Sophocles in one pocket and Keats's poems in the other, doubled back, as if the reader, in the act of reading, had hastily thrust it away.' Trelawny carefully washed and dried the pages. It would never be a good copy, or even a fair copy; but what a copy to possess!

Some Shelley first editions have come our way and Mary Shelley's four volumes of his *Collected Poems*, with her notes and introduction, add much to one's appreciation of the poet. Coleridge is a delight to collect. There is so much of him and so much to him. 'Kubla Khan' is the very epitome of romanticism with its simple but powerful language, elaborate rhyming, entirely irrelevant woman wailing for demon lover and compulsory bathos. It's only about the building of a brothel but the shackles of classical restraint are shattered forever. Coleridge's *Poems,* 1796, and 2nd ed., 1797, with Charles Lamb's first published poems, were not vastly expensive. *Lyrical Ballads* though not impossibly scarce has always been impossibly expensive. Coleridge leads to numerous additions; his delightful daughter and his impossible son. We even acquired the sermons of his father.

We never sought Byron first editions with much enthusiasm, but acquired a few; Southey similarly. Leigh Hunt, however, has almost too dominant representation on our shelves. His bibliographies remark that he is easy to collect and the sale of Horace Pym's books at Sotheby's a few years ago allowed us to just about complete our holding. Of the Victorians we have targeted Tennyson – an easy target for the most part but *Poems Chiefly Lyrical,* 1830, in boards, is not easy; nor is *Poems,* 1833, similarly attired. We have not been able to beat the millionaires to a copy of *Poems by Two Brothers.*

Poetry was never our only quarry. Sixty-five years ago Arnold Muirhead inscribed a copy of Salzmann's *Gymnastics for Youth,* 1800, to Joan. The plates are now agreed to be by Blake. Ten years ago Simon Finch catalogued a copy for £950. This is a small field but not unrewarding. Our collection starts with *De Arte Gymnastica,* Mercurialis, 1601. I can't speak for the text but the plates are fairly terrifying (unlike Salzmann's of balancing on the seesaw and trundling the hoop). This collection also includes dancing and early children's education.

In 1970 I left the RAF after twenty years, settled in Suffolk and we decided to try our hands at bookselling. It was then that the Kipling collection began to grow rapidly. It was a good time to collect Kipling. His prewar popularity had waned. He was absurdly seen by many as a racist: his sort of poetry had dated and it was not generally realised what a master he was of the short story. Once I had secured a copy of *Plain Tales from the Hills,* Calcutta, 1888, that collection was keenly pursued.

Soon after our move into Suffolk, our eldest son, after many years at Oxford, took up a post at the University of Sydney. This, and our regular visits, gave rise to an Australian collection (transferred to Sydney several years ago) which was particularly nurtured by Joan who was fascinated by the Aboriginal people and

154   JOAN AND CLAUDE COX

their art. It was further stimulated by the discovery that the Kidman family had emigrated to South Australia from our Suffolk farmhouse in the 1840s.

Suffolk opened up several new areas for collecting. It is an interesting county with an irresistible wealth of topographical items. More particularly we were now only a few miles from Woodbridge where the translator of my early favourite the *Rubaiyat* of Omar Khayyam had lived for most of his life. FitzGerald died in 1883 but it is remarkable how a hundred years later his books still turned up at local auctions. An early boost to our FitzGerald collection came from Tom Cook, the Ipswich bookseller who sold us his shop and business in 1983. Professor Terhune, the great FitzGerald scholar, who with his wife published the invaluable four-volume collection of Fitz's letters, had recently died leaving his books to his university. The Librarian, no doubt awash with books as librarians always are, noting that many had come from Cook's shop, offered them back to him. He kindly passed the offer on to us.

The first edition of FitzGerald's *Rubaiyat* was privately printed and given to his friends. The rest of the 250 copies were offered for sale, with little success, by Quaritch who eventually put them in the penny box outside his shop where they were discovered by Swinburne. The story is well known and that edition is now strictly for millionaires only. The exact facsimile by Mosher is worth having but also limited to 250 copies. My copy of the third edition (bought at auction in Woodbridge) has an intriguing ms. translation of four verses from Omar Khayyam signed 'E. B.' apparently in the hand of Prof. E. B. Cowell who had taught FitzGerald Persian and introduced him to Omar's quatrains.

Suffolk has added three more poets to our collection: George Crabbe, Robert Bloomfield and Bernard Barton, and in each case local opportunities have provided interesting copies. We even have B. B.'s silver and mother of pearl snuff box which played a vital role in meetings of the 'Woodbridge wits'. But this short account has already belied its description. One last intriguing item must suffice. George Crabbe's son, also George Crabbe, was vicar of Bredfield near Woodbridge and a close friend of E. F. G. One of the three Crabbe daughters (who delighted Fitz) kept an album which was purchased by a Suffolk bookseller at a house sale before my time. I coveted it for years and finally bought it when he retired. Its pages are full of sketches, poems (including Barton of course), riddles (E. F. G.'s is in verse) and Victorian exhortations to virtue. Not the least appealing is a series of watercolour sketches by his friend and Cambridge contemporary Thackeray with whom E. F. G. corresponded all his life. While letters were personal documents for his eyes only, Fitz was prepared to save for this album the watercolour sketches with which Thackeray embellished his correspondence, before destroying the text.

I hope these notes demonstrate in some measure how life shapes and is shaped by a collection – a subtle interaction. There is more to book-collecting than wrapping up new novels in cling film, like poor old Cyril Connelly, hoping that they will appreciate in value.

Ipswich

Drawing by William Thackeray from the FitzGerald album

JOAN AND CLAUDE COX

Derek Deadman

Leicestershire Private Presses

The initial spur to my collecting of Leicestershire Private Press material came from Michael Collinge. I have always been a collector of something or other but about four years ago I was between collections and looking for a new area. At that time I was flirting with private press books and Michael asked what I knew about the private press productions from my own backyard. Despite living in Leicester for over thirty years I had to admit to never having heard about them. Within a couple of weeks of this meeting, a local bookseller offered me a collection of about 350 Phoenix Broadsheets for about 50p each, and I was on my way. My collection now contains well in excess of 90% of all the books and broadsheets of the Leicestershire private presses known to me as well as a substantial amount of the ephemera – for example Christmas cards, prospectuses, menus, advertising leaflets, exhibition sheets and catalogues, postcards, bookplates, posters, instruction sheets, calendars and headed notepaper – that form an interesting and little known aspect of the printing activities of these presses.

I have always preferred to collect in an area where I could both research and make some kind of contribution to the literature to help other collectors. I have done this in the past with a book on cricket cigarette cards and with articles on the Victorian stamp box. Apart from Roderick Cave's account in *The Private Press*, the only significant publication relating to the Leicestershire presses as a whole appeared to be that by Ann Morris published in 1976 by the Plough Press. Ann Morris had been a student of Geoffrey Wakeman at Loughborough Technical College. For a student project she had interviewed a few of the persons connected with the local presses and produced a list of books and broadsheets to go with this information. My original intention was simply to update this listing but, as often results from such innocent beginnings, the project took on a life of its own and has snowballed to an unimaginable extent.

I blame a chance meeting with Rigby Graham at the Goldmark Gallery for the explosion of activity. Anyone who has ever met

Rigby Graham will be aware how easily this can be a life changing experience. Faintly amused to meet someone with an interest in 'the rubbish' produced from Leicestershire, in his own inimitable way he urged me to meet and quiz as many of the people involved as quickly as possible before they were dead. And what a wonderful group of people they turned out to be, uniformly generous in the giving of their time to revive memories hardly considered in some cases for the best part of fifty years.

What was common (and what is particularly attractive to me) about the Leicestershire Private Press material was the combination of an original text with original illustrations. Though many of the presses had a connection in some way with the Leicester College of Art, they were very independent presses and produced a wide range of productions and for a variety of reasons. Generally they did not take themselves too seriously and this sense of fun in the making is the dominant feeling generated by their efforts. This fun is self evident in *A Paper Snowstorm: Toni Savage and the Leicester Broadsheets* by Rigby Graham and myself that has just been published by Graham Moss at Incline Press. A second volume from the same press giving accounts of the origins and details of the work produced by each of the Leicestershire presses and containing a bibliography and illustrations of Leicestershire Private Press books, broadsheets and ephemera will follow in about a year's time.

Leicester

Drawing by Rita Foreman from *Behaviour,*
Phoenix Broadsheet 405, Toni Savage, 1994

DEREK DEADMAN

Robin de Beaumont

Sheila Markham, in her *A Book of Booksellers,* 2004, interviewed a total of fifty antiquarian booksellers of whom fifteen admitted to being book collectors, four of which also said they had started collecting at school. I am one of those in both categories.

Not only was my devious collecting path chronicled in this book, but it had also appeared in Paul Goldman's *Victorian Illustrated Books 1850–1870* headed, not very originally as I later found out, 'Collector's Progress', to accompany the exhibition of my collection of 1860s illustrators' books at the British Museum in 1994. So there are already two full accounts of my folly – but if another one is called for, then here goes.

I caught the collecting bug at school with any contemporary accounts of the French Revolution in contemporary bindings. These were easy enough to find and cheap, the reason for which I discovered later when I moved on and found them quite impossible to sell.

In 1944 I went up to Cambridge on an R.A.F. short course and with a school friend, who was also interested in architecture, started to collect early copies of classics such as Vitruvius, Vignola, James Gibbs, or Pozzo's *Perspective,* which had lain in the dusty Cambridge bookshops throughout the war. At between two and five guineas they weren't cheap but we broke ourselves. Later, married and working as an architect in Mason's Yard, St James's, I sold most of them to Marlborough Rare Books who were also in the Yard, making enough money for a holiday with my wife on Elba, having a new suit made, some bookshelves – and still with something left.

With the advent of a first child I started, not very originally, to collect Victorian children's books. But when the Osborne Collection catalogue first appeared in 1958, I realised I would have to be a millionaire and live in a castle to compete. At about the same time, Heywood Hill *gave* me a copy of Forrest Reid's 1928 *Illustrators of the Sixties* and from the checklist at the rear I realised that many of the books I already had came into that category. One lunch hour I was in Thorp's in Albemarle Street talking to

Robin de Beaumont

Mr Harris about sixties illustrators, to find he had the most as-
tounding collection in the basement with all the major books in
brilliant condition. I never found out exactly whose they had been
but think they might have been John Leighton's. Over the next
couple of years I used to buy one, or perhaps two, every pay day
and so started a sixties collection of my own.

By 1980, in my mid-fifties, and after a brief spell starting an
antiquarian book side to the stamp dealers, Stanley Gibbons, I
found myself redundant. This meant starting as a bookseller on
my own and issuing catalogues, of which there were thirteen up
to 1990, the last I find, rather sinisterly, being coded 'Calamity'.
In 1991 I received a letter from the British Museum Prints and
Drawings Department saying they were interested in adding to
their collection of 1860s illustrators and would I put them on the
mailing list. There were two or three shelves of such books in
stock and I was glad to think that, at last, they might have found
such a suitable home. As a result I visited the curator, Paul
Goldman, at the B.M. and it became obvious that here was a truly
knowledgeable devotee of the subject, no other institution in
Britain, including the V. & A., having shown the slightest bit of
interest. It was not long before I was considering whether an
offer to give my own collection might be accepted, particularly as
I had always made a point of upgrading condition wherever possible. In the current financial climate it seemed unlikely that they
would be purchased outright and in any case the actual cost over
the thirty-five odd years it had taken to accumulate them was
not great as they were deeply unfashionable (despite the fact that
they were eminently collectable, and expensive – in the 1890s with
publication of Gleeson White's *English Illustration 'The Sixties'*
1857–70 and in the 1930s with Forrest Reid's book). Once the
new head of Prints and Drawings, Antony Griffiths, had paid me
a visit and had subsequently shown me round his Department, I
found my books would be located in the same room as the Dalziel
Brothers', the major wood-engravers of the period, own archives.
So now they are in the right place, beautifully conserved with
each book in its own 'cosy' (card wrappers made by the ever
public spirited members of NADFAS) and used in exhibitions
about the world. They were given an exhibition between January
and April 1994 accompanied by Paul Goldman's book and even

received an untypically favourable review from Brian Sewell in the *Evening Standard*.

Now I have various mini-collections of such variety as T. N. Foulis envelope books, books illustrated by Thomas Lowinsky, nineteenth century colour printing, any nineteenth century illustrated book in original cloth in exceptional condition – and one collection in particular, details of which I withhold so that prices do not increase! Once a collector, always a collector and, hopefully, a hobby one can continue to the end. . . .

Chelsea, London

'St. Agnes' Eve'
Wood-engraving by Dalziel after design by
John Everett Millais,
Alfred Tennyson, *Poems*, Moxon, 1857

ROBIN DE BEAUMONT

David Dexter

On Natural Selection

The origins of my collecting habit can certainly be traced to the public library. Because there were few books in my childhood home, I have to assume that the impulse was primordial. Saturday mornings, I was at the door of my local by opening time; at closing, I staggered home with the maximum number of books allowed. Ultimately I came to realize that I wanted some books always to be at hand.

The first item in my permanent collection was a one-volume trade edition of the complete Sherlock Holmes novels and stories, a simple treasure that required three weeks of school lunch money to purchase. This sacrifice confirmed my essential nature – if there was any money available, it would probably go to getting books.

So my personal library began to grow – but without system, and usually without resources. In defence of the former failing, I must plead that editing the books of others and rearing two future bibliophiles somewhat diffuses my focus. There is no defence for the latter, which is often a fact of life. Yet I still gather instinctively, though subject to practical realities: very often paperback copies serve for placeholders, reprints stand in lieu of firsts, and damaged copies are better than none. A facsimile edition of the Kelmscott Chaucer must substitute for the real thing, probably for a long time.

But even in this rough manner, some dominant tendencies have asserted themselves – reference books of all kinds; John Donne, Robert Graves, and Aldous Huxley; England, Greece, and Italy; the Bronze Age; ancient science and religion, mythology, Cycladica, classical and preclassical literature, the history of physics; and (with my wife Patricia, a graphic designer) children's books by authors who usually write for adults; garden design; miniature books; fine printing; and the book arts. The titles arrive when they can, or when they will, but all have their shelf space.

Out of these general interests a few specializations have begun to emerge: from reference books, the evolution of the type; from Greece / Bronze Age / Cycladica, Cycladic artifacts and pre-Greek culture; from children's books, artists' books in the genre; and

David Dexter

from fine printing, the wood-engravings of Miriam Macgregor and the work of the Whittington Press. There are quite a few more rungs to climb on the evolutionary ladder before such a thing as a monograph could appear, but it would be satisfying to eventually make some contribution to the book community's gene pool.

Over the years, alas, my collecting method has only slightly matured. Rather than delineating an area and exploring it thoroughly, I have instead followed lines of interest across categories, favouring associations and connections and the worthy one-off. But during this same time, my enthusiasm has not lessened. Receiving a new book is always a cause for excitement. No matter what it is or how it comes to me, each is a treat (more or less) for the mind and senses.

And with only a slight mutation of perception, I can appreciate as well the numinous quality of the volumes on my shelves. Each book is a partial embodiment of its creators, a tangible blend of knowledge, artistry, and technique. All who contributed to the making of a book are conjured every time it is held and opened. Collecting – even if unrefined – and enjoying one's library is a lively occupation. And thus the impulse endures.

Mill Valley, California

DAVID DEXTER

Brian Donaghey

Boethius

Although coming from a family scarcely bookish at all in Queensland, Australia, I took to books early in life, starting my collecting habit when at age 15 I paid 5s. for my first old (1790s) tome, still adorning my shelves nearly fifty years later.

My favourite collecting interest began when as an undergraduate studying medieval English, I found that Chaucer had been influenced by, and translated, the prison work called *The Consolation of Philosophy* (CP) by the late Roman writer A. M. T. S. Boethius (*c.* 480–524). Most of his works were studied in the Middle Ages and beyond, but the CP was the best known, the object of many commentaries, and translated by King Alfred and Queen Elizabeth I, to name only two from a host in various languages. Sadly, Boethius' career declined from being a trusted official of the Ostrogothic king Theoderic the Great, to the accusation of treason and eventual execution. He was sometimes regarded as a Christian martyr, though his adherence to Christianity remains in doubt.

At that time I was lucky to find in an obscure bookshop in Brisbane a copy of the 1671 Variorum edition of the CP. It amused me that a work written in sunny Italy was being read in such an old edition in tropical Australia, on the verandah of my grandparents' house; but it helped determine my future course. I went on to travel to England and become an academic, with a high proportion of my published work relating to Boethian studies, including articles on King Alfred's translation, the medieval commentaries on Boethius, Caxton's printing of Chaucer's translation, and a census of the post-medieval English versions. Even before leaving Australia I had begun to collect Boethius material (financial restraints have, however, always ruled out acquiring manuscripts or incunabula).

Among the thousands of books I now have, although the core of the Boethius collection takes up only one bookcase those few shelves remain closest to my heart. No doubt I was fortunate to start collecting before book prices started to soar – several desiderata are beyond my reach now if they ever appear. Some are curiously unobtainable, like the Teubner edition of 1871: from the hundreds of copies printed I have never seen one outside of library copies.

Brian Donaghey

The CP survives in hundreds of medieval manuscripts, a measure of its popularity and influence. It has never been out of print, with at least half a dozen twentieth-century English translations, one now circulating in Penguin Classics and added to the Folio Society list. There are at least four unpublished English versions from the sixteenth and seventeenth centuries (a project for my retirement?).

Of course I started before the internet made book-searching easier, but the thrill of the chase was also greater. My first visit to what was in 1968 Blackwell's Antiquarian Department in Oxford left an impression on me, for my name was already familiar to the chief man there, who remarked he had been keeping a Boethius for me. I was touched that he had taken an interest in such a young inexperienced man as I was then.

Surprisingly, despite the number of English translations after 1500, the only printing of the Latin text in these islands until modern times was the Foulis Press edition of 1751, a bare text with no apparatus or notes. It seems everyone depended on Continental editions. Of these I have a number, though not all: two Florence editions by Giunta, 1513, 1521; Venice, Gregorius, 1516; Cologne, Cervicornus, 1535; Pulmann's editions, Leyden, 1581, 1590; Bernartius, Plantin, Antwerp, 1607; P. Bertius, Leyden, 1633; R. Vallinus, Leyden, 1656; that Variorum edition, Leyden, 1671; Cally's Delphin edition, Paris, 1680, reissued 1695; Vulpius, Padua 1721 and 1744; the Foulis edition, Glasgow, 1751; and subsequent Victorian and modern editions.

Many translations have appeared; I have concentrated on English ones but shelving has been found for others. Apart from modern editions of those by King Alfred, Chaucer, John Walton, G. Colville (1556), Queen Elizabeth (1593), J. Bracegirdle (1604) and 'I.T.' (1609), I have original copies of versions by Edmund Elys (Oxford, 1674), Viscount Preston (1695, 2nd ed. 1712), W. Causton (London, 1730), P. Ridpath (London, 1785), R. Duncan (1789), W. Warburton (1789, a reprint of the 1724 first edition), and those from 1900 onwards.

Space is short so perhaps the French, Italian, Spanish and German versions should not be listed, but they cover from the 1550s onwards. In addition there are many books about Boethius, editions of medieval and later commentaries, microfilms of manuscripts, and oddities such as the life of Boethius in Nicolas Caussin's *The Holy Court* (4th edition of the English version, London, 1678). The iconography of Boethius, derived from medieval precedents, is also exhibited in the illustrations to editions and translations, often copied one from another.

Many of my treasures are in contemporary or near-contemporary bindings so it is a pleasure to handle them as well as to re-read the text now familiar to me. Funding permitting, I shall continue to acquire where possible, although retirement and moving will force me to downsize my library as a whole. Boethius himself warned against the vanity of worldly possessions, but these mere accumulations of paper, leather and cloth on my shelves do provide a spiritual uplift and an aesthetic pleasure which I hope to enjoy for many years.

Sheffield

BRIAN DONAGHEY

Anthony Dowd

Modern Bindings

In 2001 I placed on long loan to the John Rylands University Library of Manchester, one hundred from my collection of modern bindings. The University published the catalogue in the following year, which has been illustrated by a remarkable series of colour photographs of each of the bindings. The collection will be housed in the library building that was donated by the widow of John Rylands in 1900 and which is currently undergoing a £15,000,000 refurbishment to bring its conservation and display facilities up to twenty-first century standards. The Special Collections of the library include the two Tregaskis collections of 1894 and 1994 and the prospects for major exhibitions of modern bindings in Manchester are exciting.

I started collecting books in the 1960s and was interested in those illustrated by Robert Gibbings and then the publications of the Golden Cockerel Press of which I built up a large collection. But in 1967 I was shown by Charlie Broadhurst, a well-known book dealer in Southport, a binding by Arthur Johnson of the Essex House Press *Wren's Parentalia* in full white vellum tooled in gold on the upper board with an outline of St Paul's Cathedral. This was my first introduction to a modern individually designed binding and the concept of having a binding designed to reflect the text and illustration of a book appealed to me.

In 1970 I attended the sale of the modern bindings collected by Major John Roland Abbey and was fortunate to be able to acquire eight books including two by Edgar Mansfield, one being the *Shorelands Summer Diary*, a copy of the limited edition signed by C. F. Tunnicliffe and with a binding by Mansfield that is well-known for its brilliant and complex design. It was not until 1986 that I first commissioned a binding and this was from Philip Smith who produced an impressive treatment of some Anglo-Saxon poetry illustrated with powerful colour etchings by Shirley Jones. I found the exercise wholly satisfying and enjoyed my discussions with the binder and showing the resultant binding to the artist. After this I decided to learn more of the binder's craft and attended a series of courses over four years and this taught me

Anthony Dowd

how difficult it is to create a binding without errors, particularly when using gold tooling. This training has made me very critical of a binder's work and perhaps enabled me to build a better collection.

I have so far commissioned twenty-three bindings from fifteen binders and presently have some 130 modern bindings, including those on loan to the John Rylands Library. These include a number of special bindings commissioned by private presses such as the Fleece, Incline, Old Stile and Whittington Presses, and Gwasg Gregynog where I was a member of the Board from 1994 until retiring in early 2005. I introduced and wrote an illustrated catalogue for them in 2004 of the nineteen special bindings that the Press had produced since the University of Wales revived it in 1976. James Brockman who was largely responsible for enabling the bindery to be reopened after George Fisher's occupation ended with the outbreak of war in 1939, wrote a memoir of his year as the Gregynog Arts Fellow in 1983 and has also bound fifteen copies to an exciting abstract design.

A major part of the enjoyment in commissioning bindings comes from the contact established with the owners of the Private Presses as most projects involve binding sets of unbound sheets that most presses are pleased to supply on request. Knowledge of the styles and preferences of binders enables commissions to be offered to match the artistic style of the illustrator or of the subject matter of the book. A discussion with the binder takes place and often alternative treatments are suggested. All this results in dialogue with the binder and adds to the appreciation of his work. Understanding the processes involved in the design of a book and its binding and of the nature of the materials used – paper, ink, typefaces, the printing of illustrations and the many skills of the binder – all add to the enjoyment of the finished book. I have mainly confined my collection of bindings to those bound in Britain during my lifetime but do have a few slightly earlier ones as well. I also have a small collection of the better private press books of the same period and add to these and modern bindings as opportunities permit.

Alderley Edge, Cheshire

ANTHONY DOWD   171

Robert Drake

Robert Drake

My book collecting started purely by accident. As a teenager my main interest was shooting, and wildfowling in particular. After taking the weekly *Shooting Times* magazine for a while I decided to buy a book on the subject. My first book was *Fowler's Moon* by Nigel Thornycroft. This collection of fowling trips fascinated me and caused me to seek out and read anything and everything on wildfowling. I bought mainly from an ABA bookseller, B. M. Gilbert, who worked from home locally. I built a comprehensive library between 1970 and 1980. About this time, 1980, Mr Gilbert, with whom I had become friends, said he wished to retire and as I obviously had an interest in books would I be interested in learning the second-hand book trade and maybe take over his mail order business. To cut a long story short I ended up buying his entire stock of 5,000 books which I temporarily stored all over the house, garage etc., and became a part-time bookdealer from 1982 onwards in a rented shop in Grays, Essex, where I traded until October 2004, when I decided to retire.

During my twenty-three years of bookselling my interests broadened and I made a varied collection of what interested me at different periods. I have made a small collection of the rarer local history books, a collection of books on Thames Barges and related subjects and latterly a collection of about eighty Golden Cockerel Press books and a few other private press books including a small collection of private press ephemera, plus a selection of books on bookbinding and fine printing. The highlight of my fowling books is *Snowden Sleights* by W. Smith of which I have two of only seventy-six known copies, the rarest of fowling books until a limited edition of 500 was published recently.

My local history highlight is *Alice of Fobbing* by W. Heygate, 1868, a rare novel of local interest which after thirty years of searching was found on the internet in Canada. I have heard of only one other copy of this book apart from the British Library copy. My favourite Golden Cockerel is *The Glory of Life* by Llewelyn Powys, illustrated by Robert Gibbings, also two firsts of H. E. Bates. Another favourite is *The Book of Thoth* by Aleister

Crowley, limited edition of 200 copies, signed and very nicely printed on handmade paper by the Chiswick Press. I retired from full-time bookselling at the age of 66 and have taken up another previous interest which is road cycling, and no doubt will soon be looking for classic cycling books to extend the library still further. Another as yet unfinished project is to write some reminiscences of the second-hand book trade between 1980 and 2005.

Stanford-le-Hope, Essex

Wood-engraving by Robert Gibbings from
A. E. Coppard, *The Hundredth Story*, Golden Cockerel Press, 1931

John Dunn

The Evolution of My Book Collecting Interests

In my mind's eye I can still see that book on the shelves of Mr Miles's antiquarian bookshop in Leeds, *Some Diversions of a Man of Letters*, 1919, by Edmund Gosse. At the time, I knew nothing of the author, but the title had an air of the literary dilettante about it which appealed to me. I bought the book, made space for it on the bookshelf in my bedroom and so began my collecting journey.

John Dunn

Any amateur book collector can relate in some way or other to Edmund Gosse. A self-taught, late Victorian man of letters and book collector in his own right, he contributed to the development of the field of 'Eng lit', only to confront it in later life as a discipline and the preserve of the universities and professional

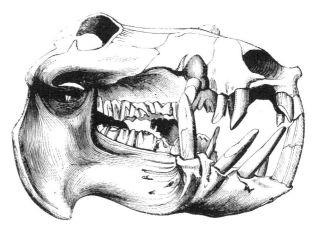

SKULL OF HIPPOPOTAMUS.

Skull of a Hippopotamus
from *Omphalos*, P. H. Gosse, 1857

academics. The still common, popular editions of his works lured me into the labyrinth of his countless short-run editions and presentation copies – and then on to his father. Similarly self-taught, this time a pioneer in the field of natural history (he invented and coined the expression, aquarium), Philip Henry Gosse wrote books that fascinate on a number of levels. For example, he fought a rear-guard action against evolutionary theory in his controversial book, *Omphalos: An Attempt to Untie the Geological Knot*, 1857. His works of popular science covered themes as varied as Jamaican bird life, the American South and, above all, marine zoology. Then there are his own illustrations for his books, often hand coloured and always fine pieces of art in their own right. With Freeman and Wertheimer's bibliography in one hand, I collected all P. H. Gosse's works on natural history, almost always in the first edition, together with many of the variant bindings of each work, though I have not yet acquired any of his religious tracts. My favourite acquisition of Gosse the father was the *Illustrations of the Birds of Jamaica* as a set of unbound plates, including the rare plate XXXVI, 'Sylvicola canadensis', one of only four known copies. I also treasure a number of signed autograph letters, including those shown in the above bibliography to illustrate Gosse's handwriting.

JOHN DUNN

Great though my passion for P. H. Gosse's works became, as a collecting interest, he led me into a cul-de-sac. I collected P. H. Gosse for my interest in the man, not the natural history. My book collecting interests meanwhile continued to grow, organically, from the son not the father. Edmund Gosse's biography of Algernon Charles Swinburne led me to an interest in the books both by and about the fiery republican and atheist poet and controversialist of his day. Edmund Gosse and the infamous Thomas James Wise collaborated in the publication of Swinburne's posthumous works, now a fascinating minefield of editions, bogus and genuine alike. Alfred Noyes, the more sober, so-called imperialist poet and, in later life, Roman Catholic, worshipped Swinburne, despite the latter's politics and atheism. He wrote in his autobiography (*Two Worlds for Memory*, 1953) of a visit to the great man at The Pines in Putney, the home Swinburne shared with Theodore Watts-Dunton and from which Noyes left with a gift of the fine Florence Press edition of *Songs Before Sunrise*. This led me to collect other poets of his time, now no longer read. William Watson was one and learning about him led me to an interest in his mentor, James Ashcroft Noble, self-made Victorian man of letters and an author of collectable works in his own right, a few of which I own and a few I covet. From here I was led to collect the works of another poet, only this time very much in vogue, Noble's son-in-law, Edward Thomas. Famous for a burst of composition, inspired by a famous encounter with Robert Frost after years of dispiriting hack work, his poems were first printed in the early pseudonymous Edward Eastaway volumes, which now hold sway over my collecting interests, together with Frost's early works. Edward Thomas has also spawned an interest for me in the Georgian poets, especially Gordon Bottomley, which is likely to keep me collecting for years to come.

It was my interest in poets, major and minor, that led me, long ago, to pick up a *History of English Poetry* by Kenneth Hopkins. Himself an innovative book collector of note (I have a copy of his charming *Book Collecting for the Financially Unstable*, and Anthony Rota makes an affectionate reference to him in *Books in the Blood*), Hopkins was yet another self-taught man of letters and author as well as self-publisher of books to snare the collector, me included. In his formative years Hopkins famously met

Llewelyn Powys, which in turn led to correspondence (later published) and an association with the other Powys brothers. Inevitably, the enigmatic brothers Powys and their circle now interest me and provide a myriad of special signed first editions and *ad hoc* first American imprints both to absorb and entrap me.

I think three things distinguish my book collecting habit. Firstly, my choice of books always coincides with a literary interest and I mostly buy books to read. I say mostly, because this feature of my collecting did not always apply to P. H. Gosse's works on natural history. However, I rarely waste space with 'reading copies'. Secondly, I do not only enjoy books as objects in their own right, I also value their association with a past age, author, previous reader or recipient of a presentation copy. Finally, I collect strictly for pleasure, never with an eye to profit.

In addition to all the above, I have an interest in postwar private handpress books, stimulated by a passion for printing, in the John Ryder tradition, under my own 'Study Press' imprint.

Loughton, Milton Keynes, Bucks.

JOHN DUNN

Margaret Eaton

Powys Collection

In the mid-sixties while chatting in our shop with Mr Howlett, always the most interesting, intelligent and charming of runners, he mentioned that he occasionally corresponded with John Cowper Powys. At that time I had recently greatly enjoyed reading *Wolf Solent* and *Glastonbury Romance* so when he offered to give us an introduction to John and Phyllis Playter, Powys's companion and amanuensis, I made sure that we would have time to visit them on our next trip to Wales.

The journey to Blaenau Ffestiniog was somehow appropriate as we entered the village via the menacing mountain pass containing the slate mines and found the cottage cowering under the mountain side. I learned later that he always picked the site of a new home for its accessibility to mountain or wilderness for his daily walk with his dog 'the black'. We were made extremely welcome, John Cowper was on a day bed at the end of the small downstairs room and despite his ill-health talked at great length with enthusiastic gesticulations while Phyllis gave us tea and very sophisticated French biscuits, the latter somehow terribly out of place in the pared down simplicity of the surroundings.

A few years later we made another visit. By that time I had become very enthusiastic about his brother Llewelyn's books and talked to him a good deal about them. He offered to give us an introduction to Alyse Gregory (Llewelyn's widow) who was living near Dartmoor. Our next visit to that part of the world was in the February of one of the coldest winters of the decade and I remember sliding down hills and battling through three feet high snow in the sunken Devon lanes in our ancient car. I was determined not to miss the opportunity to meet that distinguished lady who in addition to having published several fine novels had been the first woman editor of *The Dial*. We were greeted with tea, home made cakes and fascinating conversation. I so admired her and wished subsequently that I had recorded her conversation. However my abiding memory of the afternoon is my abject shame at her amazement that I had not read Proust. It has taken me another forty years or so to achieve that wonderfully rewarding task.

Margaret Eaton

It was through reading *Welsh Ambassadors* by Louis Wilkinson, friend and contemporary of Llewelyn that I learned of the extent and varied talents of this remarkable family. John Cowper, the eldest was a prolific novelist and essayist and spent many years travelling throughout the United States in the twenties and thirties delivering his universally renowned lectures on literature. When we exhibited at U.S. book fairs and included some of his books it was not unusual for an elderly man to stop and enthuse at length on his memories of the unique occasion when he attended one of these memorable theatrical occasions. Theodore was also a novelist but of a quite different type, his books being of a completely different style as also were Llewelyn's essays. These three achieved considerable fame during their lifetime and each still has a small

MARGARET EATON

worldwide coterie of enthusiasts. Two of the younger brothers, Littleton as headmaster of a public school and Arthur, an architect, both wrote and were well known in their own fields. Of the four sisters, one was a novelist and poet, another an accomplished artist and illustrator and another a world authority on lace.

By the time one added to these family members, wives, lovers and friends including Alyse Gregory, Gamel Woolsey, Elizabeth Myers, Louis Wilkinson, Ann Reid and others there was enormous scope to start a collection and I never regretted launching into it. I was fortunate that when I started there were so many of John Cowper's books available in the United States and every trip produced a number of exciting parcels to open when we returned home. I sometimes think that the twenties and thirties must be the most fruitful period to collect. I can think of no other time when there was so constant a stream of 'little magazines' appearing, not always for very long – in fact I can think of only a handful, such as *The London Mercury* and *The Dial* which had a long life – but nevertheless there was always another one for the writer to try with his latest piece of work. No wonder writers in this period were so prolific; in my collection was Llewelyn's notebook in which he detailed his various payments. The amounts were pitiful and one could only imagine the amount of work that went into essays, short stories etc. in order to receive a cheque for £2. 2s. or a similar sum.

In addition to the books and manuscripts I was also able to buy a few pieces of memorabilia including John Cowper's death mask and the pen with which he wrote *Glastonbury Romance*. I had more than twenty years of pure enjoyment in building the collection and was able to help with both the bibliography of John Cowper and that of Llewelyn. When the time came that the chance of finding something that I did not already have occurred less and less frequently, I decided that I would keep all my reading copies and sell the collection, just owning it was not enough, the real fun was in adding to it. I considered selling it *en bloc* but in the end thought that selling the items individually would be my choice so that I could imagine the pleasure given to the new owners. I have not regretted this decision and recall with great pleasure the years of happy hunting.

London

MARGARET EATON

Hans van Eijk

Did I ever want to be a book collector? I remember still building model boats and trains while one of my friends already collected postage stamps at the age of six – the collection was kept in his trouser pocket and so never was in a 'mint' condition. He would thrust out a handful of crumpled bits of paper at you, asking 'Do you want to see my collection?' With this excellent example I also began collecting, my father thoughtfully supplying a small album. As a result somewhere in the attic of my house a collection of cigar bands is still languishing, and a stamp collection is taking up much needed space on a bookshelf. However, the chemicals I acquired in my teens have gone – we invented gunpowder and nitro-glycerine, but never dared use them. Much of this collection was dumped in Rotterdam harbour.

As a student I realised books were there to be read and used, and had to be readily available at home when needed, without time-wasting trips to public libraries. And although the amount of English literature on my shelves continued to grow it could never really be called a 'collection'. This changed when I happened to find a few pamphlets from small presses and publishers in the mid 1960s. The printing was usually of a low quality and the poetry often not much better, yet it was always a pleasure to receive a new pamphlet. Most of these presses have disappeared now and can only be found in back issues of *The Private Library* or *Private Press Books* – Keepsake, Wild Hawthorn, Mandeville, Priapus, Poet & Printer, and so many others. More expensive books, seen on the shelves of antiquarian bookshops in London and Oxford, were beyond my means for a long time.

Equally primitive, though far more interesting, was the stream of publications coming from Leicestershire: the Pandora Press was still trying to sell off its least successful items, the New Broom Press was giving a new interpretation to book design and the Brewhouse Press was trying to move away from producing mere pamphlets. Moreover, I was no longer very much interested in the texts these presses printed, but rather admired the weird drawings and linocuts by Rigby Graham – I am told that for a long

Hans van Eijk

time I must have been unique in this respect. Eventually this became the nucleus of my collection of Toni Savage's pamphlets and broadsheets, and of Rigby Graham's graphic work contained or reproduced in books and magazines, on posters and broadsheets. I admit that I myself have contributed to the spread of Graham's work by printing many of his woodcuts at the Bonnefant Press in Banholt, and by compiling a bibliography.

Over the years I have now collected examples of the work of many private presses, mainly British. I admire much of Francis Meynell's work for the Nonesuch Press and Will Carter's at his Rampant Lions Press. There are also single titles from the Kelmscott and Doves presses, which I kept for the use of their private typefaces, just as a few titles printed by Oxford University Press in the Fell types. But what has really interested me most over thirty-odd years as a typographer and a collector are the books printed by Giovanni Mardersteig at the Officina Bodoni since the nineteen-twenties. I bought the last few volumes that appeared before his death in 1977 and have allowed myself two or three books every year, in spite of increasing prices. These are what I consider the most perfect private press books, such as a small printer like myself can only handle with admiration and jealousy.

But one cannot always go through the same books, however much one likes them. So for the evening hours I still have a collection of that very readable World's Classics series – the original series of course, although they were always surpassed in quality by their Swiss imitations published from 1944 on by Manesse.

Banholt, The Netherlands

Ballynalackan Castle, drawing by Rigby Graham from
Postcards for Murphy, In de Bonnefant, 2004

HANS VAN EIJK

Richard Faircliff

Surrey Topography and Vernacular Architecture

At the age of six I announced to my parents that I wished to become an architect on the basis that I thought that I would then be able to draw and design houses for the rest of my life. It has not been quite like that although I did become an architect, went on to design some houses and many hospitals, and have now reached the end of my career after forty-three years in practice. More time for books.

My interest in buildings and books was first stirred by childhood holidays in Devon and the Cotswolds, and the Batsford series of illustrated architectural / topographical books (I now own some seventy of them) and A. & C. Black colour plate books of the early years of the twentieth century, all borrowed from Sutton Public Library.

The first books I acquired at this time, among them a number of school prizes, included A. H. Gardner's *Outline of English Architecture* (1947), from the Batsford series, and a slightly tired copy of the three volumes in four of T. H. Turner & J. H. Parker's *Domestic Architecture of the Middle Ages* (1851–1859) given to me by an uncle who had obtained them from a deceased client, on the basis that he thought I would find them of interest. Indeed I did and they still grace my shelves, but regretfully in a somewhat more decrepit state.

My real interest in book collecting developed in the early 1970s and centred on topographical books relating to the county of Surrey, where I had been born, educated, and still lived (my collection now includes first editions of nearly all the major county histories dating back to 1736 and most of the standard town histories of the nineteenth and early twentieth century). Additionally I purchased a number of the A. & C. Black colour plate topographical books at that time for about £5 each.

Topographical and architectural interests led me into vernacular architecture, then a relatively new area for study, and the books were cheaper than architectural books *per se*. Interest in both these topics perhaps sprang from the subject of my BA Thesis '*The Architectural History of Guildford*'. Professor R. A. Cordingley

Richard Faircliff

at Manchester University was my examiner and we found we had a number of interests in common, among them 'mathematical tiles', and we corresponded on this subject until his untimely death quite soon after. He gave me a copy of his text on *British Historical Roof Types* – still a standard authority. At that time Manchester University was the centre of academic research in the field of vernacular architecture. Some of Cordingley's students went on to become well known authors in this field and included Raymond Wood-Jones (*Traditional Domestic Architecture in the Banbury Region* (1963) – now difficult to find), and R. A. Brunskill who developed the now universally accepted codification system for traditional house plans and has published many books on the subject in the last thirty years, of which a considerable number are included in my library.

But I digress. My book collection paralleled my interests and has continued, rather spasmodically at times as a result of family and financial constraints, to the present. It comprises many nineteenth century books, including about forty from the first half of that century, and twenty from the eighteenth century, the earliest being Strype's *Life of Whitgift* (1718) (founder of my old school) from the library of the Earl of Portsmouth.

In the last twenty-five years I have moved into the pure architecture field (admittedly from the lower cost end of the market), which was really my first love, and these books now form a considerable part of my library – largely on English architecture from the first half of the twentieth century, but with a sprinkling of earlier and more recent ones.

Other areas of interest are watercolour books, both history and practice, which reflect my second main spare time activity, and books about the book trade. My interest in the first category was sparked by the gift, from a grateful client (and architects don't often have these!) of Martin Hardie's *Water Colour Painting in Britain* (1967–8), in three volumes. Subsequently I bought a copy of Samuel Prout's *New Drawing Book* (1819), at a Sotheby's auction, and later added a copy of his *Easy Lessons in Landscape Drawing* (1820) with forty plates, in contemporary half calf. Books about the book trade are largely the standard works and of course include all the Private Libraries Association members' books since 1976.

A more recent discovery is in the diaries of James Lees-Milne, whom I first came across as an architectural historian and writer about country houses. In the last six years I have built up a collection of nearly all that he published (and continued to have published posthumously) – probably just in time as his books have recently shot up in price. A by-product from this subset is a small group of books by or about Robert Byron, a brilliant travel writer and architectural critic and a contemporary and friend of Lees-Milne, who was tragically killed in the Mediterranean in 1941. Unfortunately first editions of his works are now very hard to find and expensive.

My key interests remain in Surrey and vernacular architecture books. The real problem has been that my collecting interests have been too often diverted to new subjects so that no part of the collection has been developed to its full potential. But I like it that way and that is what really matters.

Bledington, Oxon.

Vernacular cottage at Cranleigh, Surrey, from R. Nevill,
Old Cottage and Domestic Architecture in South-West Surrey, 1889

RICHARD FAIRCLIFF

Gwenda and Gerald Fischer

We were born in the 1920s, Gwenda in Melbourne and I near Adelaide, and we met in 1959 when Gwenda came to work and live in Adelaide. There were not many books in the homes of our childhood and youth and our parents were not book collectors. In the 1930s we both found clerical work in Melbourne and Adelaide offices though some of the latter were still affected by the Economic Depression of the early 1930s. With hindsight perhaps a few signs of bibliophily can be discerned even in these early years of our lives. One office in which Gwenda worked (not a publisher's or bookseller's) somehow came to hold a few books and when she left to go to another position she was permitted to choose one item as a parting gift. She chose *The Works of William Shakespeare*, a set of twelve 16mo volumes in a small glass-fronted decorative wooden case, published by Frederick Warne and Company in 1888.[1] The set was something of a talisman for the rest of her life and even while working in London in the early 1950s she would remind her mother by letter to keep the books and case secure. I worked in the office of a small furniture factory and though I owned only two high-school prize books and a few early Penguins I recognised that books, however few, do furnish a room, and I was able to buy some reject planed timber and get a friendly factory hand to make me a small three-shelf bookcase. I have it still.

The war years 1939–45 widened our reading horizons and prompted us to buy a few newly published books but service life and limited civilian housing did not encourage any collection building. In the postwar years our university studies in the humanities made us aware of the vast world of Australian, English and foreign books and by the 1960s we could afford to buy some of these – both new and old – that interested us. Marriage in 1964 and the setting up of a home brought together our small and varied collections and with it the recognition of shared or related reading interests.

It might have been a likely outcome that with our professional backgrounds – Gwenda a university law librarian and myself an

Gerald Fischer, standing, with his late wife Gwenda,
and a friend, Jeff Scrivener. Lyndoch, South Australia, 1993

archivist – our book collecting could have been directed to those fields. But excepting a few specialised historical or text books our book-buying while frequent was quite general in scope – simply whatever interested us to read. In this rather care-free way over thirty-four years we acquired about four thousand hard cover books and perhaps more than half that number of paperbacks many of which in content and size made formal distinction rather meaningless.

Each of us did, of course, have some particular reading interests and in pursuing these as opportunity and chance allowed we were incidentally, but not quite unknowingly, practising some collection building. But we did not pursue bibliographical completeness exhaustively nor search patiently for first editions: if these qualities sometimes by chance proved to be practical possibilities that was an unexpected but welcome bonus.

In our early years of collecting our books were stored on library-type lightweight adjustable metal shelving which made moving house simpler. In 1981 with the construction of a new house for retirement living one large room was designated as a library and equipped with handsome adjustable wooden shelving and there was room for several free standing bookcases and one revolving book stand. This arrangement at least allowed us to make some broad classification of our books – biography, history and politics, literature, philosophy, science, with our special interest collections in the bookcases.

Gwenda's special interests included the works of the Australian novelist Patrick White and she made a complete collection of his novels starting with *Happy Valley* published in 1940. As an admirer of Virginia Woolf she acquired all her novels and much biographical and critical writing and this led to an interest in the publications of the Hogarth Press though her collection includes only one work hand set and hand printed by the Woolfs – *Pharos and Pharillon* by E. M. Forster, published in 1923. Interest in the Woolfs led on to works of Vita Sackville West and Harold Nicolson though few copies of their early books were found in Australia. Gwenda's interest in art encouraged her over time to acquire the rare first eleven issues of *Art in Australia* published by Sydney Ure Smith during 1916–21. She also brought together all but a few of the series Britain in Pictures published by William Collins

1941–50, and which have been the subject of a detailed survey in *The Private Library*.[2]

As the grandson of a Swiss emigrant to Australia I have collected books about Switzerland, also not a very rewarding field in Australia, but once it yielded up *The History of the Helvetic Confederacy* in two large quarto volumes published in 1800. The author was Joseph Plants of Swiss descent who had been in charge of the Manuscripts Department and was later Principal Librarian of the British Museum Library. I have over a hundred titles (not all read) and perhaps I am straining its bounds a bit when I say it includes *Lenin in Zürich* by Alexander Solzhenitsyn published in 1976.

In the 1960s I began collecting two series of rather small books: Thomas Nelson's Popular Editions of Notable Books many of which were issued in highly decorated blue hard covers roughly over 1910–1920s and The Travellers' Library published by Cape / Heinemann in the 1920s and 1930s. Nelson's Notable Books have perhaps some surprising titles, for example *The English Constitution* by Walter Bagehot, and an edited version of *The Journal of the De Goncourts*. Some of the travel books by lady authors in the series have pleasantly unassuming titles – *The Simple Adventures of a Memsahib* by Sara Jeannette Duncan, and *By Desert Ways to Baghdad* by Louisa Jebb (Mrs Roland Wilkins), with its enigmatic dedicatory page saying only 'To X'. I have acquired over seventy of the series mostly in Australia, but this is probably less than half of all that were published. I have acquired about the same number of The Travellers' Library but these have been collected with some discrimination with the notion that we might both – one day – actually read them and enjoy vicariously the pleasure of their type, design and limp blue covers that they must have given to their original readers. The series has also been the subject of an article in a past issue of *The Private Library*.[3]

In the early 1950s I became aware of The Novel Library, published by Hamish Hamilton and very pleasantly printed and bound, and I bought and read a few of them. Rather late in the day and since reading that one ducal collector in England has the complete series and regards it as 'something of a collectors' item' I rather regret that I did not pursue bibliographical completeness in this field.[4]

As an amateur private printer I have through the generosity of and exchange with other private printers formed a small collection of private press work which includes almost all of the books from the Brindabella Press and many items from the Duyfken Press, both presses located in Canberra.

Gwenda died in November 1998, her planned computerised author catalogue of all our books, alas, unrealised. The collection is now held in a final retirement house in a beachside suburb of Adelaide, and mostly on the re-erected wooden shelving and bookcases made in 1981. Arrangements have been made for the eventual gift of the whole collection to a university in Adelaide.

Adelaide, Australia

1. 'The 'Bedford' Edition' according to title-pages.
2. *The Private Library*, Autumn 1986.
3. *The Private Library*, Winter 1971.
4. *The Englishman's Room*, ed. Alvilde Lees-Milne, Massachusetts, USA, Salem House Publishers, [1986], p. 41.

Aldgate Pump Hotel, South Australia, *c.* 1870,
drawing by E.M.S. from a photograph,
Coaching Days at Aldgate, Pump Press, 1964

Donald R. Fleming

A display of Clipper Ship Sailing Cards in the small history window of the old Union Trust Company Bank at the corner of Montgomery and Market streets in San Francisco caught my eye. The accompanying notes revealed it was placed there courtesy of The Book Club of California and that the headquarters were just

Donald R. Fleming

DONALD R. FLEMING

a few blocks away. Curious, I made my way to the offices to be greeted by the then secretary, Betty Downs – coat and purse in hand and obviously ready to leave. Would I care to join her and a few friends for lunch with Robert Frost at the Palace Hotel?

A few minutes later and I was seated between Carroll Harris, Master of Mackenzie & Harris, Typographers and Typefounders, and that legendary collector and bon vivant, Ted Lilienthal. Good food, great wines, intriguing conversation and I was soon a member of the Club and invited, as the guest of Harris and Lilienthal, to that evening's meeting and dinner of the Roxburghe Club. That fortuitous event put me, a rank amateur, into the serious 'Pursuit of the Golden Dream', leaving a wonderful circle of friends which expanded rapidly to include such book people as the Grabhorns, the Kennedys, the Allens, David Magee and John and Warren Howell, all of whom seemed bent on inoculating me with their wonderful 'bug' – the association with and collecting of fine books. Needless to say, I was soon spending any and all of my spare time in the pursuit of everything bookish, even to the birthing of our 'Press of the Golden Key' with my equally enthusiastic wife Kathi as its 'Printer's Devil'.

Then came binding with Herbert and Peter Fahey as our mentors, and all other ramifications of the 'bug' received their share of our adventure into the 'book-arts'. The American west, fine press work, books about books, printing and typography, Samuel Johnson and his circle, Pepys – all kept us busy building bookcases. Then a foray into American stamp bindings of the late nineteenth century and early twentieth century usurped the walls of the guest bedroom. One side of the forty foot hallway handled novels, travel and bookish publications. Books and book people have been the focus and joy of our sixty-four years of marriage – we could have asked no more.

Orinda, California

DONALD R. FLEMING

Keith Fletcher

Mechanical Road Transport

In 1955, while still a schoolboy, and dreaming of the sports car I would one day own, I made the discovery that if, instead of buying a second-hand postwar MG, one were to go back to the 1930s, or even the 1920s, one got a very much more exotic car for one's money. I quickly decided that to identify the desirable models of the period I would need to find out what the enthusiasts thought of them when they were new: I began to seek out books and magazines that gave not only the testbed statistics but the reputations that they gained among the motoring public of their day. My first book, which I found on the shelves of my father's shop in Cecil Court, was Prince Chula of Siam's *Road Racing 1936*, printed by the Sun Engraving Co. 'For Private Circulation'. Having read the tales of derring-do, and been seduced by the fine printing and exotic imprint, I put it on my own shelves and immediately began adding similar titles. By the time I bought my first car (a 1927 3-litre Bentley tourer) at the age of 21 I had a substantial group of books on vintage and historic cars.

Books are for reading; and although the story of the motor car is usually regarded as beginning in the last quarter of the nineteenth century with Daimler and Benz I soon discovered that most general histories of the subject begin with a chapter or two on the ancestors of the automobile and the germs of the ideas that were to contribute to its development. In the nineteenth century there were 'steam carriages for common roads' and before that, back at least to the fifteenth century, all kinds of passenger-carrying vehicles moved by cranks and levers, cogs and pedals, or windmills and sails. Although I continued to amass material on the combustion-engined motor car (to date several thousand books, over one thousand manufacturers' catalogues, two thousand postcards, as well as posters, prints, paintings, photographs, bronzes and other related objects) I became more and more interested in the 'pre-history' of the car, and when I began to focus on this early period I found that I had the field almost to myself. Certainly many of the books that I decided I needed were already 'collectable books' but I have never found a competitor in the

Keith Fletcher

market with the same reason as myself – I have never met anyone else with a fine copy of the first edition of Tristram Shandy in a transport collection (in volume 2, chapter 14, Uncle Toby and Dr Slop discuss the merits of Stevin's wind carriage).

Han[d]cock's Steam Carriage Automaton which provided a regular bus service from Islington to the City in 1836

The richest section of this part of my collection is that on the steam carriages of the nineteenth century, mainly in the British Isles but also some in France, Italy and the United States. There are all editions, and translations, of the standard works by Alexander Gordon, Walter Hancock, Sir Goldsworthy Gurney, and Col. Maceroni, as well as several by the American Oliver Evans; more than fifty separate pamphlets extolling either the virtues of a particular machine, or the new mode of transport in general, and a group of prospectuses seeking to tempt the venture capitalists of the day; complete sets of both *The Mechanics' Magazine* (1823–1872, 97 vols) and *The Repertory of Arts and Manufactures* (1795–1859, 132 vols); several portfolios of prints (with a few drawings) ranging from fine aquatints of the carriages of Gurney, Hancock, Maceroni *et al*, to endless variations of 'the exploding carriage' by the satirical cartoonists of the day. Among the ephemera are a Leeds creamware mug, an engraved pewter plate, a transfer-printed plate, a watercolour by Isaac Cruikshank, an oil painting of Dr Church's carriage and a magnificent tinplate model of a steam(?) carriage made for Sir George Cayley (1773–1857), inventor of the aeroplane, with his arms on the carriage door, to demonstrate his ideas on mechanical road transport.

The earliest printed suggestions for mechanical vehicles are those of the Italian, Roberto Valturio, whose *De Re Militari* was first published in 1472, and is the first printed book with technical illustrations. I have never been able to afford the first edition; missed my opportunity some thirty years ago to buy the second edition (Verona, 1483), and have had to be content with Weschel's edition (Paris, 1532) which includes Vegetius's text on the same subject and has magnificent woodcuts, including a siege tower moved by windmills geared to its wheels, and a 'musculus', a primitive tank, moved by pedals on the front axle. I did manage to add an incunable edition of Vegetius (Rome, 1487, unillustrated) and the first edition in English (London, 1572).

In 1600 Simon Stevin, mathematician and military engineer, built for Prince Maurice of Nassau a giant sand yacht and I bought, early on, the very large (84 × 21 ins.), and very rare engraving by Gheyn and Swanenburch of Prince Maurice demonstrating his new machine to a group of distinguished passengers on the beach at Scheveningen. With this lucky find as a starting point I have pursued Stevin's 'Windtwagen' through several centuries (it is said to have been destroyed in 1803 on orders from Bonaparte), adding other engravings of this occasion as well as eye-witness accounts. Stevin is responsible for many of the more incongruous items in my collection. I have already mentioned Tristram Shandy where Sterne talks of 'Peireskius' walking from Paris to 'Schreveling' to see the Windtwagen; I also had to have Gassendi's *Life of Peiresc* (Paris, 1641) and the English translation by William Rand (1657) which I identified for Kenneth Monkman at Shandy Hall as Sterne's source. As a young lad Grotius was a passenger on Prince Maurice's inaugural trip and wrote poems describing his experiences. My copy of his collected poems is from the Duke of Devonshire's library and has a presentation inscription from Grotius to Ellberg. Early travellers in China reported the use of sailing wagons; early Dutch cartographers, having scant knowledge of China used sailing wagons (and sometimes elephants!) to fill the space; after 1600 these were modelled on Stevin's Windtwagen and later historians deduced that he got his idea from the Chinese. It was not until William Alexander, official artist to Lord MacCartney's Embassy to China in 1797, returned with drawings of Chinese wheelbarrows with rattan sails that Stevin was cleared of the charge of plagiarism. The collection contains maps of China by Ortelius 1584, Mercator 1609, Speed 1626, and John Seller 1670, as well as Alexander's *Costume of China* 1805. The results of all this research I wrote up as a contribution to the Dutch bookseller, Anton Gerits' Festschrift ('Voor Anton Gerits', Amsterdam, 1990).

Books of 'scientific amusements' often have suggestions for mechanical vehicles. The earliest I know of is Wilkins' *Mathematicall Magick* (1648). I have all four seventeenth century editions including an unrecorded variant of the third edition. Also in this group are Powell's *Humane Industry* (1661); Ozanam's *Récréations Mathematiques*, second edition, 1696, another much enlarged edition in four volumes, 1778, and the first English translation of 1708; Hooper's *Rational Recreations*, four volumes, 1774, and the second edition, 1782–3, with all the plates coloured (as issued?); and various nineteenth century titles along the lines of *Curiosities for the Ingenious*, *The Wonders of Nature and Art* and *A Million of Facts*.

Father Ferdinand Verbiest, S.J., an eminent mathematician and astronomer, was sent to China in 1659 where he became the friend and tutor of the Emperor Khang-Hsi. In order to entertain His Majesty Verbiest constructed a model carriage, two-foot long, which was driven by steam through an aeolipile. Verbiest describes it all in his book, *Astronomia Europæa . . .*, Dillingen, 1687, and can be credited with the earliest known application of steam power to a vehicle, albeit only a model. I have dubbed him 'The Father of the Automobile'. To document the principle of the aeolipile I have Hero of Alexandria's *Spiritalium Liber,* 1575, while Branca's *Le Machine,* 1629, shows both a steam turbine and a wind-driven vehicle.

Manumotive carriages are treated in Isacchi's *Inventioni . . .*, 1579, Cornelius Meyer's *Nuovi ritrovamenti . . .*, 1689,

Doppelmayr's *Historische Nachtricht von den Nürnbergischen Mathematicis* . . ., 1730, and many of the 'scientific amusements' titles. One of the most curious figures in this genre is Lewis Gompertz. His intense love of animals, which led him, in 1824, to found the R.S.P.C.A, also forbade him to allow them to labour on his behalf. His inventions, therefore, are aimed at the improvement of working conditions for draught animals and providing himself with a mechanical means of transport. His most practical solution to the latter problem (they included a manumotive helicopter) was a manumotive carriage.

In June 1978, at the ABA Antiquarian Book Fair, I mounted an exhibition of some fifty items from my collection, called 'Mechanical Carriages in Print 1600–1850'. Ten years later Raymond O'Shea asked me to do a similar one for the antiques fair at the Park Lane Hotel, this time titled 'From Dream to Steam – the Early History of the Travelling Machine'. For each of them I issued (*c.* 100 copies) a mimeographed catalogue giving the story behind each exhibit.

I no longer add very much to the 'internal combustion engine' end of my collection, but the byways of the prehistoric part are endlessly fascinating. My latest addition, made July 2005, is a copy of Restif de la Bretonne's *La Découverte Australe* . . ., first edition, four volumes, 1781, because I discovered on pages 81–98 of volume 1 an account of 'un carrosse sans chevaux'. Books are also for reading.

Much Hadham, Herts.

Bryan Forbes

Bryan Forbes

Books, like a wayward, demanding mistress, have determined the pattern of my life. From the moment I started to earn my living, I have spent recklessly in bookshops the world over. Not content with buying books, I owned and operated two bookshops for thirty-four years until the demise of the Net Book Agreement put me out of business. I learned my trade as a result of my friendship until his untimely death with Tony Godwin, an innovative bookseller who some might remember established Better Books in Charing Cross Road post war and later went on to become Managing Director of Penguin Books. The title of my second volume of autobiography – *A Divided Life* – sums up my rake's progress through seven decades as author, screenwriter and film director, the three careers constantly swelling my library. When I was asked to write and direct a film about Napoleon and Josephine, I acquired some 5,000 volumes about the period – the film never saw the light of day, but I went on collecting. A friend in Hollywood introduced me to the American Limited Editions Club – I joined and acquired the entire backlog. I have been a member of the Folio Society from the year dot. My long and lucky career meant that I met and became friends with many distinguished authors – notably Graham Greene, Len Deighton, John Le Carré, Maurice West, Christopher Isherwood, Kingsley Amis, Daphne du Maurier, Frederic Raphael, Anthony Burgess and Raymond Chandler, whose works warp the shelves with signed first editions. My taste is nothing if not eclectic, for my library houses a vast collection of film and theatre books (including a special copy of Ellen Terry's autobiography inscribed to Dame Edith Evans – *A Girl After my Own Heart* – left me by Edith in her will, after I had written her authorised biography). Along with the Nonesuch Dickens, a collection of Ford Madox Ford (*The Good Soldier,* one of the great novels written last century), together with a range of American authors such as John O'Hara, Updike, Hemingway, Scott Fitzgerald, Brian Garfield, Nathanael West, Paul Bowles *et al*. I support private presses (especially the Incline Press) and I have always collected extra-illustrated editions of antiquarian books. At one time together with three friends I established a private press of my own (Carpathian) and we produced a handsome version of Wilde's *The Ballad of Reading Gaol* with superb engravings by Peter Forster, fully bound by Tony Wessely. I still get a 'fix' from opening a new book and smelling the print, for the joy of reading has few equals. I cannot imagine a life without a library. It matters not how large or small, what is important is that books inhabit a home.

Wentworth, Surrey

Colin Franklin

How it began

It is to school football that I owe an abiding admiration of William Morris, his books, designs, his Society for the Protection of Ancient Buildings, his whole life (except the fudge-medieval prose romances). More accurately, it is to my loathing of school football, its mud and physical nuisance and tribalism; for I could avoid such afternoons, without breaking rules, by hiring a bicycle (note from Miss Kennard, house matron) and cycling the five miles or so to Cotterstock where lived old deaf Mr Newman 'friend of William Morris' (so it was said) whose house was filled with Pre-Raphaelite treasure, such escape reckoned permissible as being educational. I don't now believe Newman was Morris's friend, rather his client. Anyway the house was stuffed with De Morgan tiles, Hammersmith carpets, Rossetti chairs, Burne-Jones paintings – and Kelmscott books. So, did the sight of his Chaucer overwhelm me? It did not. I went for the free tea, and private peace, and to hear old Newman shouting his arts-and-crafts advice, as we slowly climbed the stairs – 'another thing, remember if you buy a suit always get a good one, it will last you a lifetime'.

Ten years later I had a mystic experience with Morris. Rowing down the upper Thames in the summer of 1951, soon after we were married, I saw a house across a field above the bank and said instinctively without maps or thought 'It must be Kelmscott'. We moored the boat, walked up that field as if in *News From Nowhere* and rang. Mr Webb, caretaker, showed us round the damp and neglected place. He thought I must be a great expert, having come so far and troubled to visit. 'Do you think' he asked, as Charlotte and I descended those stairs, 'that Morris would have placed the sofa *here*, or might it have been *there*?' He seemed a worried man.

My work was at a publishing office in Carter Lane, near St Paul's to the east and not far from Chancery Lane to the west. I had never thought of attending an auction, nothing so grand, but remember noticing a catalogue dangling by string outside Hodgsons' rooms in Chancery Lane advertising a sale of books 'from the library of Mr. Newman of Cotterstock'. My old deaf

Colin Franklin

friend must have died by then, his son was selling those Kelmscotts which had saved me from football. Thus arrived my first Kelmscott book, Swinburne's *Atalanta*, limp vellum lacking one tie, thirteen pounds.

Those were the days. I loathe people who forever talk prices and bargains, but it seemed nobody was collecting that beguiling subject, private presses. I didn't nip in because they were affordable but it became a lunch-time obsession: should it be Maggs today, Francis Edwards, Quaritch, Sawyer, Bain . . .? The rot really set in when I brought home from Maggs copies printed on vellum of the first two Kelmscott books (*Glittering Plain* and *Poems by the Way*). One cost a hundred pounds, the other sixty. 'Isn't that rather going it?' Charlotte asked uncertainly.

The disease spread of course, to Vale and Doves and Eragny – and now Eastern books – helped by the merry fact that part of my job in Carter Lane was designing books, laying out pages for text and title and the rest of it; becoming acquainted with those wonderful Monotype adaptations from Baskerville, Bodoni, Aldus. Folio centred below text, no extra lead; close and even spacing throughout; 42 × 24 ems. Peaceful world, calm mornings, with Maggs beckoning at lunch-time – or should it be Quaritch?

Culham, Oxon.

Part of a carved wooden cover for a Sutra (Buddhist sacred text),
c. seventeenth century (reduced to about 70%)

COLIN FRANKLIN

207

Ursula Freeman

The Redlake Press

I do sincerely believe that there can be no more rewarding way of life than making books. I have written about private press publishing 'After the excitement and fun of deciding to produce a book, we have a honeymoon when it all starts happening, followed by the black period when author and artist find themselves up against reality in the form of this nit-picking, obstinate, dilatory, stupid, pedantic and worldly printer / editor / designer / publisher and then, suddenly, they are signing the most wonderful book ever produced, the sun shines, the birds sing, and, in an orgy of self-congratulation, we start talking about the next one.'

Seriously though, I have been fortunate in the number of distinguished and talented writers and illustrators who have wanted me to print their work, who have added immeasurably to the enjoyment I find in printing, and have subsequently become very good friends. Until I went to school, and started to learn to read, it was a reasonable assumption that blood ran in my veins. With hindsight, and considering my refusal to read any childish book whose appearance and design I disliked, it should have been apparent that my veins ran with ink.

My father kept me supplied with reading matter – a small green leather bound copy of Kipling's *If* (a verse to a page with rubrics); a particularly neat *Alice in Wonderland* with the Tenniel illustrations; Arthur Ransome (who could forget those wonderful dust jackets?). But, as happens to all of us, the happy days of lying on the nursery floor, surrounded by books, came to an end. Afternoons got shorter, book tokens from kind relatives became sparser, and all too soon I was young, impecunious, and haunting second hand bookshops. My tastes were eclectic, and dictated by content, but I always bought the best editions I could find.

Later, my life enhanced by a husband and two lively little boys, not to mention two terriers, I bought a small handpress, and The Dirty Paws Press (soon to become Ursula Freeman's Press) started to accept commissions. I attended The Leicester School of Printing, where I was allowed to write my own syllabus, and given unlimited help and support. Whatever idea flew into my head,

Ursula Freeman

some expert was found to enable me to put it into practice. When I am working in my printshop now I often think with gratitude of those printers who made me do things, often reluctantly, in the ways that have been proven to work.

So it was that a lifetime passion for books became the realization that I had the ability to make them and that this was what I wanted to do. A friend renamed the press The Unidentified Flying Printer and my first publication was a little pamphlet, *South Atlantic Protest*, a response to the Falklands War. I am pleased to think that this embodied what I consider the first principle of a private press, that new work should be published, reflecting the ideals of the proprietor.

The Brotherhood of Ruralists suggested that I should print a trilogy illustrated by their members. These were pretty little quarter bound books with a cover paper designed by Brian Partridge, now out of print. The success of these books made me feel quite grown up, and I changed the name of the press for the last time to The Redlake Press, after the river on which my house stands.

Soon after this Simon Rae, whose first collection of poems I had printed for the trilogy, rang me and asked how I would feel about another book, he had a selection of poems for each month of the year. Strangely enough I had been holding some woodcuts for each month for some time, so very excited, and feeling that this was surely meant to be, we leapt into our respective motors and drove to a pub midway between Bristol and Clun. How wrong could we be? The poems and the pictures reflected completely opposing visions of the countryside, one realistic, one romantic. However, we were both by then sold on the idea and the book went ahead with some very suitable commissioned line drawings and the title *Calendar*.

For the exhibition 'Alice in Wonderland' Brian Partridge and I collaborated in my first and only reprint, *The Gardner's Song* from *Sylvie and Bruno* by Lewis Carroll. This is a small book, 6 × 5½ inches with a bright red cloth quarter binding and a charming cover paper by Brian with weeds rioting all over it.

St Martin-in-the-Fields asked me to print poems written by homeless people. Not great poetry, but some are very moving and I felt I needed a first class illustrator to make the book work. I was lucky to find Clara Vulliamy who produced some striking and sensitive scraper board drawings. I decided to cover it with a facsimile of the Financial Times, to emphasise the sleeping arrangements of our authors, but this was not as simple as might appear. Finding the right weight and colour of paper was quite a search, because the newspaper fades quickly, and it was necessary to keep replenishing the copy for matching.

This year I started really pushing the boundaries with a previously unknown Malagasy folk story, *The Beautiful Plump Little Boy*, sewn into papyrus covers with hand plaited raffia from Madagascar. And in complete contrast I made *December*, by Eleanor Cooke, with twenty-four wood-engravings by Peter Reddick, bound in silver and red.

I have learnt over the years that the books which have proved to be the most successful are those where I have followed my own aesthetic and creative instinct. I like at least six months gestation, and then I wake up one morning with a vision of the book in my mind. Then there are decisions about the number of copies, cost, paper, page size, allotting the ISBN, working out a timetable, and

URSULA FREEMAN

the countless other routine tasks that are necessary to get it off the ground. But also there is the pleasure of the contact with writers and illustrators, which usually seems to involve the odd glass of wine, planning the launch, publicity, fliers, getting it onto my website. I design the covers in consultation with some excellent bookbinders, who are, as are all the people I have met in the printing trade, a pleasure to work with. Apart from the bindings, all the work is done by myself alone.

Most Redlake books are limited edition handmade books printed by traditional letterpress methods. I see my task as this: to translate the ideas of the writer and the illustrator into the most appropriate physical form.

Clun, Shropshire

Wood-engraving by Peter Reddick,
from *December*, 2003

Paul Goldman

Illustrators of the Sixties

I never intended to become a book collector or indeed any other kind of collector – it just happened. As a child I became fascinated by history and started a small collection of English silver coins. All my pocket money went on these enchanting pieces of the past which excited me because, in a romantic way, I felt close to people in history such as Charles I and Oliver Cromwell when I looked at them and touched them as they themselves might have done. It was the very tangibility of historical resonance encapsulated in these often worn and rubbed items which gave me such intense pleasure. At about the same time I also collected cigarette cards which similarly provided me with both pictures and information about another age. I was especially proud of a set of actresses of 1898 – it was made up of just thirty photographic pictures without any texts – apparently these cards were first invented to stiffen the packs to prevent the contents becoming crushed. These again I appreciated because although many of the women were rather matronly and remote, others were as pretty and as 'modern' as the girls I was becoming aware of around me as I was growing up. The coins and cards were mainly bought at a tiny shop run by Mr E. H. Woodiwiss in Sicilian Avenue in Holborn – it was a magical place to me all those years ago. A little later I progressed to the hallowed portals of B. A. Seaby (for coins) and began to read the informative and scholarly bulletins the firm produced. Both these institutions are now sadly long gone.

After university and jobs in a provincial museum, Dr Johnson's House in Gough Square and a commercial gallery in London, I found myself in the Department of Prints and Drawings at the British Museum. Employed primarily as an educationalist I searched for an area of interest to develop – by definition it had to be one which did not intrude on any colleague's field of research.

One day in a shop near the BM I came across a Victorian book of poetry illustrated with black and white wood-engraved illustrations. It was rather battered and looked uncared for despite its elaborate gilt binding. For some reason it appealed to me. First

Paul Goldman

perhaps it was the gold, the colour – the sheer external vulgarity
and exuberance that struck a chord. When I looked inside I discovered designs by three of the leading Pre-Raphaelite artists –
William Holman Hunt, Dante Gabriel Rossetti and John Everett
Millais, each of great imaginative power and a wonderful
example of draughtsmanship. The volume was a reprint of the so-
called 'Moxon' Tennyson and I came away clutching it with delight and amazed that at £8.50 I could actually afford it on my
extremely modest Civil Service salary. From then on I researched
these 'sixties' books and found a few in the museum collection
which I studied with interest. Although it contained many proofs
and separate impressions of the designs, there were relatively few
examples of the books themselves. Eventually the Head of the
Department, observing my interest, suggested that I make a visit
to the august Robin de Beaumont with the idea of purchasing a
few books of this type for the museum to place alongside the prints

themselves. As we talked Robin quietly said that he would like to give his entire private collection of books of the sixties to the British Museum. It was an utterly unexpected and a magnificently altruistic gesture, for his books were the finest in terms of condition to be found anywhere in the world.

An exhibition and a publication followed as well as a deep and lasting friendship. Over the years I have continued my research in the field and have collected in a modest way some of the relevant books. My interest in collecting has always been in the illustrations above all else – I have found in the designs both of the Pre-Raphaelites and in those of their followers such as George Pinwell, Frederick Walker, and John William North a fastidious and refined approach to drawing as well as a profound sincerity and attention to the texts.

The books in my collection have come because it is so much easier for me to have the images to hand rather than always needing to travel to libraries and public collections. So I might be called a collector 'in denial' because I like to rationalise my purchases with the thought that I am holding them chiefly for research purposes and not for the simple pleasure of ownership. I only add to the collection occasionally now – the book has to be something very special or rare. One such is Henry Gordon Hake's *Parables and Tales* published by Chapman and Hall in 1872 and illustrated by Arthur Hughes. The binding design is by Dante Gabriel Rossetti and is one of his most extraordinary and distinctive. Hake wrote to William Michael Rossetti (the brother of the artist) 'Your brother has made me a most beautiful design for the cover of parables and tales – it is thought to be the finest that has ever been produced. The spade laid across the empty cradle is certainly a touch of pathos no one else would have conceived.' So I have already contradicted myself, for here is a book which I like just as much for the outside as for the illustrations.

Am I a true collector I wonder?

East Orchard, Shaftesbury

PAUL GOLDMAN

Richard Goulden

The Kent Book Trade and the Goulden Family

Since 1840 the Gouldens have been booksellers and printers, spreading out from Canterbury to cover a sizeable part of Kent. While their presence in the Kent book trade is long gone, three decades and more ago, their books, pamphlets, music sheets and broadsides, all bearing the Goulden imprint, are mute reminders of the vitality of the Gouldens in both the Kent book trade and outside the county boundary. Such reminders are, even so, not sufficient to make solid a shadowy past: one needs to limn these long-dead Gouldens, to place on both paper and disk their lives and careers, otherwise this urgent question will always be asked down the years: 'Who were these Goulden booksellers and printers?' Who were they, indeed. To answer this insistent question, to put in perspective these Gouldens and their achievements, and to give an account of them for posterity to acknowledge their existence, I have for the past twenty years built up a research collection on both the Kent book trade and the Gouldens within it.

There are two main elements in this collection: the first covering works on various aspects of the Kent book trade covering both the eighteenth and nineteenth centuries, and the second containing publications bearing various Goulden imprints from 1840 onwards. The former element will in all probability be dispersed once I have no need for it, but the latter element is a collection added to, and handed down from one generation to another as long as respect for one's ancestors remains within the Goulden family. Both elements, though, give grist to the mill of the book historian, leading to a compilation, on which I have been engaged for the past two decades: the *Kent Book Trade Directory, 1750-1900*, which will give details on the booksellers, stationers, music sellers, printers, newspaper proprietors, editors and reporters within the Kent book trade of that period, and which will include many Gouldens from Charles Goulden of Canterbury, the first of the Goulden booksellers, to Anthony Thomas Goulden of Tunbridge Wells, my grandfather, who gives his name to my daughter, Antonia. Two sections of this compilation are in print: the

Richard Goulden

Faversham Book Trade, 1730–1900 and the *Sittingbourne and Milton Regis Book Trade, 1770–1900*.

Guidebooks to local sights were found in all Kentish towns in the stock of both booksellers and printers during the late eighteenth century and throughout the nineteenth century. The study of these particular publications throws light on both the structure of the Kent book trade and the involvement of the Gouldens in the production of guidebooks. Both Charles Goulden and his son Henry James considered the guidebook to be an important part of their

RICHARD GOULDEN

stock-in-trade, and both men published a great number of Canterbury guides between 1840 and 1910, as did many of their contemporaries in Canterbury and elsewhere in Kent. It is therefore natural that a good part of the collection contains guidebooks that represent a significant aspect of the Kent book trade; and many guides in the collection are unique or the only ones in private hands, other copies often held in local public reference libraries. A bibliography of Kentish guidebooks written by me was published in 1995: the *Kent Town Guides, 1763–1900.*

Toward the study of various aspects of the Kent book trade, the collection may be found useful. It includes nineteenth century slip-songs and single-sheet ballads printed in Canterbury, Deal and Rochester, allegedly in great numbers, but rarely found nowadays. These often have headpieces and tailpieces that help to identify the printers of other Kentish slip-songs and ballads that have no imprints but similar ornaments. It holds various difficult-to-find local almanacs, including the unique *Goulden's New Kentish Almanack,* a single sheet almanac printed in 1847. It has an affection for verse, and holds editions of two prominent Kentish poems: John White Masters's *Dick and Sal at Canterbury Fair* in dialect and the anonymous *Folkestone Fiery Serpent.* There are in the collection publications on various booksellers, printers and papermakers in Kent, and on the histories of Kentish newspapers. In this section is the *Memorandum and Articles of Association* for the firm of Parrett and Neves, printers in Chatham, issued in 1930. Such articles of association to cover limited companies were printed in very small numbers, and are, unsurprisingly, extraordinarily scarce. Also in the collection is the manuscript letter-book of John Vine Hall, bookseller of Maidstone, while in Worcester in the first decade of the nineteenth century, as well as a good number of invoices made out by various booksellers and printers, including John Blake of Maidstone's bills sent to the Chamberlain of that town in 1814 and 1815.

The emphasis in the collection, as always, is on the activities of the Gouldens. Although many known items such as Joseph Conrad's stage text for *The Secret Agent* have escaped my net, the Goulden part of the collection is sizeable. Here are, *inter alia*, several scarce Charles Goulden pamphlets of the 1850s for children, such as *Goulden's Royal ABC*; more substantial books from the shops of Henry James Goulden, including the Friends of Canterbury Cathedral's annual offerings in the 1930s and the late 1940s, these being the acting editions of established authors' plays such as T. S. Eliot's *Murder in the Cathedral*; ephemeral publications by Henry's erratic brother (more of a loose cannon) William Edward Goulden, including examples of his various albums of Canterbury views. John James Goulden of Dover and his brother Richard in Folkestone printed many of what might be called local publications: Molony's *Hougham Church*, Jenkins's *The Chartulary of the Monastery of Lyminge*, and Dover Hospital's annual reports: these are also in the collection. John James's widow Charlotte (her imprint deliberately 'C. Goulden' to avoid male discrimination), concentrated on books and pamphlets on Dover itself, a good example being Mary Horsley's *Some Memories of Old Dover*, 1892. One could go on and print a long list of Goulden publications found in the Goulden collection, but that would be hardly appropriate here. Moreover, I have not touched on the writings of the Gouldens themselves, though here I cannot resist making an exception with my grandfather's somewhat racy *Mitosis in the Spermatheca of the Honey Bee*. Solemnity began this account of the Goulden collection, and mirth ends it.

Croydon, Surrey

Rigby Graham

Living in a 1930s semi-detached house on a noisy city main road with a fifteen stone Irish wolfhound is hardly the ideal setting for someone who both collects and produces. Bookcases and shelves fight with paintings, prints and eastern rugs for limited wall space. Framed pictures stacked six deep lean against almost every available piece of furniture in every room and in hall and stairway. Persian rugs lie three deep in every room and tied in rolls under the tables.

It is against this untidy background that my ungainly collection of books sits – on shelves, in cupboards, on tables, on the furniture and in stacks on the floor. Most collectors know exactly where to find any and every book. Luckily I have never suffered from this affliction. I spend hours searching, a continual voyage of discovery and revelation, and I rarely put any books away and fall over stacks of them when I try to get into bed. Two large bedroom cupboards which once served as wardrobes are now taken up with hundredweights of books – the clothes being encouraged to hang about wherever they can, or drape themselves over the heaps of books, and rolls of Persian carpets and salt and grain bags for horse or camel.

Twenty-five years ago – in order to help subsidise research I was involved into with the work of Hans Erni in Lucerne – I sold most of my collection of T. E. Lawrence and my whole library of music biographies, and modern poetry as well as first editions. Since then, I have been unsystematically replacing many of the volumes I got rid of, thinking I could do without them. Recent years have seen a vast increase in Lawrence material and many reprints of hitherto almost unobtainable texts are easily come by compared with previous times. There have been many listings and bibliographies on the subject, of which Philip O'Brien's massive volume puts this whole collecting area into context.

Never having suffered from that affliction common to most collectors, librarians and bibliophiles, I have never felt the need to build up complete sets. Believing I could always pick up missing copies of the *Oxford History of English Art*, the *Pelican History*

Rigby Graham

of Art, *Matrix*, early editions of the *Shell Guides* and copies of *Baedeker*, I have usually managed to pick up duplicate copies because whatever lists I have made are never up to date, often left in the wrong jacket, or in the glove compartment of my dented car. The disappearance of many of the second hand bookshops in the Midlands, where I live, has not helped me in my flabby attempts to fill gaps. My tendency to live, as I think, in the nineteenth century, has meant that I still use a pen and ink, and the typewriter, the computer and the internet seem to have passed me by.

Because I taught bookbinding for some years at Leicester College of Art under John Mason, and was a colleague of George Percival (both distinguished practitioners), I bound up some hundreds of volumes of my own as well as many for my friends. Runs of literary magazines, volumes on printing and art exhibition catalogues, originally issued only in paper wraps, were all dealt with. Finally shortage of space at home, and continually being asked to bind this, that and the other, by friends who unthinkingly commit your precious hours, made me get rid of most of my bookbinding presses, blocking press, finishing tools and materials. Since then I have paid Sangorski, Zaehnsdorf and other binders to do work which I once did for next to nothing.

Many years ago, as a pottery student at Leicester, I was fascinated by ceramics. The College of Art kilns at that time could handle raku, earthenware, stoneware and enamels but porcelain was beyond them. On my journeys between home and college, I varied my route through many of the back streets of Leicester and saw many local industry workshops and specialists of various kinds. One tiny shop, which only opened one day a week, was in the front room of a narrow terraced house. In the small window of the house, against a grey velvet background, were displayed three or four pieces of Chinese, Korean and Vietnamese porcelain. Some were damaged, some were 'wasters', but these seemed magical to me and opened up a new, exciting world, even though I could afford none of them, nor any of the Faber monographs on Eastern ceramics which were being produced at that time. Fifty years later, battered copies of these volumes appeared in second-hand bookshops and at book-fairs, and pristine pieces of these ceramics are now surfacing in vast quantities, as the

salvage efforts of Captain Hatcher and his associates have re-
covered sunken cargoes from the *Tek Sing*, the *Hoi An* and the
Ca Mau. These have been appearing through Nagel's Auction
House in Stuttgart, Christie's and Sotheby's in Amsterdam. In
November 2000 the largest auction was held offering over eight
thousand lots. Because of this, I have now finally been able to
fulfil a lifelong desire to acquire several examples of these beautiful pieces.

As someone who has spent a lifetime travelling about, I have
managed to assemble a miscellaneous collection of books and
guides covering the topography of much of the British Isles and
Western Europe. These are working tools, which I have taken
with me at different times and many of them are showing the
signs of hard use and wear. Some of the Baedecker guides like
Switzerland (16th edition, 1895) or Muirhead's *North Eastern
France* (Macmillan, 1930) are covered with annotations and
underlinings from previous owners. Baedecker volumes, some consisting of over 500 closely printed pages, are extensively illustrated with engravings and maps, which fold out, up and down.
A particular favourite is one once owned by Elsie M. Muston from
Leicester, an intrepid traveller in the early twentieth century, she
excelled herself and in so doing gave her guides an extra dimension, a personal record that has almost become an original manuscript.

Shell guides, of which I have a fair number, are widely known
and appreciatively remarked upon. Murray's *Architectural Guides*
are magnificent, although only *Berkshire*, *Buckinghamshire* and
Lancashire were ever issued. Betjeman, Piper and Fleetwood-
Hesketh gave the series a flying start and then nothing. What a
series it might have been had England been covered.

Due to the nature of my work I have met a lot of collectors of
different kinds – eccentric, obsessive, enthusiastic, usually friendly,
eager to share and to explain. With some though, once an area is
complete, whether it be cricket memorabilia, silver stamp boxes
or the work of novelist or poet, interest suddenly fades and a new
enthusiasm is taken up, the urge to collect enters a new and exciting hunting field. I am not a proper collector, for the ramshackle
life I lead precludes systematic organisation. The work I do:
travelling about drawing and painting; writing and making

autographic prints; has meant that collecting has been erratic, wayward and casual, so that I have endless recordings of operas of Bellini, Donizetti and Rossini; all the biographies and histories of these composers, and of Richard Strauss, Beethoven, Wagner, Mozart; not only the music on obscure recordings but early accounts, memoirs and collected correspondence. The same has happened with Wordsworth, Coleridge, Shelley and Byron, Edward Thomas, Eliot, Larkin . . . but I have also a large collection built up over 50 years of tins of oil-based letterpress printing inks – carcinogenic and therefore thrown out by the printing industry, encrusted with a skin, which when cut back with a sharp knife reveals glowing colours. I have tins and heavy tubes of lead paints, difficult to obtain because of health restrictions. Having experienced cancer and lead poisoning I am careful but not unnecessarily worried. The same things threaten and apply to stained glass, the design of which I have been involved with. Modern regulations have spread across the European Union and one needs to chase the receding suppliers further and further east to obtain some of the historic colours and effects.

There is excitement and adventure in almost everything. Collecting, for me, has never been a pastime in itself, but a peripheral result of my other interests and activities. The glowing patterns of a Tekke Bokhara rug from Southern Russia, a small Schmidt Rottluff woodcut, or a much larger coloured one of Karl-Heinz Kliemann picked up in Berlin, a dram of cask-strength Laphroaig in an Irish crystal tumbler, a recording of a John Field piano concerto are all things which enhance my collections and enrich my life. As time moves on, these collections reflect my memories and recollections and bring a warmth and enthusiasm to the passing days.

Leicester

RIGBY GRAHAM

Frances Guthrie

James Guthrie and the Pear Tree Press

'Oh, no', I said, finding myself correcting an Antiquarian Book Dealer, 'That's not James Guthrie – that's his son John.'

When long ago they cleared out my much loved Grandfather's home, the boys had needed useful things, rugs, cutlery etc. Under the benign eyes of mother and aunt, I was delighted (being the 'arty' one) to lay my eager little hands on Uncle Jimmie's intriguing books. Working in London, and sharing a flat with two other girls, I couldn't import too much 'rubbish'. I escaped with my booty and being tidy minded I started on making a Neat List and found there was much missing.

So I started trying to fill in the gaps. Unwittingly I had become A Collector.

That sucked me into the enchanted / expensive world of second hand – er – Rare Books where I found though I knew nothing about Books (except liking to read them), I did remember something about my Great Uncle whom my brother and I had visited in school holidays with Grandfather who was his closest brother. Imperceptibly my Neat List became an amateur Bibliography linked to an even more amateur Biography in order to make sense of his story.

I attacked numerous large important institutions for information, here and abroad, and even had one glorious foray into the old Round Reading Room at the British Museum. More importantly I rattled round a number of elderly aunts who were all great fun and kindly emptied drawers of odd letters, snaps and as much information as I had wit to ask.

James had three sons, I never met the eldest who sadly died while in uniform in the Second World War, the second, Robin, who lived in London, was a well known painter. He turned up one evening and with a wicked grin emptied out a sack of letters, 'see what you can make of that'. Sadly he too died not long after. Later, I was to meet the third son, John, who lived and worked in Venice, ex artist, printer, scene painter, ballet dancer, and soldier, he was currently Professor of English at their University. He became a tremendous prop in my more wobbly moments.

The haul from Robin, expanded, once the air got into it, into lots of little piles of paper across our living room floor (luckily it was an ex billiard room), over which the flatmates had to hop-

Frances Guthrie

scotch on their way out to work. By happy chance my Landlady allowed me to use her Wine Cellar as a storeroom. It was perfect – shelves upon shelves. But office equipment is costly. How to make up filing trays? Luckily the local Woolworth's had a sale of rectangular washing up bowls. I bought three, then went back for another five, then decided to go back and take the lot. Staggering out I found myself accosted by a beady eyed Manager, 'You must have an awful lot of washing up . . .'

FRANCES GUTHRIE

I can also recommend rolls of plastic sandwich bags for smaller files.

My Neat List encompassed about 150 titles if you include magazines. Luckily my Grandfather's collection included a core of the Pear Tree Press's work. It was strange to be able to enjoy it unhurriedly, remembering Uncle as a rounder, rosier version of my Grandfather. When we visited he had ceased serious printing but let us play with some small plates, and he even made me up some headed writing paper. The size of his 'mangle' made me appreciate what strenuous work printing was. My mother said that it was strange to think that such gnarled and work-worn hands could produce such dainty things.

That was the Accumulation Phase. It was lucky I started so long ago, otherwise all those bits of family history would have vanished. Only one person – my eldest Aunt – was able to give me histories of the brothers and sisters and identify who was who in photographs – and translate some very old fashioned writing by scratch pen.

At the same time Catalogues began to come my way and the earnest slog of capturing these elusive titles. But slowly the ticks against the titles on my List increased, and slowly, slowly the story of his publishing, his verses, his painting, essay writing, pen and ink work and his printing, emerged, leaving of course more black holes.

From time to time this relatively quiet way of life was rent by the frightening event of an Auction, which goes at nerve racking speed, one's cool reduced to meltdown, leaving one licking one's financial wounds, or if lucky racking up another completed set, or star-gazy at a Picture one has long coveted.

Nowadays, after an interim of having to provide the Chancellor with regular taxes, I am in the long drawn out Explanatory Phase, dusting the dinosaur bones of the facts and artefacts given, trusting the whole carefully collected printing animal will arise.

A few gaps still remain of course, and what when those are filled? One will, of course, need to substantiate those *alleged* Ghost Books . . .

Enfield, London

Barry Jackson

Surgery

I joined the PLA in 1962 after seeing an advertisement in *The Observer*. My collecting had for some time been centered on the Diaghilev ballet, about which material could then be obtained fairly easily and amazingly cheaply. I still have some gems which are now very hard to find. *Designs on the Dances of Nijinsky* by George Barbier, published in 1913 and for which I paid £2, recently sold at auction for £1,800.

It was around this time, too, that I started my collection of Beaumont Press books which I wrote about in the Spring 1975 issue of *The Private Library*. I have acquired several more Beaumont Press volumes since that article and the collection now comprises a virtually complete output of the Press including a fair amount of ephemera. But, of course, over the course of time, other interests emerged. Some of these were relatively short lived, for example books about books and London topography (the scope here was too wide to make real inroads into making a comprehensive collection), while others have been long lasting, such as anything relating to the Crimean War.

My principal collection, however, has been formed over some forty years and comprises books on surgery, written in English, and published before 1900. It is now one of the largest in private hands and continues to grow. Perhaps this somewhat arcane interest is not surprising when I say that I practised as a surgeon until my retirement last year.

In 1994, I gave a talk about the collection to a meeting of the Association at the invitation of my former bookbinding classmate, Frank Broomhead (then Hon. Sec. of the Association), and displayed a number of highspots as well as more standard items. The earliest volume, printed in black letter and published in 1525, is a translation from the German and titled *The Noble Experyence of the Vertuous Handy Warke of Surgeri* .... Judged by the horrific illustrations, the experience of undergoing an operation in those days was anything but noble.

Inevitably, in view of the large number published, eighteenth and nineteenth century volumes predominate but perhaps the most treasured volume is a vellum-bound seventeenth century book (1617) by John Woodall, a St Bartholomew's Hospital surgeon, titled *The Surgions Mate*. Admittedly, two leaves are missing but it is excessively rare some sources claiming only five copies in Great Britain, and I am exceedingly fortunate to have acquired it at auction before its rarity was fully appreciated.

However, despite the somewhat recherché antiquarian interest of early surgery, I still have an interest in modern fine printing and the private press movement. My collection of Simon Lawrence's Fleece Press is complete all bar a few very early items, and I eagerly await each succeeding volume as it appears.

Surbiton, Surrey

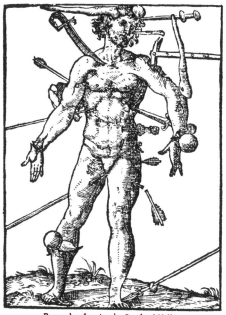

Certaine Workes of Chirurgerie, 1563

Shirley Jones

Red Hen Press

I publish my own books, in the tradition of the French 'livre d'artiste'. My first book was produced as a post-graduate printmaking student at Croydon College of Art and Design, a course I took after an English Literature degree, seven years of teaching, three children, and part-time courses in etching, lithography and sculpture. Since setting up my own studio in 1977 I have produced a further twenty-two artist books, adopting the imprint Red Hen Press in 1983.

That year was an important landmark for me. I had published six books by then but had no real idea of how to market them, mistakenly and unsuccessfully trailing them around London galleries. Basilisk Press and Bertram Rota were my outlets. Charlene Garry at Basilisk and John Byrne at Rota's were equally encouraging, but sales were not. I had just published my first translations of Old English poetry, *Scop Hwilum Sang*. I set the text in Baskerville and printed the translations in dark green alongside the Old English in deep red, keeping to these two colours for my illustrations, all aquatints. It was the most challenging book I had attempted; it was certainly the most successful, being out of print within a year. But it didn't sell itself. Shortly before I was to accompany my husband on a business trip to the United States, Colin Franklin wrote to me. He had just acquired copies of all of my books from Basilisk Press and expressed surprised concern that they were still available, including one of my first, in an edition of six. On learning that I was soon to visit the United States he was extremely helpful in directing me to private collectors and institutions, his name proving an invaluable reference. He continued to be supportive for many years and wrote a review of my work in *The Private Library*.

The illustrations in my books are invariably my original etchings, aquatints or mezzotints, usually full-page and described in *A Nation and its Books* as being, 'of considerable power and haunting beauty'. In recent years I have concentrated on mezzotint, which is a bit perverse since it is the most difficult of the printmaking techniques, and gives rise to even more problems than

Shirley Jones

etchings in books. But I like to exploit the mysterious, almost meta-physical quality of simple forms emerging from the blackness of a mezzotint. My poems are usually a response to an experience, recorded in isolation from anything else I was experiencing at the time, the isolation of the image in a mezzotint can work as a per-fect counterpoint.

Blind-printed etchings have also become something of a signa-ture with me. These are heavily bitten into zinc rather than cop-perplate, which is what I would normally use. The zinc plate is often cut to shape and impressed into thick wet paper and printed, without ink, at high pressure. The result is white on white and satisfyingly three-dimensional.

The texts in my books consist of my own poems, prose pieces, translations of Old English and Old Welsh, and sometimes quite lengthy essays. My 1995 book *Falls the Shadow* was an ambi-tious multi-layered work which explored the gulf between Man's ideals and the realisation of those ideals. In my six essays I drew

SHIRLEY JONES

on historians from Thucydides to Christopher Hill; political phi-
losophers from Aristotle to Mao Tse-tung; poets from Pindar to
Eliot. It was with the last source that I came up against my first
brush with copyright laws, a lengthy problem with Faber and Faber
only finally solved with my husband's negotiating skills. I used a
blind-printed etched shell as a symbol of the ideal which gave
birth to a movement, a sepia mezzotint to shadow its progress. I
began with Greek democracy and finished with Pol Pot and the
Killing Fields of Cambodia.

Y Morgrugyn Cloff, four years later was also long on text.
I introduced and abridged seven tales from *The Mabinogion*,
careful to preserve their full flavour, and printing in italic my
own translations of passages selected to convey the humour, irony
and lyricism that permeate these stories. The images, in mezzotint, aquatint and relief etching were interleaved with Unryushi
tissue printed with the Welsh passages they illustrate. The title
means 'The Lame Ant' and is a wry reference to myself, coming
late and lame to these stories. The little character appears in that
rip-roaring story, *Culhwch and Olwen*. One of the forty tasks
Ysbaddaden Chief Giant sets Culhwch as the price for winning
Olwen, is to gather in one day, nine hestors of sown flax seed to
make a head-dress for her. Help is given by grateful ants 'with
none of it wanting save for a single flax seed. And the lame ant
brought that in before nightfall'.

My latest book, *Chwedlau* is my exploration into fifteen centuries of Welsh myths, legends and folklore and their place in the
rich history of Wales. Each of the seven essays is prefigured with
a blind-printed etching or, in one case, a small mezzotint, and
faces a full-page mezzotint or aquatint. It was two and a half
years in the making because it was so lengthily researched and
there were fourteen plates to print forty times!

Since I work alone, setting and printing the text on a
Vandercook Universal Press, I now have these longer texts set for
me at Gwasg Gregynog. David Vickers is not only a very fine
printer, but generous with his help and time. An added bonus is
that the initial proof-reading is carried out at Gregynog. The paper
I use in my books is always heavyweight, handmade or mould-
made and often rough textured, chosen for its suitablity for etching or mezzotint and not always easy for printing letterpress.

Each book is a total concept, a planned integration of different crafts, involving visual as well as literary activity, which is why the binding is, for me, equally important. Bookbinding was a part of the post-graduate printing course all those years ago and I was a fairly competent binder of my own books in the early days. I was however, somewhat deflated by a helpful critic who suggested I find someone else to do my bindings. He did add, more kindly, that what was inside deserved more than what was served up on the outside. I took his advice and found good, more than competent, binders to work with me, and to my designs. John Sewell has for the last ten years met those requirements exceptionally well.

The books, usually in an edition of forty, are now bought by private collectors and over fifty major institutions including the British Library, the National Art Library at the V & A, the National Library and National Museum of Wales, the Gutenberg in Germany and Rijksmuseum in the Netherlands. The Library of Congress has the only complete collection of my work, apart from mine and it is in the United States that I still sell 80% of my books. This involves biennial, three week trips to around twenty-five universities, colleges and public libraries and lengthy advance planning by my husband. But meeting and talking to rare book librarians I know well about my work is not only enjoyable but an effective way of selling books that are inevitably expensive.

There have been many high spots in the long career of my press. I was elated by the selection of two of my books for the V & A's exhibition, 'The Open and Closed Book' in 1979. In 1994 *Llym Awel*, my translations of early Welsh poetry, won the British Book Design award in the limited edition category. Almost as satisfying was the inclusion of my work in the New York Center for Book Arts exhibition, 'Masters of their Craft'. And although there was an exhibition of my books and some of my prints at the V & A's Art Library in 1993, more satisfying were the two major retrospective exhibitions of all my books and over 100 prints from them, beautifully mounted. Both exhibitions were in Wales. The first, in 1995 was held in the Gregynog Gallery of the National Library of Wales, the second in 2004 in the main gallery at Newport Museum and Galleries. Newport also produced a superb catalogue in which was quoted a comment by Katherine Reagan, Curator of Rare Books at Cornell University, U.S.A:

SHIRLEY JONES

Shirley Jones is not only an artist and printer, but an eloquent writer and storyteller. Her books achieve a harmonious balance between text and illustrations seldom seen in the work of contemporary fine printers.

After thirty years of striving to reach all of those goals, no accolade could be more appreciated.

Llanhamlach, Brecon, Powys

Mezzotint by Shirley Jones
(the feather printed in dark emerald)
engraved for *Matrix* 9, 1989

Philip Kerrigan
(Photograph Nicolette Wilson)

Philip Kerrigan

Omnium Gatherum

My interest in books started at an early age. They were at the top of my Christmas list. In 1936, when I was fourteen, I was given Cecil Lewis's *Sagittarius Rising,* an autobiography of a First World War pilot. In his review, Bernard Shaw wrote, 'This is a book which everybody should read. . . . The boy had all the noble tastes and qualities, love of beauty, soaring imagination . . . he is a thinker, a master of words, and a bit of a poet.'

At that time, aviation was really still in its infancy, but living in Southampton made it possible to see a variety of aeroplanes from nearby airfields. There was a great deal of propaganda about the need for everyone to become 'air-minded'.

Flying had not produced many outstanding books but one other title made an impression on me: *Wind, Sand and Stars,* by the French author, Antoine de Saint Exupéry, published in 1939.

Aviation as a subject for book collecting did not last. My insatiable desire was to buy books of literature and biography. At home we had a diverse collection most of which had come from my paternal grandfather who was a voracious reader. It is to him, I believe, that I must owe my long-standing interest in book collecting.

In December 1939, on a rare visit to Foyle's in the Charing Cross Road, I came across Arnold Bennett's *Literary Taste: How to Form it with Detailed Instructions for Collecting a Complete Library of English Literature.* This ambitiously titled book of 143 pages seemed to give the sort of guidance I had dreamed about. It served me well for a few years until I saw *An English Library: A Bookman's Guide* (1964) by F. Seymour Smith. This comprehensive guide I still use in conjunction with the Oxford Companion to English Literature.

My mother came from Dorset and I suppose this could have influenced me when I started buying Thomas Hardy. One of the first titles was *Tess of the D'Urbervilles,* a nice edition published by Macmillan in 1926 with forty-one wood-engravings by Vivien Gribble, bound in buckram bevelled boards.

In 1935 a lot of publicity was given to T. E. Lawrence following his death after a motor cycle accident. I can remember our form master giving a short account of his life. I was intrigued. The local library had a copy of the 1935 edition of *Seven Pillars of Wisdom* which I tried to read without much success. It wasn't until many years later that I came to appreciate it. Winston Churchill said that we should leave the reading of some classics until later in life. For me, this was one of them. Conversely, reading *T. E. Lawrence by His Friends*, edited by A. W. Lawrence (1937) and David Garnett's edition of *The Letters of T. E. Lawrence* (1938) developed my taste. Although I retained an interest in Lawrence over the years it was not until I retired in 1982 that I started collecting him seriously. Lawrence produced only three major books, *Seven Pillars of Wisdom, Revolt in the Desert* and, posthumously, *The Mint*.

Seven Pillars of Wisdom had a very complicated inception, but suffice it to say that between 1919 and 1926 Lawrence had completed four drafts. The third draft was printed by the *Oxford Times,* limited to eight copies, and called the Oxford (1922) edition. The fourth draft was an abridged version, cut by 84,000 words, 25%, and known as the Subscribers' edition (1926) limited to perhaps 170 copies, with another thirty-two lacking some of the plates. It was this text that was printed shortly after Lawrence's death in 1935 by Jonathan Cape for general circulation. The Oxford 1922 edition was published by the Castle Hill Press in an unlimited edition, but not until 1997. This version is considered by many to be the better.

Two translations were made by Lawrence. *The Odyssey of Homer* was printed and published in 1932 by Sir Emery Walker, Wilfred Merton and Bruce Rogers in an edition of 530 copies bound in full leather. There is justification, we have been told, for a classic to be re-translated every ten years or so. Since 1932 several versions of *The Odyssey* have appeared and have been enthusiastically received, but Lawrence, I believe, still has his place. It is fascinating to be able to hold the first edition and read Bruce Rogers's detailed description in *Paragraphs on Printing* of how he set about making this book. Each chapter is headed with a roundel, three and three eighths inches in diameter, with a gold leaf background overprinted in black with Homeric figures from Greek vases. To achieve this required seven printings. The gold

PHILIP KERRIGAN

leaf and the smell of the ink are still there after 73 years. It has been described as one of the finest books, typographically, of the last century.

The other was a translation from the French of *The Forest Giant* by Adrien le Corbeau, first published in 1924 by Jonathan Cape. The second edition from the same publisher in 1935, is illustrated with wood-engravings by Agnes Miller Parker.

Lawrence was a prolific letter-writer and so far seven volumes have been published, with more to come, from the Castle Hill Press. Especially in later years, he took 'immense care over the literary quality of his letters, which were sometimes redrafted more than once'.[1]

Because his published writings were few, a collection is bound to be made up mostly of books about Lawrence and those of a peripheral nature, such as Doughty's *Arabia Deserta* and the biographies of General Allenby.

As one of the most colourful and well-known personalities of the twentieth century it is not surprising that Lawrence has attracted a great deal of interest resulting in the publishing of numerous biographies. In my opinion there are two that stand out above the rest, *The Prince of our Disorder* by John Mack and *Lawrence of Arabia: the authorised biography* by Jeremy Wilson.

At the time of Lawrence's death his library was at Clouds Hill and it is fortunate that we have a fairly accurate catalogue of its contents. This provides an opportunity to read those books which influenced his thinking and writing.

His appreciation of books was not confined to fine writing but included fine printing. The library contained private press books from Ashendene, Doves, Kelmscott and Gregynog. It was his ambition to set up a private press and hand-print the classics of his choice. This he never achieved, but he did design and supervise the printing of the 1926 Subscribers' edition of *Seven Pillars*. I was much influenced by his enthusiasm for fine printing and for many years I thought of having a press of my own. When John Ryder published his book, *Printing for Pleasure*, in 1955 I was one of many who saw it as a godsend.

But setting up a press is not to be undertaken lightly, and it was not until ten years later, in 1965, that I was able to produce my first hard-backed book with the imprint of the Tabard Press.

The object was to print books about books to as high a standard as I was capable. So it was necessary to obtain books on printing and examples from the Ashendene, Doves, Gregynog, Shakespeare Head, Golden Cockerel and Nonesuch presses.

I have difficulty in remembering why I started to collect Horace Walpole. Perhaps it was because he was another prolific letter-writer who operated a private press. His name, of course, will always be associated with Wilmarth Lewis. Between the Wars Lewis regularly visited England and purchased as many books and manuscripts as he could lay his hands on at a time when British collectors were apathetic about Walpole. His collection became the most comprehensive ever assembled in private hands. Yale University produced a new edition of the letters edited by Lewis. This was started in 1933 and completed in 1983 and has been described as 'the greatest editorial achievement of twentieth-century publishing.' I have only nine of the forty-eight volumes published. It has the advantage of, *inter alia,* including letters from Walpole's correspondents. I do have the complete Toynbee edition of sixteen volumes, published in 1903–5, which Lytton Strachey referred to as 'the Palladian beauty', and in which Walpole's own letters are arranged in chronological order.

This interest led me to the eighteenth and nineteenth century novelists: Defoe, Samuel Richardson, Laurence Sterne, Peacock and Walter Pater.

When asking for contributions to this book the editor, amongst other things, suggested that members should give the main thrust of their collection. For most this will prove no problem. I am reminded of some collectors (few in number, no doubt), whose ambition is to possess every edition of one particular title. The reader, if he has got this far, will now appreciate that I am not one of those. My collection of something between 2,000 and 2,500 books is diffuse, the very antithesis of the single title collection. To comply with the editor's wishes I suppose I could say that my main thrust is to acquire books of my choice.

Arundel, West Sussex

1. *Lawrence of Arabia: The Authorised Biography,* Jeremy Wilson (Heinemann, 1989), p. 715.

PHILIP KERRIGAN

Bill Klutts

A direct descendant of Sir James Tyrell (alleged assassin, for Richard III, of the 'Princes in the Tower'), I was born in Ripley, Tennessee (north of Memphis, almost in Arkansas), June 26, 1928, and have spent my life there, except for two periods away. I was four years at the University of Chicago, Illinois, on one of two full-tuition / expenses scholarships offered in a state-wide competitive exam taken (among distracting sirens and fireworks) on VE Day. There later followed two years of active service in the Army during the Korean War (drafted as private, rising to sergeant-major, 318th Heavy Tank Battalion, serving thereafter for 25 years in the Army Reserve and later the Naval Reserve, until retirement as lieutenant commander).

Editor of my high school newspaper, I began writing for our weekly community newspaper, *The Lauderdale County Enterprise* (of which my mother was bookkeeper and 'society editor'), and I was on the staff of the University of Chicago weekly *Maroon* while working thirty hours a week in the Chicago *Associated Press* bureau. After taking my B.A. in 1947, and two years of graduate work (in History), I returned to Ripley to purchase a half-interest in the *Enterprise*, acquiring sole ownership in 1965.

As a collector of American art pottery I was responsible for most of the Second Series of *The Collector's Encyclopedia of Roseville Pottery,* 1980). Since the mid-1980s I have served as Membership Secretary in the States (for a period including Canada) of the PLA.

The *Enterprise* was for many years printed on a Miehle No. 2 press, from four-page forms of metal type (from a mid-1940s Model 32 Linotype, display types hand-set). When printers turning to off-set dumped hot metal equipment, I scrounged it from as far away as New York, for spare parts for our plant. With this stuff came printers' manuals and type specimen books (which I had never noticed), sparking an interest in the book arts which built a collection of more than 2,000 volumes, dispersed in two sales at Christie's East, New York, in 2001.

I have kept a few gems: Haebler's three volumes of incunabula

Bill Klutts

leaves; Ratdolt's *Appianus,* 1477 (described to the Bibliographical Society by G. R. Redgrave as 'Magnificent . . . there are few printed books of any age which can be compared'); Baskerville's personal and inscribed copy of his *Book of Common Prayer*; one of twenty-five copies of the Officina Bodoni *Sentimental Journey*, 1926 (I bought two sleeping in a mixed lot at Sotheby's in London; Hans Schmoller flew to Ripley to cajole the other); Gill's own specially bound copy of *Typography*, two prospectuses laid in, 1931; and Stannard's *Art Exemplar*, *circa* 1860.

Stannard, a retired London lithographer, who also called himself 'Harry Sanders', for reasons unknown, listed and explained in detail, in 220 pages, 156 methods of printing, from Acrography to Zincography, but with duplications, only about forty-three. He bound in examples of each method of printing (examples not uniform in various copies). His supply of examples limited his edition to four large paper (22 × 14½ inches), six small (11 × 14½ inches).

Of the four large paper copies: Stannard's copy (lot 340 in estate auction, 1880) is in the British Museum Print Room (re-bound, *circa* 1965, in buckram with morocco spine, no record of original binding, some pages re-margined / re-mounted). Two other copies were last recorded as owned by H. M. The Queen and the Lord Chief Baron Kelly. The fourth copy, owned by the Earl of Bridgewater (Lord Ellesmere), was not included with the books he sent in 1917 ('discarding duplicates', de Ricci, 1930) to the Huntington Library in San Marino, California. Elizabeth Harris (*JPHS*, 4, 1968) is in error (page 21) that the Ellesmeres still held this copy in 1967–8. Ruari McLean bought it (with Bridgewater bookplate) in a North Kensington bookshop, about 1954, and later donated it to the University of Toronto.

Of the six small paper copies, one is reported in the Bodleian, one in the Victoria and Albert Museum, and one (ex Howard Levis, 1911) in the U.S. Library of Congress. One, sold by Hodgson's in London in 1926, has not been traced. My copy (original binding gilt, all edges gilt, with the large paper title-page folded in) was listed for sale in *The Antiquarian Bookman* (U.S. equivalent of the UK *Clique*) from an Oregon(!) bookstore for $80. I sent a telegram for it. I have ever been astonished that Questor Rare Books offered a small paper copy (re-hinged, hinge partially cracked) for sale (1991) at $25,000.

Ripley, Tennessee

BILL KLUTTS

David G. Lewis

Gregynog Press Special Bindings

In 1963, I inherited from my father sixteen books, in the case bindings, that had been published by the Gregynog Press between 1923 and 1940. In 1982 I wrote to the Warden at Gregynog, Dr Glyn Tegai Hughes, and asked him to send me a complete list of the books the Press had published. Dr Hughes responded with a list of the forty-two books and recommended that I acquired Dorothy Harrop's book *The Gregynog Press*, which had just been published by the Private Libraries Association, and which became my constant inspiration..

I had two alternatives: either I should sell the sixteen books or try to acquire the remaining twenty-six books. I decided on the latter and I completed that set in 1998. However, three of the books which made up my collection were in the special binding as I was unable to find those titles in the case binding. Consequently, I was faced with a further dilemma: should I now try to acquire a complete set of the special bindings and continue to pursue the remaining three titles in the ordinary bindings?

I was not sure it was possible to complete a set of the special bindings as the Press only published a limited number of copies for each title. I turned to Ed Maggs of Maggs Bros for advice, and he was in no doubt that it would be possible, but then cynics would say that was in Ed's interest. Ed is a great enthusiast and if anyone could help me achieve my objective, it was Ed and his colleague Sophie Schneideman at Maggs.

I researched the Press archives at the National Library of Wales to establish how many special bindings had been produced and where they might be found today. There were 980. I have located over 600 of which I have seen over 500. This gave me an indication of how many remained in circulation. The majority of these special bindings were bound by George Fisher: the remainder by his assistant John Ewart Bowen.

I am writing a history of these special bindings which will show who bought them (with a short biography of each) and where they can be found today. Some of the original purchasers were: George Bernard Shaw, Major Abbey, Thomas Watson (founder

Gregynog Press

of IBM), Edward Wilding (who actually designed the S.S. Titanic), Sir Stephen Gaselee, Henry Davis, Albert Ehrman, and Viscount Astor. I have now collected forty-four of these special bindings (thirty-five titles and nine variant bindings). So I still require a further seven titles. In addition, I have amassed a large quantity of the ephemera. All the books are kept in solander boxes made by Sangorski & Sutcliffe or Zaehnsdorf/Shepherd's.

The Gregynog Press closed in 1940 when the staff were called up for military duties. The Press was re-established in 1978 under the name Gwasg Gregynog in the same premises as the old Press where it continues to flourish to this day. I own a complete collection of all the Gwasg Greynog publications and I am also a Trustee of the Press.

London

Pressmark, Gwasg Gregynog
designed by Keith Holmes

Bernard C. Lloyd

Sir Walter Scott

The collection of over 6,000 volumes was started in 1972 with a chance meeting with a retired antiquarian bookdealer who lived next door and from whom I used to buy books. I had always collected books since a child – somewhat eclectically – and it was put to me that there should be a theme to my collecting. In fact, it so happened that he had eight first editions of the Waverley novels in original boards. So that became the beginning of thirty years of collecting books by and about Scott. The collection now resides at the University of Aberdeen. I felt that Scott would have wanted it to go somewhere in his native land and to an institution, led by an enthusiast, Professor David Hewitt, that had a passion for Scott.

The collection is the most comprehensive ever assembled of Scott material. It comprises all the Waverley novels; all his poetry; most of his miscellaneous prose; most of his many submissions to various periodicals; song sheets and books of his words put to music; plays and playbills from his novels; chapbooks and parodies; numerous illustrations; manuscript material. It includes almost all of his works in original paper boards; most of the various British editions, e.g. most of the twenty-five editions of *Lay of the Last Minstrel*; a number of presentation copies; many foreign editions in both English and the local language; over 500 books about Scott. The recent bibliographers of Scott – Professor William B. Todd (a Past President of the PLA) and his wife the late Dr Ann Bowden – in reviewing the collection stated 'Beyond question the whole assemblage, as well as the manuscripts continually acquired, established this collection as quite beyond compare'.

However, it is not Scott the writer that intrigued me, it was Scott the person who was extremely secretive in his commercial dealings. He was the main shareholder in the Ballantyne Press, that was not known publicly until its bankruptcy in 1826. He wrote the Waverley novels but did not acknowledge them publicly until 1827 after most of the novels had been written. When he went bankrupt himself in 1826, it transpired that he had transferred

Abbotsford – his home – into the name of his son thereby avoiding the necessity of a forced sale. It is not unreasonable to believe that he had some inkling that he was in financial difficulty at the time and his legal training would have suggested this course of action. Nevertheless, Scott was an astute business man and a man of integrity. He personally went bankrupt in 1826 in the sum of £120,000. He agreed with the Trustees that he would work to pay off this sum. During the period until his death in 1832, he had repaid most of the debt. Within eight years the balance was repaid by his Trustees from the copyrights to all his works

On the other hand, Scott is a milestone in the history of English literature and made the novel popular – albeit with an affluent segment of the population. Scott originally came into prominence as a poet. In about 1812, Byron's poetry was in its ascendancy and selling well whereas Scott's was starting to decline. Scott had an expensive lifestyle which needed an income above his wife's and his own as the Sheriff of Selkirkshire. So, in 1814, he found an uncompleted manuscript of a novel that he duly completed. This became a bestseller starting the 'series' of his twenty-three novel outpourings that came to be known as the Waverley novels.

I have been indebted to many book dealers over the years. Four come to mind and supplied (or sold to me) a substantial part of the collection. Spike Hughes of Innerleithen – a leading and discerning dealer whose personal Scott collection I bought. Brian Lake of Jarndyce, London – a dealer whose knowledge of eighteenth and nineteenth century English literature is second to none and who is greatly respected and acknowledged by dealers and collectors alike. James Burmester of Bristol who when he was in New York with Ximenes helped me acquire some choice Scott material. Alan Grant of Grant and Shaw, Edinburgh, whom I first knew when he was at Blackwell's in Oxford.

I will not bore the readers with specific details of the collection. It can be seen on the web site of the University of Aberdeen (abdn.ac.uk) by searching for Bernard C. Lloyd or Sir Walter Scott.

In 1992, I started collecting comic books relating to the works of Scott. Whilst in America I mentioned my collection to someone who told me that a number of Scott's works had been put into comic book format. This whetted my appetite and my comic book collection was born.

BERNARD C. LLOYD

Comic books have been around since 1842 when *The Adventures of Mr. Obadiah Oldbuck* was published by Wilson Company, New York, illustrated by George Cruikshank. It was created by Rudolphe Topffer a playwright, novelist, artist and teacher from Geneva. As early as 1827, he began producing 'picture novels' – published privately in Geneva, sharing them with friends and students. The American artist for the 'masthead' comic book was D. C. Johnston – highly influenced by Cruikshank. Johnston went on to illustrate many of that era's comic books. However, it was Frank Bellew who is credited as the father of American comic book art. Born in India, educated in France and England, he emigrated to America in 1850. He was influenced by Richard Doyle and his art graced numerous American periodicals in the 1850s to 1870s.

In the twentieth century, the main medium for comics based upon the classics of literature was the Classics Series that began in 1941. This series was the brainchild of Albert L. Kanter whose company, Gilberton Co., published the comics. He saw – in this new comic book medium – a means of introducing children to the classics. Over the next six years, Kanter published thirty-four Classics Series (plus numerous reprints) such as – *The Adventures of Sherlock Holmes, Lorna Doone, Oliver Twist, Robin Hood, Gulliver's Travels, Robinson Crusoe, Frankenstein, Moby Dick, Uncle Tom's Cabin, Huckleberry Finn, The Three Musketeers* and *Ivanhoe. Ivanhoe* alone had over ten million copies issued, which included twenty-five reprints over a twenty-year period.

In 1947, the search for a classier logo resulted in the Classics Illustrated Series. Because of the higher quality image, this series flourished in the 1950s whilst other series were reeling from outside competition. This later series included *The Lady of the Lake, The Talisman, Rob Roy, Castle Dangerous.* However, production finally ceased in 1962 as the publisher lost its 2nd class mailing permit.

The Classics Illustrated Series had a veritable plethora of foreign variations in twenty-five languages in twenty-seven countries with over 4,000 foreign editions. The British Classics Illustrated Series was published by Strato Publications / Thorpe and Porter of Leicester from 1951 to 1963. The Series was not issued in the US Edition's numerical order as initially the title numbers were issued randomly and then missing numbers were filled in. The Scott publications were *Ivanhoe, 1952, Rob Roy, 1955, The Talisman, 1956, Lady of the Lake, 1957 and Castle Dangerous, 1958.*

There were other US & UK 'classic' comic book publishers. Dell Publishing Company, New York, produced 1,350 comics mainly based upon movies from 1939 until 1963. Fawcett Publications Inc., Greenwich, produced twenty Movie Comics from 1949 to *Ivanhoe* in 1952. Marvel Comics Group, New York, produced thirty-six Classics Comics from 1976 to 1978, with *Ivanhoe,* 1976. Pendulum Press, New York, published sixty Pendulum Illustrated Classics from 1973 until 1978, with *Ivanhoe,* 1978. King Features Syndicate, New York, published twenty-four King Classics in 1977 and 1978, with *Ivanhoe,* 1977, and reprints in 1979. Acclaim Books Inc., Greenwich, produced the Classics Illustrated Study Guides from 1995 to 1998. Amex Co. Ltd, London, published twelve Classic in Pictures Series during 1949, including *Ivanhoe.* The Amalgamated Press (later Fleetway), London, published 450 Thriller Comics / Picture Library from 1951 until 1963, with many Scott items.

Also, these Classics were translated into many languages. In the Scott collection are comics from Denmark, Netherlands, Germany, Sweden, Belgium, Mexico, Greece and Spain. In my opinion, Kanter was right when he stated that he wanted to 'introduce' children to the beauties of literature. His intention was not to educate, but to 'whet the appetite' of children so that they would read and appreciate the real thing. We live now in a graphical world and the graphical format of comic books as an educative tool has not been fully understood and appreciated. My collection of Scott 'comics' continues to grow including now over eighty examples.

Shrewsbury

Marc J. Loost

Herbert Ingram & Nathaniel Cooke

This part of my collection consists of the titles (exclusive of newspapers and periodicals) that Herbert Ingram (1811–1860) and Nathaniel Cooke (1810–1879), at first together and later separately, published in London during the period 1847–1855. During this period, they published some 165 titles, nearly all illustrated, involving a multitude of diverse illustrators, engravers, printers and binders

There is much here to attract the inquisitive collector. Little is known about their book publishing business, which is one of the reasons that led me to commence the collection. No records of the business have apparently survived. No complete list of their published works has been found, although partial lists and extensive advertisements do offer some guidance.

Like other publishers at the time, they classified and promoted some of their books in series called 'libraries', e.g. *National Illustrated Library*, *London Biographical Library*, *Illustrated London Library* and *Universal Library*. These series' names, however, differentiated their components more in format and style than in content.

A number of factors can make it difficult to identify, date and locate their titles in repository libraries, where, even if found, the original publisher's bindings have often been replaced. They initially published under imprints that did not disclose the names of Ingram and Cooke and that confusingly identified the publisher only as the 'Office' of the particular series. In some titles, the publisher's imprint consisted only of a street address. Some titles, although running into several editions, were issued without dates, and some in parts not in immediate sequence.

Biographical data about Ingram and Cooke is also scant, although enough was known concerning Herbert Ingram (who was a Member of Parliament for Boston, Lincolnshire, from 1856 to his death) to enable a recent biography by Isabel Bailey. Nathaniel Cooke is said by some (mistakenly I believe) to have designed the eminent 'Staunton' pattern of chessmen that first appeared in 1849.

Cooke and Ingram (whose sister Cooke had married in 1835) were the main members of the partnership of 'Ingram, Cooke and Co.' This partnership had commenced in Nottingham as 'Ingram and Cooke' in 1840. In 1849, it became styled 'Ingram, Cooke and Co.', when William Little (1816–1884) was added as a 5% partner. Ingram had married Little's sister in 1843.

Through their partnership, Ingram and Cooke were the principal owners of the *Illustrated London News,* the renowned illustrated weekly newspaper that they had founded in 1842. In 1853, Ingram, who was the dominant 70% partner, split off the book publishing business, for which, after October 1853, Cooke took sole responsibility and carried on in his own name for nearly two years. Ingram nevertheless also continued to publish some of their books under his own name in direct competition with Cooke. In 1855, most of the remaining inventory and copyrights of the business were sold – ending the business nearly as mysteriously as it had commenced.

The aim of this collection is not only to assemble all their published books in original condition but also to prepare a descriptive bibliography and provide biographical information that has not been furnished elsewhere. The collection currently comprises 397 volumes. They have been acquired during the past fourteen years mainly by browsing at London book fairs, where I have often benefited from the knowledgeable enthusiasm and generosity of Robin de Beaumont.

As might be expected of the owners of the *Illustrated London News*, most of their books were amply and imaginatively illustrated with frontispieces, plates, vignettes, and ornamental devices. The illustrations and devices were by artists such as Cuthbert Bede [W.T. Minor], J. R. Clayton, George and Edward Dalziel, Edmund Evans, Henry Fitzcook, Birket Foster, John Gilbert, H. C. Hine, Henry Noel Humphreys, W. H. Kearney, Charles Keene, John Leech, T. R. Macquoid, William McConnell, Kenney Meadows, 'Phiz' [Hablot K. Browne], George Thomas, William L. Thomas, Henry Vizetelly, and Joseph Lionel Williams.

Many of their books also featured distinctive decorative bindings. At the lower end of the price scale, they were among the first to publish so-called 'yellow-backs', 'railways books' or 'one-shilling books' in striking coloured paper wrappers. Most of their books, however, were bound in distinctive publisher's blind-embossed cloth that was ornamented with gilt spines and vignettes (some signed by John Leighton and William Harry Rogers). They published four titles in bindings blocked in silver leaf.

Their books could also be obtained in gilt-embossed publisher's morocco, or bound in decorated calf with marbled boards. Their extraordinary *carton-pierre* bindings designed by Henry Noel Humphreys for his own works on the *Origin and Progress of the Art of Writing* and the *Coinage of the British Empire* in themselves merit more commentary than space here permits.

Ingram and Cooke pioneered in the publishing of new illustrated editions of earlier works to bring world literature and education to a wide popular audience at the cheapest prices. They included popular biographies of Samuel Johnson, Alexander Pope, Edmund Burke, the Duke of Wellington, Napoleon Bonaparte, George Washington, Martin Luther, and Toussaint L'Ouverture, and histories and travel books concerning a wide variety of countries, including India, Siam, Iceland, Russia, Australia, etc. Their profusely illustrated educational works offered popular instruction on drawing, engraving, mathematics, geography, astronomy, geology, electricity, chemistry, cookery, microscopy, medicine, railways, animal husbandry, and forestry. They published their own edition of Webster's *Dictionary of the English Language* (Goodrich 3rd) and of the New Testament (authorised version).

Their literary works included new illustrated editions of works by Homer, Milton, Goethe, Schiller, Bacon, Emerson, Alexander Pope, Charles MacKay, Harriet Beecher Stowe, Emilie Carlen, Frederika Bremer, and Mikhail Lermontov. There were also a few works for children by Jacob Abbott, Maria Jacob and Elisabeth M. Stewart and some books of humour or light leisure reading by authors such as Cuthbert Bede, Angus B. Reach, Shirley Brooks, William Jordan, Horace Mayhew, and Sarah P. Willis Parton.

London

Frances and Nicolas McDowall
(Photograph: Bernard Mitchell)

Nicolas McDowall

The Old Stile Press

I cannot remember a time before I loved books. As a child I hoped to be given books for Christmas and I would visit bookshops, especially second-hand ones, with excitement from an early age. I am ashamed to remember that, as a teenager at boarding school, I worked out a foolproof method of pilfering from my favourite warren of a bookshop. It involved visiting the shop dressed for tennis and carrying a racquet and box of balls. The clever thing was that there were no balls in the box. I think that I was much too scared a lad to have carried out the scam but I did emerge from that shop with many legally acquired treasures such as five leather-bound volumes of Pope's *Iliad* which cost 15s. and how I can remember the smell and the thrill as I opened one of those romantic objects . . . books which had been made and actually handled by people living in the eighteenth century.

I cannot remember a time before I read books. Had I started this piece thus, rather than as above, few might have noticed any difference but the fact is that the latter is as untrue as the former is true. I was, and remain, a very slow and unhappy reader. I simply cannot concentrate on the words. If I am trying to read for pleasure I soon nod off, even if I am not reading in bed. If I am reading because I have to, or need to, I find myself thinking about something else after a couple of sentences . . . just as I did in prep while trying to read the designated chapters about the Thirty Years War. It is the equivalent of the small boy in class who keeps looking out of the window and, indeed, I was that very child. So, if I did not devour pages of text, for study or stories, like the usual sort of bookworm, why did I like books so much? The simple answer to this conundrum is . . . pictures. The best books of my childhood had gobbets of text on each page but these were surrounded by images in which I could be lost, worlds in which I could wander and in which I could be more alive than in the atmosphere of fear at school and of boredom at home. Actual illustrations (magical line drawings by Heath Robinson, John Minton and Mervyn Peake or summery lithographs from Curwen and other presses transferring drawings of Babar and Orlando to metal plates from grained plastic sheets, for example) were marvellous in themselves but my favourite books were those which used the double-spread like the stage of a theatre or the wide-angle viewfinder of a movie camera. Swirling vistas of imagery cover the page and the paragraphs of text sit safely surrounded by the scenes they describe. In some artists' work it is the all-over tapestry of the treatment that is satisfying while in others (and these appealed more and more) the effects were achieved by artist and book designer with less rather than more. I would let my eyes wander round an expanse of land, sea and sky and suddenly realize that it consisted largely of white paper and the magic of an artist. Pope's *Iliad* wouldn't have had many pictures in it, I hear you comment. No, but it did have glorious initial capitals and stretches of large italic type and ligatures and long ʃes and all sorts of exciting ways of placing stuff on a page which, as a schoolboy, I found intriguing but did not understand (like sex) and certainly did not know that it was called typography.

For a time after becoming an educational publisher, I attempted to collect old schoolbooks but soon found that most of the Victorian period ones, which were available on the shelves, either had no pictures in them or were unimaginatively laid out with 'improving' engravings. Sadly, lovely ones from earlier times, which I had seen photographed in books, were fiendishly rare and expensive. Carefully locked away in glass-fronted bookcases, posh 'limited editions' are all preserved, while books made for children are now rare, having been loved, scribbled or torn to pieces by the little monsters.

I soon began to concentrate on illustrated books of the first half of the twentieth century. There were the Pre-Raphaelite wood-engravings, Beardsley, Laurence Housman and early Heath Robinson at one end and, crucially, at the other end, the wonderfully inventive post-war publications (so often from Houses run by European refugees) on war-economy paper with no margins and, if you were lucky, a dust-wrapper with another on the back, liberated from the over-long print run of some other title. The very best of these, for me, were those illustrated by the neo-romantic painters with whom I had been fascinated since exploring the various Cork Street galleries as a teenager. At that time I could not afford the paintings (lost time has been made up

NICOLAS MCDOWALL

for to a certain extent now, I am happy to say!) but often the images by Keith Vaughan, John Piper, Graham Sutherland, Edward Bawden *et al* in these volumes took the form of autographic lithographs and, thus, represented (and still do, of course) a wonderfully inexpensive way of acquiring original prints by my favourite artists.

In those early days, mine was an unfashionable area for collecting. In special cabinets, booksellers would prize Rackham and Dulac books but these, to me, were simply books of text pages with reproductions of paintings glued in. My quarry, with the help of my 'shopping lists', John Lewis's *The Twentieth Century Book* and Rigby Graham's PLA booklet, *Romantic Book Illustration in England, 1943–1955*, could be found anywhere and picked off the 'ordinary' shelves. I would spend an hour in a new shop and come out with a cardboard box full. This honeymoon period was not to last, of course, and I am happy that I did not let up while the going was so good. I did lash out on some major treasures when funds allowed. When we moved out of London to our paradise in Wales, I was moved when the irreplaceable Alan Hancox sent a postcard to wish us well, saying that he was pleased that his copy of the Gill Four Gospels had ended up so close to Tintern Abbey!

Active collecting ended when we started to produce books of our own. The Old Stile Press had started when I was still a full-time publisher and developed over a number of half and half years before becoming all-consuming when I was able finally to bid farewell to London. Our pattern (almost from the beginning) of working with artist / printmakers on books in which image was as important as words and the design of the book as a completely integrated whole was foremost, has developed over the years. We are going strong, with an eager following among librarians and collectors across the world and, as I write, I have exciting projects being worked on by artists which will keep me busy hand-feeding sheet by sheet well into my dotage. It is a happy and satisfying thought that, had that fifteen year old snuck into that bookshop, all those years ago, and found one of the books we are now producing, he might just have liked it enough to slip it into his empty tennis ball box!

Llandogo, Monmouthshire

NICOLAS MCDOWALL

Richard Martin

The Comfort of Books

I have a septic-tank-emptier friend who collects erotica. He says that his books take his mind off the job. Quite the opposite, and rather geekishly, my book collecting reflects my work, for the growth of my library of sheep, wool and textile books has grown, over thirty years, with my woollen weaving business.

It is a working library, and illuminates everything that we do. Whether designing, manufacturing or marketing, at some point in the process we will pull down a volume to see how they did it in 1870s Yorkshire, or in ancient India, or in modern Peru, and find that it helps us in 2006.

Unlike my book collector friends who collect the first editions of a specific dead author there can never be a completeness about my collection, and, because it is a practical working library, we will buy new books as well as old. So the number of books keeps growing. If the library was in the mill, this would not be such a problem, but because I can not bear not to have my books about me, they must be in our relatively small house. Every collector who is one half of a couple will know exactly the problems this can cause.

Not only is there never enough room to house and use the books, every time a section of the collection is re-organised, more shelves are required. Sometimes it seems that releasing a book from the close confines of the shelf makes it fatter. Or maybe it's just time that makes books grow! In any event, my books have long since blossomed from the room my wife calls 'the office', and I call 'the library', and found niches in every room in the house. Mill architecture is on the landing outside a bathroom, Australian sheep-breeding is in a guest bedroom, and South American weaving is behind a settee in the living room.

It is not a particularly big collection, but, as I said, it's not a particularly big house. There are probably about five or six thousand books and pamphlets relating to textiles from fibre to fabric, with a bias towards wool and woollen cloths. So I start with agriculture, sheep and wool growing, gather pace with analysis of fibres and their uses, and plunge headlong into the intricate and multifarious world of spinning and weaving. Then there's a canter through books illustrating cloth designs and techniques from here and everywhere, and the finishing post is in sight with cloth marketing and costume. Then there is silk and silkworms, 'new' fibres (cashmere, mohair and synthetic, depending upon what 'new' meant to the authors of different centuries), and the topography of wool and weaving areas.

These are pretty obvious byways, but of course there are also the big detours beloved by all 'proper' book collectors. Many eighteenth century copper tokens show textile tools or techniques, so there are books on these, and of course books on architecture because of mills, economics because of the once proud place of the wool and weaving trade in the wealth of the nation . . . and a host of other sub-collections. I started a section on the spiritual aspects of weaving after buying a mid-seventeenth century book of prayers for weavers during a PLA picnic-visit to Lilies some years ago.

There is one big subject that runs almost in parallel with the story of textiles, and that is books on the history of textiles. My background was originally in engineering, in so far as that is what I set out to read at university. I chose engineering because it fascinated me, and I still think that apart from directing a film, turning the design for a motorway or shopping centre into something concrete rising from the mud of a construction site is a wondrous thing. I am definitely with those who see Brunel as one of the greatest Englishmen. However, after a year or two at university, I realised that engineering is a vocational subject rather like medicine: the course was not designed for gawpers at the wonder of it all like me, but for the budding Brunels of the late twentieth century. So I changed to read history, and there's the rub. I am a practical chap, and can cheerfully fettle a shed full of Dobcross looms, but I'm also fascinated by not just how techniques have evolved over the centuries, but what each age thought about how their forefathers had fared. There is the history of change, and there is the history of the history of change.

So, there are shelves of books on the history of textiles, written by men who surveyed the past from the viewpoint of their particular age. A man who looked back at the medieval gild system from the late-nineteenth century, when the mighty mills of Imperial

Britain truly were the 'workshops of the world', was likely to see ill-equipped, inefficient individual weavers scrabbling for a crust, whereas historians looking back from the rather grey, multi-national, corporatist present see proud craftsmen, with the dignity of self-employment, yet working in harmony with each other.

And of course it is not just the opinion that changes. Facts themselves are bent by the use to which they are put. As Aldous Huxley almost said 'facts begin as heresies, and end as superstitions.'

I think it was the great bibliophile John Arnott who reacted in horror when he was asked if he had read all his books. 'Certainly not!' he said. And I certainly haven't read all mine. No true collector ever has. Two books a week throughout a seventy year reading life amounts to only about 7,000, vastly less than the output of UK publishing houses in one year, let alone a lifetime. (It explains why I buy mostly novels by dead authors; if they are still in print they are probably worth reading.) And anyway, books are not just the contents. Anthony Rota was spot on when he wrote about all the other aspects of a book in *Apart from the Text*.

There is the association; I have a splendidly splenetic pamphlet published during the mid eighteenth century railing against the iniquity of those who sought to smuggle raw fleece out of England to the detriment of the English weavers. The margins are filled with equally splenetic notes from a contemporary English wool-grower wanting the higher prices to be obtained on the continent. At times he is so filled with bile against the anti-smuggling pamphleteer that in his rage his quill has scratched through the page. No doubt the value of the pamphlet is thus compromised, but as an object it is priceless.

And then there are the idiosyncrasies of authors. Sheep roamed English pastures for a thousand years before any sort of systematic exposition of sheep and sheep-keeping appeared, with *The Complete System... on Sheep, Grass Lambs and House Lambs* in 1749. William Ellis was the man who wrote it, and does he start his ground-breaking tome with some sort of overall synopsis of the breeds, or their uses? No, his first chapter is about the virtue of employing a lame shepherd and a lazy dog 'because these necessarily drive [the sheep] leisurely [and] give them their due time of feeding.' Wonderful and absurd stuff! In fact, Ellis wrote with great force about all sorts of country matters, and contemporaries beat a path to his farm to see how things should be done. Alas they found that he spent so much time writing, his own farm was a complete muddle.

What of the feel of books, the smell of books, the sheer pleasure of being surrounded by books? I walk into my library, look about me, and at once am transported to L. P. Hartley's 'other country where they do things differently'.

And did ever a man have such power as a book collector? There they are, shelf upon shelf of books, each distilling the erudition of a thousand authors who never met in life, but now are brought together by the collector-impresario to put on a show entitled 'My Library'.

But no true book collector should collect only for himself, collect just for the ownership. When the great library at Alexandria was destroyed, it was not just the books themselves that were lost, scholarship suffered too. On a far, far humbler scale, there is nothing I find more satisfying than being able to show someone, especially someone who would normally contend that the past can teach us nothing, the power of an old book to illuminate a new problem.

So there is something doubly satisfying in old books that have very obviously already solved many problems over the years. I have row upon row of nineteenth century weaving textbooks, well thumbed, annotated, and sweated over by generations of textile students learning their craft. What wonderful patterns must have grown out of studying the very books I now love and use?

And 'well-thumbed' reminds me of a particular favourite. One so often judges a book by its title, its edition, its condition. But I have a *Wool Dealer's Calculator*, a bound set of tables, converting the various local 'stone' to legal stone, used by a merchant buying fleece in the early-nineteenth century in the West Riding of Yorkshire. Every page is blackened by the wool-greasy thumb of the merchant as he ran it along the lines of figures in search of the right price to pay, while bargaining with the farmer. And every mark brings vividly to life the human round of 200 years ago.

Give me books, and give me life!

Cotswold Woollen Weavers, Filkins, Lechlade, Glos.

RICHARD MARTIN   259

Jim Maslen

Wood-engravings

My wife feels that the best way to describe my collection is monotone; the dominant feature is certainly monochrome. I have collected books illustrated with wood-engravings for over thirty years, with occasional excursions into the more colourful worlds of Albert Rutherston, the Ariel Poems, French illustrated books, Marc Chagall *et al.*

My interest in natural history and the countryside brought me into contact with books with wood-engravings and my collecting was relatively indiscriminate to start with. I came inevitably across books by Robert Gibbings and realised that I was beginning to build up useful collections of his work and that of the great names of the twentieth century – Joan Hassall, Gwen Raverat, Eric Ravilious, Agnes Miller Parker, John Nash, Paul Nash, etc. I began to focus on the work of Gibbings and Hassall and to extend my collecting by buying ephemera and prints. I had the immense good fortune to buy a considerable amount of ephemeral material from Joan Hassall's estate, which set me on a more rarefied course, that of signed and inscribed material. My usual routine in bookshops and at fairs had been to walk past shelves saying 'got that, got that' and sometimes saying 'I would love that, but it's too expensive'. Now I examine every copy that I see of a book by Hassall or Gibbings in the hope that it will be inscribed.

Joan Hassall seems less inclined merely to sign books and normally inscribed books to family or friends. Books with signature or inscription are both relatively uncommon. Her hand is neat and readily recognisable and she may sign as *Joan*, *Joana* or *Joanna*. I have books inscribed to *Topher* (her brother Christopher), *Mums*, F. Ernest Jackson and a number of friends. She was a natural and obliging letter writer and I have a number of letters written by her. One copy of *The Strange World of Nature* produced two letters written on behalf of a friend to solicit advice on a painting; a copy of *Theatrical Figures in Porcelain* has a letter turning down a commission for a bookplate on the grounds that it would take her years to get around to it, which seems a familiar story. A recently purchased leather bound copy of *Cranford* pro-

Jim Maslen

duced a most charming thank you note with an engraving to Elfreda, who had invited her to a Beatrix Potter party. Elfreda then passed the note on to Leslie Linder, the Beatrix Potter expert, with the following comment *Joan Hassall is a very considerable person in her own field, a considerable scholar and a musician – she plays the harp. She was the dumpy white-haired lady in a cloak and I first met her doing aqua-tinting at a party given by the Association of Painter-Etchers.* Such material brings a person to life (it also satisfies the sheer acquisitiveness of the collector). Her inscription to Ernest Jackson is *with admiration and gratitude*, a typical inscription which reveals the humanity and openness of her character.

My collection of books is largely complete and my collection of commercial work and ephemera extensive. I was rather irritated that David Chambers, in his book on Hassall, allocated a number to *Fairy Tales*, which was never produced, as it means that I can never achieve a complete Chambers listing collection. I have all the Saltire chapbooks, six of them signed, but not their fore-runner, *A Little Book of Tailpieces Engraved on Wood*. I have a signed copy of *Lancelot & Elaine* (slightly deceitful, in that the signature is on a tipped-in bookplate) and a possibly unique book – a proof copy of an alternative setting of *Portrait of a Village* that had belonged to Francis Brett Young. More important than that, I have a postcard from Joan Hassall, her reply to a letter that I sent her simply addressed *Joan Hassall, Malham* when she received her OBE. I have touched her life vicariously through correspondence with other members of the PLA, but the kindness of that reply brings her to life.

My Gibbings collection differs slightly in character, in that there is significantly less ephemera. There are books that I will probably never buy, the more expensive Golden Cockerel books and the portfolio of engravings from *The Seventh Man* (I do have the equivalent portfolio for *Erewhon*), but they are not rare; if I overcame that Calvinist streak that makes life difficult for a collector, and if I could sneak them past my wife, I could buy them all tomorrow. The £500 that I paid for *The Glory of Life*, which Gibbings considered to be one of his best two books, seemed a small price to pay, as does the £750 that I paid for a beautifully crisp inscribed copy of *Twelve Wood Engravings*. If a copy of that mythical beast *The Zoo* ever came onto the market I would have no problem raiding my savings. My quest for Gibbings has focused on inscribed and association copies, which tend not to be overly expensive, but which have to be hunted down. I have forty-six books that fall into this category, plus limited editions signed by Gibbings on a routine basis. My wife thinks it strange that I have six copies of *Sweet Thames Run Softly*, five of *Coming Down the Seine*, four of *Till I End My Song*. They map out the life that emerges from Martin Andrews's book. There are inscriptions to childhood friends – *Greetings and Happy Memories of Kinsale – to May Emerson* and *a long time since we met. Must be about fifty years – at Myrtle Hill I think* – and friends of youth, Colette O'Niel, the daughter of Mabel Annesley. There are books inscribed to Norman Howard, who helped build the *Willow*, to Alix (sic) McLachlan, who typed his manuscripts, to his colleagues at Reading University, Charles O'Donoghue and Ian Crichton – *another drop of water* – and others to Augustus John *who liked Over the Reefs* and Mario Toso *with appreciation of his art*. There are inserted letters and cards – *I'm in the final throes of preparation*

before setting off on another expedition from which I hope to com-
plete a book entitled 'Disguised as a Willow' (the working title for
Sweet Thames Run Softly). One recipient carefully cut out a small
part of a letter and pasted it into her copy of *Over the Reefs* –
Now I must stop & engrave a paddle and perhaps a fish hook for
the spine – along with a pen sketch and a copy of the photo reproduced on page 271 of the Andrews book (if only she had kept the
whole letter). His character emerges from his self-portrait carica-
ture – I have one ordinary version and another in *Beasts and Saints*
with an added halo – and his less serious inscriptions – another
copy of *Beasts and Saints* reads *Oh God, make me a saint – but*
NOT YET.

I have copies of his books inscribed by his second wife, Elisabeth,
and his sister, Aimée, and a number from the library that he shared
with Patience Empson. He gave her a copy of *The Radium Woman*
(*Patience from Robert*) and of Slocum's *Sailing Alone Around the*
World (P.A.E. from R.G.), which he then read and annotated himself (he marked vigorously this quotation *I had already found that*
it was not good to be alone, and so I made companionship with
what there was around me, sometimes with the universe and some-
times with my own insignificant self; but my books were always
my friends, let all else fail.) Gibbings's treatment of books would
make collectors despair; a book to him was something to handle
and even mishandle. I have an appalling copy of the eighth
edition of Darwin's *Voyage of the Beagle*. The binding is going,
the hinges are cracked, there are notes in pencil, ink, red, blue,
purple and green crayon, the corners of about thirty pages have
been turned down and chunks have been cut out of five pages. It
is, however, the copy that he used to prepare the Limited Editions
Club edition of the *Voyage* and has provided me with many hours
of pleasure as I try to follow the creative process. Gibbings's handwriting can present some difficulties to those unused to it; some
signatures degenerate into an R, a series of vertical strokes and
an emblematic flourished gs which is readily recognisable to those
familiar with his handwriting.

My collecting is wider than this suggests. The wood-engraving side has recently focused on the transitional period 1915–1930.
I normally buy books that I like, and I do try to read them all, but
the stamp collector mentality of the little boy has led me to buy

some appalling books. The two worst are a 1928 edition of *Epithalamion* with engravings by Maud Wethered (I shudder when I open it) and *The New Book of Trees* with engravings by C. Dillon McGurk. Raverat, Hassall, Farleigh all produce trees which can be readily identified; McGurk fails abysmally. I do sometimes feel the need for colour, which was satisfied by the lithographs of Chagall when I was single and is now satisfied by the work of Albert Rutherston. My collection is not a grand collection, but, as was the case with Gibbings, my books are my friends.

Hull, Yorkshire

Coronation Invitation,
scraperboard drawing by Joan Hassall, 1953,
reduced from 180 mm high

JIM MASLEN

Mark Mawtus

I have always been something of a collector, and one with a great interest in books. It is only in the last decade, however, that I have started to build something approaching a collection of what might be described as fine, rare, unusual, old, or just plain collectable books.

Being somewhat eclectic in my collecting (or accumulation), undertaken with limited funds, I have nevertheless managed to acquire a number of interesting items. The main themes of the collection include English history, with a special interest in Yorkshire, well printed poetry, books-on-books (inevitably) and some private presses (past and present).

In writing this essay at another time, I'm sure other examples would be selected, but as it must be short I simply give some good examples with relevant comment. I found a copy of Sir Thomas Browne's *Hydriotaphia, Urn Burial* (edited by Sir John Evans, Charles Whittingham, 1893) in my local bookshop some years ago. It included the bookplate of Alban Dobson with a blue label stating 'From Austin Dobson's Library'. It sparked an interest in both the Chiswick Press, and books written or owned by Austin Dobson.

Of Dobson items I have quite a number, though not rivaling that of the late Claude Prance. Probably most worthy of mention is a copy of Andrew Lang's *Specimens of a Translation of Theocritus*, with Austin Dobson's bookplate (one of less than forty copies, without a title-page, printed by the Chiswick Press *c.* 1879).

Another book I am very pleased to have is Evelyn Philip Shirley's *The Sherley Brothers* (Pickering, 1848) printed by Charles Whittingham, which has a beautiful title-page in black and red containing a pleasing dolphin and anchor device. The book was done for the Roxburghe Club, but my copy is inscribed to his wife 'Mary Clara Elizabeth Shirley, From E. P. S. April 1850.'

On two occasions I have dug a little deeper into my pockets to acquire a book printed on vellum. One of these is *Verses Written During Forty Years* (privately printed, 1879) by Sir John Duke Coleridge, which appears to be the author's own copy. A Lord

Chief Justice of England, he was a grandson of a brother of Samuel Taylor Coleridge. In looking through the book I note a thought provoking comment suitable for inclusion here, 'This book perhaps may linger in a few libraries when I am gone, and many of its later pages may seem to chance readers to express only foolish fondness'.

Much of the fun of book collecting comes from hunting for interesting books. It was very pleasing to find very cheaply a copy of *The Gledstones and the Siege of Coklaw* by Mrs Oliver (Edmonson & Co., Edinburgh, 1878, for the Hawick Arch. Soc.) inscribed 'Dr. Murray with Mrs. Oliver's kind regard' with extensive handwritten notes in a small neat hand. These can only be the work of the future Sir J. A. H. Murray, best known as editor of *The Oxford English Dictionary*.

Books printed and published by private presses from the late nineteenth century onwards have continued the tradition of creating books to the very highest standard. A favourite of mine from my collection is *The Works of Edmund Spenser, vol. 8: A View of the Present State of Ireland* etc. (printed at the Shakespeare Head Press for Basil Blackwell, Oxford, 1932), with a beautiful printed and coloured frontispiece and title-page.

Letters of Sir Walter Scott (J. B. Nichols, 1833, 2nd ed.) is probably my favorite Scott item with its mix of poetry and history including the introductory lines of the Rev. Polwhele 'Twas then, on topographic lore, Some evil genius bade me pore; Borne on swift steed of keen research, Hunt out a ruin or a church; Unfold, tho' faint from wan disease, By lurid lamps, dull pedigrees'.

Finally what collection would be without a copy of J. H. Burton's *The Book-Hunter* (my edition one of 1,000 copies, Blackwood, 1882, with wonderful illustrations)? A fantastically witty and intelligent text.

Tunbridge Wells

John Morris

Provincial Printing

My Books have been acquired for pleasure rather than for profit, so it is a bit ironic that the first book I can remember buying is now one of the most valuable that I own. It was Mervyn Peake's *Titus Groan* (in first issue dust wrapper, as it happens) which I bought (when I was aged twelve) as a discard from McLelland's Lending Library in Larne, County Antrim. That was in 1960, and books have come and gone in my life ever since. Domestic and financial upheavals over the years mean that my custodianship of many has been only too brief.

Nevertheless I still own a few thousand books which I receive great pleasure from, and the one part of this library that could properly be described as a collection rather than an accumulation is the several hundred British provincial imprints that I put together during the 1970s and have been adding to sporadically ever since.

During that period I worked as an assistant and cataloguer for several antiquarian booksellers, and in the course of this work I came across a pamphlet printed by J. W. Morris in Clipstone in 1799. I was curious to know where Clipstone was, and became curious too about other imprints that passed through my hands. Bungay-printed bibles often turned up, and I wondered when printing started in Bungay. Soon I was scouring local history journals, specialised monographs and library catalogues, and started compiling a card index with a view to producing a gazetteer of the spread of printing throughout the British Isles, a modern version of Cotton's pioneering *Typographical Gazetteer*. I still have that card index – and how I wish that there had been personal computers in those days.

I started buying the odd item that I could afford, trying to get the very earliest imprints from as many places as possible, at the same time never able to resist buying an inexpensive Milner of Halifax or Nicholson of Wakefield printing. I even came to terms with the products of the Welsh presses, and am the proud owner of several Welsh 'incunabula'.

So amongst my other books I now have a dedicated bookcase

John Morris

of mainly eighteenth and nineteenth century books and pamphlets of interest largely as productions of the local press. As far as I know I have copies of the first (or earliest known) books printed in about twenty-five towns, including Batley, Bolton, Bramley, Bridlington, Burnham, Clipstone, Driffield, Hartland, Honley, Ironbridge, Kettering, Milton Ernis, Newcastle upon Tyne, Newport Pagnell, Pateley Bridge, Romford, Rotherham, Tunbridge Wells and Walton, and early examples from many other places. There is a human story behind each one.

These pioneering local productions are still (2005) out there to be bought, although probably not for much longer, and although this aspect of printing and social history is now a subject of growing academic interest, it still remains a rather despised and neglected area of book collecting. I think it is absolutely fascinating and wish I had had the resources of a Heber or a Phillipps to take advantage of my expertise in this area.

Discussion of Milton's description of the printing press as 'that mighty engine of liberty', and the conceptual links between Gutenberg, Caxton, Tim Berners-Lee and the internet I leave to others. I now collect and make badges (in America they are called buttons) since it is a cheaper hobby but reflects the same impulse. They are also easier to store, and are more accessible in the so-called 'age of the sound-bite'.

If you happen to be reading this on Mars, do keep an eye out for the first Mars printing – you really ought to have it in your private library.

York

Paul W. Nash

Printing and Bibliography

My library is a relatively young one, begun in 1988. At that time I was employed at the Bodleian Library in Oxford, and working with rare books inspired me to begin collecting. At first I was indiscriminate, gathering first editions, fine printing, antiquarian and illustrated books of all sorts, and for a while I even considered becoming a bookseller. But soon I developed a particular interest in printing and bibliography, and decided I could not part with the finely-printed books I had gathered. Private presses thus became the main focus of my collecting. I also decided to become a printer myself, bought a small press and a few founts of type and continue to amuse myself by printing and publishing small books. Ephemera interests me too, and I have found it rather easier to acquire the prospectuses and advertisements of the great printers than to buy their books. I am attracted to the more unusual and out of the way presses, and to those which experiment with type and paper, even if unsuccessfully. An early passion was the Corvinus Press, on which I published a small book in 1994. Joining the Private Libraries Association in 1992 was a turning point, as I quickly became involved with the society, and joined David Chambers as co-editor of the journal in the following year.

My collection now consists of some 2,500 volumes plus a great many ephemeral pieces. I probably have the second best collection of Corvinus Press books in private hands (although I should be happy to be corrected about that), and also have most of the volumes published by its rather more quotidian successor, the Dropmore Press. A recent acquisition which pleased me very much was *More Papers Hand Made by John Mason* (dated 1960, but my copy was completed in 1965); it has sections printed on Mason's visceral papers by several contemporary artists and presses, including the Samson Press, which I am now researching. Another on-going project is a new bibliography of Guido Morris's Latin Press, and I have slowly been gathering examples of the books and ephemera he printed, in fits and starts, between 1935 and 1973. More recently, under the influence of Guy Powell, my interest in Loyd Haberly has been reawakened, and I have

Paul W. Nash

acquired many of his curious hand-made books. In addition to
private press printing, I also have small collections on book-
design and production, printing history, early publishers' bindings, Georgian and early Victorian architecture, and what I call
'bibliographical curiosities' (which allows me to assimilate more
or less anything into the collection). I also enjoy bad poetry, and
have a couple of shelves of books and pamphlets fit to make the
muses weep.

Witney, Oxon.

PAUL W. NASH

Adam Naylor

I started collecting books with my wife, Marianne, when we were students in Edinburgh in the 1970s. The first book we bought was an A & C Black Colour Book on Edinburgh and gradually we amassed nice copies of most of the standard works on the history and architecture of that most beautiful of cities. When we graduated, I returned to university to do research in nineteenth century Irish history and started collecting related material. Even in those days, good Irish books were much harder to find than their Scottish equivalents: a first lesson in comparative scarcity!

In the early 1980s we bought Compton Mackenzie's house in the New Town of Edinburgh from his widow. We decided to try and make a comprehensive collection of his works, the first editions but also all the reprints and the many books to which he contributed. Mackenzie was a prolific author, writing to sustain his lifestyle, and his oeuvre encompasses everything from his highly regarded early novels to a history of the Gas Board. He was generous in inscribing books and we managed to find a reasonable range of presentation copies. I wrote a short account of our collection for *The Scottish Book Collector*, volume 1, number 3.

A move in the 1990s took us to the Lake District and the house of another writer, Arthur Ransome. Again we started to amass his books. Our collecting interests have always been wide, too wide I fear to have made any real in-depth collections apart from the Mackenzies. Marianne has always enjoyed collecting interesting covers and bindings: Talwin Morris, the Cranford series, indeed Victorian decorated cloth in general. She has designed two bindings which were executed for us by a local binder, one for a first edition of *The Adventures of Sherlock Holmes* bought in a grim library binding.

Like many collectors, we have a weakness for books about books and also for series. The former is now represented by a whole wall of bibliographies, booksellers' reminiscences and histories of publishers and libraries. The latter has seen us collect King Penguins, the first ten Penguins and 'Shown to the Children' for example. Architecture and country houses are another pro-

Marianne & Adam Naylor

ductive area, as are favourite authors: Trollope, John Buchan, George MacDonald Fraser, Cunninghame Graham. In the end like most collectors it is probably the association copies that we treasure most: interesting inscriptions, books from the libraries of the distinguished. I enjoy having a copy of Trollope's *The Prime Minister* in a superb binding from the library of the 5th Earl of Rosebery, who was of course himself Prime Minister in the 1890s. Likewise, our copy of West's *A Guide to the Lakes*, the first important Lake District guide, was once in Wordsworth's library. Marrying together our two biggest author collections is a copy of one of Arthur Ransome's children's books enthusiastically inscribed by Compton Mackenzie to a young friend.

Lowick, Ulverston

ADAM NAYLOR   273

Alan Neatby-Smith

My Pathetic Collection

As one guilty over the whole of my life of the socially unforgivable sin of poverty, as a result of which I can boast of no First Folio, nor even a modern first edition, I may be adding to my guilt by my membership of this august Association. Not being a natural bookworm in my early years – village cricket, and visits to Trent Bridge to watch Bradman & Co predominating – I was nevertheless almost in awe of my parents' well-stocked bookshelves. I think I can date the actual start of my collection to just before the war when I learnt that a new book club was about to commence operations with my (then) hero Lawrence of Arabia's *Seven Pillars of Wisdom*. How could I possibly resist joining? At that time many excellent books were issued, albeit in standard buckram covers, and I was grateful that my mother kept my subscription going right through the war. So when I got back from overseas RAF service, I found an extremely neat set of books lined up for me.

But as the problem of getting back into civilian life, and picking up the threads of my previous life left no time for books, my collection remained static for some time. As my articles to a Derbyshire chartered accountant were bedevilled by two almost fatal illnesses which effectively put paid to qualification, and my five years in the RAF as an engine-fitter had given me a rest from pen-pushing, on resuming my profession I thought I would benefit from London experience, and sampled three jobs over two years. In this time I had married a London girl who was dying to get out of it, so I put an advert in *Taxation* for a 'Situation Wanted' in the 'West Country' and received thirty replies from Oxford to St Austell. I had almost agreed to a job in St Austell when I got a telegram from a Penzance firm, saying one of their partners was in London, and would it be possible for us to meet. This we did, in the subway at Piccadilly, and as we liked the look of each other I was taken on in 1948, and stayed with them for twelve years. This happened to produce two substantial additions to my collection.

Living in a village some miles out, I took sandwiches for lunch, and in my lunch hours I explored the town. Somewhat towards the

Alan Neatby-Smith

end of the twelve years, I chanced to go into the principal auction rooms and found that in a forthcoming sale there was to be quite a number of books. As I would not be able to attend the auction, I asked a salesroom attendant if he would bid for me – though I don't recall giving him any special instructions. When I went round to find if I had been successful, it transpired that I had had knocked down to me 300 books at (you won't believe this!) one (old) penny each. This rather staggered me because practically all these books were very similar to those I had admired on my parents' shelves. I don't recall whether it was before or after this auction-room business, but in the cellars of the large house in which the practice was run, there was an old collection of books which had been used as the library for a war-time youth club, of which the senior partner was in charge. When I had located this hoard I spent my lunch hours investigating it. This came to the attention of the senior partner who, possibly seeing an opportunity to clear the cellar, sensed that this was a heaven-sent opportunity. Eventually a deal was struck whereby for the princely sum of £2. 10s. 0d. I was permitted to clear the cellar of all the books, plus the substantial book shelves, collection index book, two substantial metal bowls and odds and ends. Most of these were 'improving' books, and included a wide range of youth classics.

The remainder of my collection has largely been fuelled by regular close inspection of charity shops and car boot sales, where I am still open to 'improving' books on technical matters, such as *Sewage Treatment: Basic Principles and Trends* (Bolton & Klein, 1961). Since giving my unused Myford lathe to my son-in-law recently, my collection is now minus some engineering books.

Hayle, Cornwall

ALAN NEATBY-SMITH

Derek Nuttall

I suppose that my interest in books began around the outbreak of the 1939–45 War when my maternal grandfather's library was sent off for salvage: an act that I regarded as wanton vandalism, and have since wondered what treasures might have been repulped.

Then, in 1946, being at the time an enthusiastic philatelist, I decided that my future must be in printing and I embarked upon a seven–year apprenticeship with a small Lancashire firm of general printers (where everything was still hand-set). It was there, at around the age of 16, that I found a mutilated eighteenth–century folio of John Bunyan's *Works* which was being used for pasting on by the bookbinder. The proprietor kindly let me have this volume (which I still have) and this marked the beginning of a life-long passion for printing history and bibliography. Whilst still an apprentice I began collecting examples of printing by buying sackfuls of books from a local auctioneer – ten shillings for a bag of octavos and £1 for a big bag of quartos and folios!

An even better 'scoop' was a first edition of Foxe's *Actes and Monuments* (lacking title-page) obtained from a well–known Manchester bookseller for the sum of just one pound. This was around the time when, as a full-time student at the then Manchester College of Technology (later to become UMIST), I joined the Manchester Society of Book Collectors. Through membership of this I met and made friends with many of the leading book collectors and book sellers of north-west England in the 1950s. Membership of this rather elite society proved valuable to me later when I was invited to return to Manchester College of Technology as a full-time lecturer in the Department of Printing and Photography, where one of my specialities was lecturing on the history of printing and typographic design. I now began to build up examples of early fine printing to show to students, such as books printed by Baskerville, illustrations by Bewick, and examples of private press productions. Through the Manchester Society of Book Collectors I made useful contacts with the staffs of John Rylands, Manchester Central, and Chethams libraries and often had privileged access to their collections of early printed books.

Derek Nuttall

Later, my interests expanded into historical bibliography and for many years I was an active member of Liverpool Bibliographical Society, which was based at the University. Indirectly this led to my writing *A History of Printing in Chester* which, in its turn, resulted in my obtaining an M.Phil. at the University of Leeds. By this time I was acquiring a sizeable collection of books and other material related to typography and bibliography. For many years I was a tutor on the annual SCONUL courses and it was through these that I made lots of good friends in various libraries, universities and colleges of librarianship – which all helped to extend my knowledge of books.

A spell in industry, at Lund Humphries Ltd, in Bradford, prior to returning to Manchester as a lecturer, resulted in my acquiring a collection of *Penrose Annuals* and several rarities, such as a bound volume of *The Imprint*, Furst's *Wood-engraving*, etc., when the firm decided to have a clear-out of its file–copies and offered them free to staff.

My library has been very much a 'working tool', particularly when researching for my M.Phil. and later for a Ph.D. at Reading University. Even after some twenty years of retirement, my collection continues to grow and now numbers some 700 items – not to mention long runs of various technical or bibliographical journals. Since I retired, I have tried to make use of my knowledge of printing and historical bibliography by becoming the honorary librarian of the Chester Archaeological Society's *c.* 11,000 volumes as well as being 'curator' of the early printed books at Chester Cathedral Library (some 2,600 works dating from 1476 to 1800).

My love of books and fine typography has given me much pleasure, but apart from technical books I have long had a soft spot for works illustrated with wood–engravings, as well as the productions of private presses, old and recent. I also have a collection of some 200 books on the local history and archaeology of Lancashire, Cheshire, and North Wales. The big problem is where to keep putting them all.

Dodleston, Cheshire

Wilfried Onzea

Aesthetic and Textual Arts of the Book

Growing up as the youngest child of a large family in a prudish and catholic environment doesn't seem to be an ideal breeding ground for a book lover. Yet my parents had a stationer's shop and later a printing firm so perhaps the smell of paper helped me on the way? As my father died when I was eleven and we moved elsewhere, the link with paper and printing was severed but somehow I always liked to have books around me.

I was not a brilliant student and I had to work hard but fortunately I had a gift for languages and I avidly read books in Dutch, French, English, and later in German.

That my career should be in books was clear: my first job was in a large bookshop in Antwerp. . . . Later on I worked for six years in a Documentation Centre as a librarian and editor of a bilingual technical periodical. The contacts with the printing firm and the making of the layout stirred up my interest in books and printing. I followed the course on books and printing in the famous Plantin-Moretus Museum (three years on Saturdays) and this started me on a book collecting trip which lasts to this day. A few years later I wrote to the then Director, Dr Voet, asking whether there was a vacancy in his Museum. He kindly sent me a reply mentioning an exam for the City of Antwerp for 'Assistant Books & Documents'. Of course I participated and after some time (April 1974) I indeed worked in the library of the Plantin Museum and later on in the Antwerp City Library. I ended up these last fifteen years in the museum library of the Middelheim Open Air Museum of Sculpture (modern and contemporary art).

As a young man I combed the antiquarian bookshops in Antwerp looking for fine bindings and printing and I gradually developed an interest in English book printing, book illustration, colour printing and publisher's bindings, William Morris being my great hero.

Gradually I started buying from English antiquarian booksellers. The contacts were always congenial and familiar and in the case of Tony Cox we crossed the Channel to meet him and see his bookshop in Ipswich.

Wilfried Onzea

At that time I was also very interested in the great eighteenth century writers, Swift, Sterne, Johnson . . . The result of that is a beautifully bound first impression of Sterne's *A Sentimental Journey* in my collection!

Another important meeting was with Joe Lubbock in 1983: the contacts have remained close and I have most of his books in my library. I have also collected the work of the French poet, painter and printer Alain Anseeuw about whom I wrote an article in *The Private Library*. Modern private press books have remained a main interest, mostly English and German. During recent years I have become interested in artists' books: I have unique copies of two books written and 'constructed' by the German artist Gerhard Multerer, made in editions of a single copy only. Since I got interested some fifteen years ago in Russian language and literature I bought books by the artist and bookmaker Michail Karasik.

As a whole my collection reflects my literary tastes and my interest in the arts of the book with an emphasis on aesthetical aspects.

I am a founding member of the Flemish bibliophilic society

'Literarte' which publishes a book each year for its members. Apart from the essay on Alain Anseeuw in *The Private Library*, I have written a few articles for the Belgian periodical *Arte Grafica*, and one, in *Ons Erfdeel*, on the private press in the Flemish part of Belgium since 1980, and a pamphlet on the printer Edward Burrett.

Antwerp

Ex Officina Plantiniana
Apud Franciscum Raphelengium, 1597

Alan Painter

My Interest in Africa: How it all Began

Way back before the days of television, there was a programme on the radio that used to broadcast the novels of H. Rider Haggard, and after listening to the radio adaption of *King Solomon's Mines*, that was enough to inspire me to get to know more about Africa. So I went into a good bookshop in Salisbury and bought a copy of the novel and read it through. Eventually I bought the complete set of Haggard's African novels. However, there was something missing. This material was basically fiction and fancy. I wanted the true facts. My aim was to build a collection relating to the true facts regarding Africa, its history and its people.

I bought a copy of *Shaka Zulu* by E. A. Ritter and from that first book of fact I started my small collection of knowledge of the Zulu people, their history and social system. Such ceremonies as the 'Ukubuthwa' when all the might of the people came together for a common cause.

Then later on with the making of the film 'Zulu' that finally convinced me that the Zulu people and the Bantu in general were a great people and a subject worth studying, I started collecting seriously. This must have been about 1964.

My collecting initially was centred on the Zulu nation and kindred tribes. However, other indigenous people came into focus, so I began to buy books about all sorts of subjects e.g., history, anthropology, ethnology, ethnography, etc. All strictly based on the continent of Africa. It became a very serious subject of study for me. So I came to the final decision to form my own private library, and so during 1998 African Studies was founded.

So what exactly is 'African Studies'?

Basically it is a small collection of Africana material that at the time of writing amounts to some 2,000 volumes. However, 'African Studies' is not just a collection of books about Africa. It is a serious study of the history of the continent and what's more important it is a study of all the various types of people that inhabited this vast area of land.

In the early years my intention, due to lack of space, was to limit my collection to an area from the Cape-Province northwards

Alan Painter

to the limits of the Zambezi River. However, over the years various other people offered me material based on more northern territories so that now my library covers the whole of the African continent.

Of course there are many people who are dealers and collectors of African material. However, I consider my library different as I try to concentrate and specialise on the study of the African indigenous people, their history from the earliest times of their evolution up to the present day. I specialise in social anthropology, ethnology, archaeology, pre-history, languages, religious studies, missionaries, the social sciences and much more.

I don't collect books as people collect rare material e.g. antiques or first editions. I will buy anything that is serious and interesting, but *fact* only. I am not interested in novels of any sort. Neither will I buy books on hunting, big game, wildlife or safari. It is the people that I am interested in.

Now what I would like to make clear to all the readers of this note is that although African Studies is basically a private library centred in a small first floor flat here on the outskirts of Bournemouth, it is open to all serious collectors and those interested in the subjects it covers, by appointment only. All my books are for sale but it is not run as a business and is non-profit making. That is to say, if I buy a book for say £20, I am quite willing to sell to any interested person for £20.

I buy books from bookshops, car boot sales, jumble sales and of course book fairs. However, most of my material comes in from overseas, mainly of course Africa itself but also from all over the world, through catalogues or via book search companies. I will buy anything that relates to my subjects in any condition as long as its text block is readable.

I consider 'African Studies' unique as it specialises in material that is rare, scientific and academic. I have a large collection of rare journals and periodicals that the general book dealer won't handle. I have them here because it is from these journals that most modern authors over the past fifty years have obtained their information. They are very important to the students of history and anthropology etc. and therefore valuable, but not in monetary terms as they are cheap to buy ranging from £1 to £5 per volume and complete runs can sometimes be obtained for under £100.

Other very important material to the historian are the records produced by the Colonial Government Office, generally referred to as 'Blue Books'. These come to me in all sorts of conditions from just a few ragged pages to complete leather bound volumes, but all are expensive. Prices start at about £35 way up to £450, many of them rare and important to African Studies.

So there we are; that's the African Studies library here in Bournemouth. I am semi-retired now and I am free for consultation any Monday afternoon and all day Tuesday. I can be contacted by email at alan.painter@african-studies.com or by Tele-Fax 01202 528678.

If you are in Bournemouth, do come and see me for a chat about your interests over a nice glass or two of good Dorset cider and who knows, perhaps do a bit of business.

Bournemouth

Zimbabwe warrior
(courtesy Zimbabwe National Archive)

ALAN PAINTER

John Porter

William Pickering

Why does one person collect and another not? The difference sometimes seems as fundamental as that between the sexes. I was first aware of this as a child before the war, collecting the plastic caps from toothpaste and other cream tubes, which were then of surprising variety and colour. I never heard of anyone else doing this, which was perhaps why it got me into trouble when other guests at houses to which I was taken, complained of tubes which had inexplicably lost their caps. The vermilion Euthymol with a small chain fixed to the tube was a lovely catch, like extricating the hook from a perch.

I suppose I first became aware that books could be more than just repositories of words, with the row of G. A. Henty's gripping tales in my father's bookcase. He would occasionally read to me from one of these, although I was too young to follow what they were about, but it was perhaps mainly for his pleasure. I was, however, fascinated by their distinctive pictorial coloured and gilt stamped cloth bindings.

I bought my first book when I was nine, and have it still, remembering the grip of pleasure when I first saw it in the window of the bookshop – long gone – just below Palace Gate in Kensington. Collins Clear-Type Holy Bible, 'Ruby 24 mo.' 1937, on India paper. I believe I read Genesis, but I wanted it for the way it looked, chaste and untouched in ivory morocco-grain cloth, spine with raised bands, lettered in gilt, wrapped in cellophane in a blue box for 7s. 6d. I knew I could not live without it.

The seeds of book collecting, dormant throughout the years away at school, began to germinate as the scales of war and schooldays fell away. From Kensington there were buses to Paradise: the Beauchamp Bookshop at South Kensington; Peter Eaton in Church Street; Times Bookshop in Wigmore Street; Bumpus in Oxford Street; and of course Charing Cross Road. Only later was I to discover the great West End booksellers. The geography, however, was established. National Service in 1947 followed by training to be an architect was a fallow period for collecting old books, although the Orders of Architecture propelled me to Foyles, then

John Porter

a bookshop of extraordinary stock and management principles, where one would find Isaac Ware, Colen Campbell, Gibbs, Vignola, and perhaps Serlio in first or early editions for shillings. Bought, they would be dismembered; texts discarded, and the engravings shared around the studio for producing rendered isometric projections of classical buildings, with little sense of barbarity. Charing Cross Road and its environs, with 'Bunjies' the hub, became part of the curriculum.

For the student, modern architecture was largely experienced through the lyrical publications of The Architectural Press, Verlag für Architektur and others, where we thought we understood the work of Le Corbusier, Mies van der Rohe and Alvar Aalto. The kindest dealer for these was John Zwemmer, who, when his father was absent, would reduce the price of a volume and was generous in exchanging or buying, unlike the frosty despatch to the basement if one tried to sell at Foyle's. With the start of professional practice, followed by marriage, came the chance to search the bookshops and acquire some of the things one liked. In 1946 I had found in Cecil Court an odd volume from a set of Chaucer published in 1830 by William Pickering. It intrigued me by a certain elegance and character, and I was now able to look for other books which he had published. The search became compelling, and I have now spent much of the last fifty years collecting books which he had produced and researching them for my forthcoming bibliography. Whilst the books produced by Pickering and his inseparable printer, Charles Whittingham, have been central to my interest in nineteenth-century books, they have been paralleled by interest in his contemporaries, L. A. Lewis, Talboys and Wheeler, and Francis Macpherson of Oxford. I am particularly interested in works edited by Samuel Weller Singer and the strong typographical influence he had on his printers.

Working in London in the decade following 1956 was a now vanished experience for a book-collector. Lunch times would be a round of visits to Thorp of Albemarle Street, where each week one would be greeted by vast new piles of books on the floor, from a country house sale, or Hodgsons. Other days it would be to Quaritch or Sawyer in Grafton Street, Maggs, Francis Edwards, or the first floor at Hatchard's. Always new experiences to be had, and affections forged, which I still retain for anything from the libraries of Theodore Williams, Joseph Haslewood, E. V. Utterson, J. W. K. Eyton, E. C. Hawtrey and Jonathan Rashleigh.

The search was the fun, and where there were no bookshops, good things could be found in antique shops as 'props' in breakfront bookcases: never considered, or priced (having no doubt been taken as 'clearance'). In those days any offer for a volume was likely to be accepted, perhaps into the assistant's pocket. At Notting Hill I found two fifteenth-century Aldines, perfect in the original vellum bindings for ten shillings, for which Maggs gave me nearly two months' salary. At Phelps in St Margaret's, Twickenham, where Anne and I lived in Turner's small villa after our marriage, I found a copy of Stanfield's *Coastal Scenery*, pristine in green goatskin for fifteen shillings, in what subsequently proved to be the earliest recorded binding by Joseph Zaehnsdorf.

JOHN PORTER

It is now in the British Library at Howard Nixon's request.

The best times were the stolen Saturdays with my dear friend Robin de Beaumont, usually as directed by Robin's sensitive antennae. Sutton, Surbiton, or Norbury; to Baldur Bookshop on Lower Richmond Hill, the proprietor ever wary lest the Thames should engulf his stock; Alec Fletcher at Windsor; Brown's at Eton; and countless small shops now lost in memory. The return invariably with something we had never seen before, and the feeling that we bibliophiles must be blessed.

The quest goes on . . .

Bath

Pickering device, 1828

JOHN PORTER

R. Guy Powell

It would be reasonable to say that my book collection began before I did, as my father purchased two small books (*Peter Rabbit* and *The Flopsy Bunnies*, naturally) ready for me when I appeared on the scene. One of my earliest memories therefore is 'reading' them to my little sister – probably upside-down. Charles Kingsley's *Heroes* (illustrated with line drawings from Greek vases) was used to teach me to read and bred in me a love of myths and legends and to a collection of Greek and Etruscan antiquities including some Attic vases of my own. Later it was *Swiss Family Robinson* in a fine Victorian binding with chromo-lithographs and numerous steel-engravings to fire one's imagination. This and others like it were upstairs books for weekdays but on Sundays there were the drawing-room books. Some had pictures of the life of Christ but more were on art and artists (with coloured reproductions from the old masters) a large volume of Fra Angelico in black and white from my grandfather's collection and the 'Told to the Children' series of Dickens. Lamb's *Tales from Shakespeare* and Scott which we loved to hear our mother read to us long after we could perfectly well read for ourselves.

Public School days in wartime were not conducive to book collecting: but in 1945 I inherited the library of a cousin: no great treasures there but his long shelf of Baedekers came in useful in 1949 for my Grand Tour of ltaly, as so many pictures were still hanging in the same places in the galleries and churches as in 1909 and his Austro-Hungarian Empire volume was unrivalled for Yugoslavia, just opened to western tourists in 1953.

1946 saw me begin collecting in earnest at Oxford with Everyman and World's Classics (in their elegant blue cloth bindings and Bell types) to the fore. They were within my pocket and a good excuse not to buy the cigarettes that so many of my contemporaries consumed. Hakluyt's *Voyages* in eight volumes, Gibbon in six, Lamb's *Letters*, and later the novels of Anthony Trollope. The purchases continued apace when I reached the City though at thirty-five shillings a week the scope for an articled clerk was not wide. Looking back, there were two significant points – one was to find a copy of *Cockalorum* at Saunders narrow little book-shop at the foot of Chancery Lane – which opened up a whole new world of private press books, past and future.

R. Guy Powell

The other was to visit W. J. Bryce in Museum Street where Mr Chambers sold not only new books but also periodicals such as

Book Handbook and *Antike Kunst* from Switzerland which fuelled my Hellenic studies. Sadly I did not take up Mr Chambers' recommendation to buy *The Lord of the Rings* as it came out in parts, but many other volumes from his shelves I still have including a volume of the Trianon Press *Blake*.

About this time inspired by the Private Libraries Association I began to think I ought to collect in a more ordered way. I chose Walter de la Mare, Christopher Fry and John Betjeman – none of whom are sought after now – but also after the National Book League's Exhibition of Wood-engravings from 1920 to 1951 to pursue some of the titles represented, as many of these proved to be within my means and expanded my collection of private press books including the Golden Cockerel then being re-issued in simpler bindings.

As my nieces and the contemporary children of my friends began to reach 'book age' Edward Ardizzone began to play a big part in my collection and has remained so ever since. All these books I have mentioned I still have: looking round I find I have tended to collect by publisher or printer as much as by subject: the set of Lion & Unicorn Press subscription volumes; a long line of Dent's Temple Classics with its useful texts not available easily elsewhere such as the *Golden Legend* in Caxton's translation; Trevor Hickman's Brewhouse Press books, with others mostly illustrated by Rigby Graham all from the Leicestershire area; Simon Lawrence's Fleece Press; and the Cambridge University Printer's Christmas books.

Law books do not feature as largely in my collection as I suppose they should. The two principal items are both printed by Richard Pynson (1515 and 1520) so they are special in their way. Brian Cron thought I should aim to collect early printed law books, but I am afraid I did not take that suggestion any further. Loyd Haberly I have collected more assiduously with great help from Paul W. Nash in recent times. *Book Handbook* led me to him and the late Lord Kenyon, who had known Haberly while he was still at school, encouraged me so that I now have examples from the collections of many personal friends of Haberly while in England together with a few of his American volumes.

I have always had a penchant for illustrated books, Lucien Pissarro, Gwen Raverat (both friends of my grandfather), Edward

Bawden, Ravilious and David Gentleman spring to mind. Latterly I have looked more to bindings as my eyesight deteriorates – but except for a series of bindings for Gregynog Press and Gwasg Gregynog specials, again inspired by Lord Kenyon, these are a somewhat random collection. Having been a member of the Hellenic Society for many years, there is a section on Greek vases including Sir John Beazley's five volumes on *Attic Vase Painters*, the index of which provided me with useful holiday locations for several years.

Drawing by Edward Bawden
from *Tea and Tea Cakes*, [1947?]
Courtesy The Estate of Edward Bawden

Finally I must acknowledge the part Sir Allen Lane has played in my collecting. King Penguins as they came out, the Buildings of England series similarly (to which I probably refer more often than any other books in my library), Penguin Classics in translation, the first hundred titles, so elegantly designed and printed and the many history books and art books which he inspired for our better education.

Leatherhead, Surrey

R. GUY POWELL

John Randle

The first proper book I bought was Ruari McLean's *The Wood Engravings of Joan Hassall,* from the White Horse Bookshop in Marlborough in 1961. I still think this is one of the prettiest and most satisfying books I own. From then on I wanted to print books with wood-engravings in Bell type on smooth cream paper.

Not surprisingly, many of the books I subsequently bought contained wood-engravings. In the early days of the Whittington Press quite a lot were from the private presses, partly to see how it was done, and partly because I felt that printers should put themselves in the shoes of their would-be customers and experience the pain of parting with money for a book. I bought quite a lot of American press books, and avidly collected ephemera, especially prospectuses, now, after a recent turn-out, in the John Johnson Collection at the Bodleian. Looking around, books on printing and typefaces also seem to proliferate.

Photography being an early interest, I have many books of photographs, and am particularly interested in their reproduction, partly the result of working in commercial publishing in the sixties when every halftone came in a washed-out grey. The reproduction of a photograph is just as important as the initial pressing of the button, since this is how the world will see it, and this is why the reproduction of photographs takes a high priority at the Whittington Press. One of the saddest lost processes of recent years (far more so than the over-rated collotype) is sheet-fed gravure with its wonderfully rich, mezzotint-like blacks, and I have many volumes of these published by Thames and Hudson and Phaidon, which are absurdly cheap and plentiful.

Few volumes manage to escape, my excuse being that, living far from St Bride's, I need them for reference. However one did recently, in unusual circumstances. It was Charles Jacobi's worthy *Some Notes on Books and Printing* of 1912 (described by William S. Peterson as 'especially influential'). It is inscribed 'G. B. Clark, Esq. From Chas. T. Jacobi'. It next went 'To Charles Ede – a more deserving owner, from Adam Maitland c/o The Chiswick Press 1946–1960.' Next stop 'For Bernard – passed on

John Randle

down the line. CE, 14.7.79'. Then '. . . and on to the Randles, still printing by letterpress, as God intended. From Bernard Roberts'. It must have sat on our shelves (unread, I regret to say) for a good many years, where I stumbled upon it and read it with a pang of guilt, and sent it on its way. 'And now for Simon Lawrence, who doesn't need it anyway (at least there's some Caslon on the frontispiece), 1.1.05'. I rather like the idea of books that go round in circles. Who next, I wonder?

Another reason for not disposing of one's books cropped up at a seminar in Delaware recently. Someone from the floor suggested that if the classic private press (or whatever) books could be re-produced at a reasonable price, far more people could enjoy them at home. But I disagreed, suggesting that even if one had just one volume from a certain press and only looked at it every ten or twenty years, the comforting presence of its spine gave off certain vibrations that I like to feel affect me as I go about my business at the Press. Rather expecting to be shot down in flames for this stupid and quite unsupportable notion, I was pleasantly surprised when a murmur of approval flickered around the hall. Perhaps there is still room for romance in the pursuit of keeping a library, however modest.

Risbury, Leominster, Herefordshire

Wood-engraving by Hellmuth Weissenborn

Ann Ridler

I am so frequently confused with the late Anne Ridler, the poet, that I must emphasise that I have no connection with her. I am the widow of William Ridler (1909–1980), whose collection of over 4,000 items of fine printing is on permanent loan by me to Birmingham City Libraries and may be seen at the Central Library, in the care of Mrs Pam Williams. I am also Chairman of the George Borrow Society and editor of its Bulletin.

My book collection flies in various directions, doubtless representing its owner's multivalent personality. I first realised books were objects to be collected as well as read (or not always read!) in 1953, in the nine months before I went up to Oxford. I was earning four guineas a week in Hackney Central Library, and had no other money. Among my most influential acquisitions was Joyce's *A Portrait of the Artist as a Young Man*, the second edition, but first English edition, of 1917. It lacked its front free endpaper and cost me one shilling from a bookseller's outside box in Charing Cross Road. That started me on a Joyce collection which I have now largely sold. Another acquisition, alas unread, was a tiny Elzevir Ovid of 1664, picked up from Fletcher's outside box in Cecil Court. It cost me four shillings. In general I don't collect pre-nineteenth century books, but some have a special appeal. I must include Cicero's *Epistolarum ad Familiares, libri XVI*, published 'Typis Joannis Gatti', Venice, 1788, which I bought for its enchanting publisher's woodcut emblem of four playful cats. Other striking acquisitions were part of an embryonic collection of Gray's *Poetical Works*. My Strawberry Hill copy of Gray's *Odes* (1757) was my twentieth wedding anniversary present to my husband in 1979. Another notable edition, printed for Joseph Wenman in 1785, bears on its flyleaf the admonition 'REGARDEZ, ET SOUVENEZ VOUS [Look and Remember]. Sep. 11th 1794' – surely a reference to some horror of the French Revolution. My other passion among older works is to collect William Penn's wonderful *Some Fruits of Solitude*. I have fourteen editions so far, the earliest being the seventh of 1718.

Ann Ridler

George Borrow has occupied a large part of my time and attention since 1975, and I have a reasonably comprehensive collection of his published works and related critical material, as well as some twenty-five manuscript items. I am also particularly interested in the dialect poet William Barnes, one of the highlights of my collection being a copy of his *Poems of Rural Life in the Dorset Dialect. Third Collection*, of 1863, with the ownership signature of the Lancashire dialect writer Edwin Waugh. Apart from these author collections I have spread into the twentieth century with an extensive collection of works by, illustrated by, or with dust-wrapper by Michael Ayrton (I also have three of his bronzes, two lithographs, a multimedia seashore painting and the last aquatint on which he was working before he died). E. M. Delafield is another interest – she was quite a prolific novelist yet is only known for her 'Provincial Lady' works, and surely deserves much more attention. I have nearly all her novels, from 1918 to 1943. Other modern writers of particular interest to me are Roy Fuller, James Kirkup, Patrick White, Ruth Pitter, and James Fenton. The most prolific of these was, and is, the poet, autobiographer and travel writer James Kirkup – I have over seventy of his first editions from 1943 to the present, and several items of ephemera, including a large press-cutting collection of the obituaries he writes regularly for *The Independent*. Highlights of this collection are undoubtedly the rare and exquisite Circle Press publications: his *Zen Gardens*, with original prints by Birgit Skiold (1973), one of ten Artist's Proof copies of an edition of seventy-five printed in English, signed by the artist and the poet; the same in Japanese, one of five Artist's Proof copies of an edition of twenty-five printed in Japanese, signed by the artist and the poet; and *The Tao of Water*, a poem by James Kirkup with prints by Birgit Skiold (1979), one of twenty Artist's Proof copies of an edition of 200, signed by the author and artist. I also treasure a framed poster-poem with a photograph of a fine twelfth century Japanese wood carving of a 'semi-Buddha', and a moving poem by Kirkup beneath it, 'Enlightenment', dated 1978.

In the case of the poet Ruth Pitter (1897–1994), on whom I wrote an article for the *Oxford Dictionary of National Biography*, I have acquired not only all but one of her published works (though I still lack a couple of American editions), but what I

ANN RIDLER

believe to be a fairly comprehensive collection of anthologies in which poems of hers have appeared. Currently the collection includes at least sixty-two anthologies, and I feel there is a study worth doing of precisely which poems were most frequently selected. Indeed it was quite an eye-opener to discover just how many poetry anthologies had been published between 1933 and 2003. This raises the tormenting question of how one can determine 'completeness' or 'comprehensiveness', especially if one wishes to include translations, photographs, Christmas cards, musical scores, LPs, audiotapes and CDs, newspaper and magazine articles and reviews, prefaces and other contributions to the works of others, not to mention a huge wealth of associated biography, criticism, works on or by friends of one's author, part of his or her circle, and works in which one's author was interested! I am not a terminal case as a collector, and I don't spend all my time scouring the internet for missing items, or haunting charity shops, but I do try to be an opportunist and am a diligent, if tardy, reader of booksellers' catalogues.

What else do I collect? I am a bit of a sucker for series. I have a complete run of King Penguins all in nice condition, a nominally complete set of the Travellers' Library, a nearly complete set of the Oxford Miscellany series – the ones with the attractive dark green bindings and gilt spines, a growing run of the New Adelphi Library published by Martin Secker in the 1920s and 1930s, a burgeoning run of Society for Pure English Tracts, and a shelf full of that nice series of the 1890s, produced by various publishers, generally in dark green cloth with highly gilt pictorial covers and lavish illustrations. The trick is to find them in bright condition. When I first started collecting these, they were around 7s. 6d. (38 pence) and now one is lucky to find them for £30–£35.

I have probably not paid more than £350 for any of my books (Penn's *Fruits of Solitude* in the beautiful Essex House Press edition comes to mind), but manuscripts, I'm afraid, are a different story, and George Borrow, though so unjustly ignored by academia, still commands high prices in the saleroom. For me there is nothing comparable with handling pages over which Borrow himself laboured, and I have examples of his handwriting from 1826 to 1878, the last being the most moving. In this connection I have to say how much I owe to my first husband, Will Ridler, who in the 1970s fed my passion for Borrow, finding me many of the highlights of my collection including Lord Esher's copy of Borrow's translation of Klinger's *Faustus* of 1825, purchased from Deighton Bell in Cambridge for – wait for it – £15, and Lord James Butler's copy of Borrow's *The Talisman*, published in an edition of about 100 copies in St Petersburg in 1835. I also owe to my husband the lovely suite of bookcases he had made for his own collection, as well as some fine antique bookcases.

Currently, I am rather slowly endeavouring to create a dual catalogue – one a short-title catalogue logging basic details of edition, association, etc., and the other an item by item text-based descriptive catalogue. The wood-engraver Sarah van Niekerk engraved a beautiful bookplate for me and I am at the same time trying to catch up with book-plating the significant items. So far I have listed just over 1,250 titles and feel I have barely scratched the surface. I have sometimes thinned out my collection, and always bitterly regretted it. After all, for every collector, one's collection is the story of one's life. Interests of earlier years have a way of coming full circle and tying up with interests of later years. Book collecting surely helps one to make sense of one's own identity. I still remember the yearning I felt in about 1946, at the age of eleven, seeing an early film of *Pride and Prejudice*, with Mr Bennet sitting in a comfortable chair in his library, being ministered to by attentive servants. At least I now have the library, if not the attentive servants. And I haven't mentioned collecting books on cats, sculpture, local topography, wild gardens, or wood-engraving.

Warborough, Wallingford, Oxon.

Epistolarum ad familiares, libri XVI, Joannis Gatti, 1788

ANN RIDLER

Neil Ritchie

Italian Travel

My interest in collecting Italian travel books grew seam-
lessly, almost automatically, out of my youthful reading of
D. H. Lawrence and Norman Douglas. I was introduced early to
D. H. Lawrence as my mother had copies of *Sons and Lovers* and
Women in Love on her shelves as well as *The Tales* (1934), a
composite volume of his shorter fiction. I think she felt some affinity to D. H. Lawrence as a fellow Midlander just as she rejoiced
in Arnold Bennett and Mary Webb. She did not know Norman
Douglas but I came across *South Wind* as a schoolboy as did so
many of my generation and maybe that introduction to Italy played
some part in my decision to emigrate there on my retirement.

Once settled in Italy I set about acquiring the Italian travel
writings of these two old favourites. *Twilight in Italy* soon arrived, then *Sea and Sardinia* and shortly thereafter *Etruscan Places*.
Etruscan Places led on inevitably to George Dennis's *The Cities
and Cemeteries of Etruria* (1848), the two volumes in their
original picturesque bindings by Remnant & Edmonds with their
ticket. Dennis in his introduction acknowledges his debt to
Mrs Hamilton Gray 'for having first introduced Etruria to the
notice of her countrymen': her *Tour to the Sepulchres of Etruria
in 1839* (1840) joined the Dennis before too long.

Meanwhile I found copies of Norman Douglas: *Siren Land*
(1911), surprisingly still in its dust jacket, *Old Calabria* (1915)
which led to the discovery of Gissing's *By the Ionian Sea* (1901)
and Lenormant's *La Grande-Grèce* (1881), and finally *Alone*
(1921) which introduced me to Ramage. Crauford Tait Ramage
published *The Nooks and By-Ways of Italy* in 1868, but it
describes a journey he made all on his own on foot forty years
earlier into the heart of the Mezzogiorno, an escapade just as
eccentric as those of another Italian (and South American) traveller, Charles Waterton

Ramage somewhat smugly comments that Henry Swinburne
in his *Travels in the Two Sicilies* (1783) covered nearly the same
ground as he but with the 'attendance of high rank and protected
by a constant guard of soldiers'. This was enough to alert me to

Neil Ritchie

these *Travels*, but is not an entirely fair claim. Swinburne includes Sicily and his two splendid quartos illustrated with his own drawings must rejoice the heart of any bibliophile. My set is bound with the Beaufort arms on the spine and carries the ducal garter arms ex-libris on the pastedowns. I often wonder how it came to leave Badminton.

Few travellers wrote accounts of Sicily before the second half of the eighteenth century. John Dryden, the son of the poet, visited the island in 1700 but his text was not published in his lifetime, appearing only in 1776 as a direct result of the success of Patrick Brydone's *A Tour through Sicily and Malta* (1773). This was the first important book on Sicily and indeed one of the most popular eighteenth century Italian travel books published in the United Kingdom.

Dryden Junior was by no means the only writer on Italy to be published posthumously. Montaigne travelled to Rome in 1580–1581 but the account of his Italian journey was only discovered almost two hundred years later when it was published as his *Journal du Voyage en Italie* in 1774. Three issues appeared: a quarto, a duodecimo in two volumes and a duodecimo in three volumes. Bibliographers still cannot agree over precedence. No such problem haunts John Evelyn's diary, it, too, posthumous. Evelyn went to Rome and on to Naples in 1644–1646 but his *Memoirs* did not see the light of day until 1818 when a magnificent quarto in two volumes appeared. My set was bound for the Duke of Buckingham and Chandos with his garter arms: I strongly suspect it was sold when the second duke fled from his creditors and his library at Stowe was dispersed in 1848.

In my collecting I have tried to follow Byron's advice and 'leave topography to classic Gell'. I have not always succeeded as I could not resist his *Pompeiana* (1817–1819 and its two volume sequel of 1832) nor his *Rome and its Vicinity* (1834), but in general I eschew guidebooks. Even so, and discounting the sumptuous illustrated folios such as the five volumes of Saint-Non (*Voyage Pittoresque . . . de Naples et de Sicile,* 1781–86) which only the mega rich can afford, the field is still large enough to allow my instincts of acquisition to lure me into adding to these travellers' tales and so beguile my reading hours.

Hout Bay, Cape, South Africa

NEIL RITCHIE

Mary Schlosser

Harriet Beecher Stowe and her Family

I started my post-college career as an art historian, very oriented towards objects. It was not a far reach, therefore, to become involved with books, especially after I married a serious book collector. My husband, already a Grolier Club member, strongly encouraged me to enter the book world, first by studying book-binding and repair (in-house conservator, anyone?), and then by beginning to collect on a modest level. After some thought, I settled on what at the time seemed an inexpensive collecting focus – a nineteenth-century American literary lady not quite in fashion in the 1960s, Harriet Beecher Stowe. At this early date Women's Studies and Black Studies were only beginning to be defined fields of study in the academy.

At the beginning, there was not a lot of material on the market, so in order to keep acquiring (no true collector can repress the urge), I could not resist adding other members of the Beecher family to my list. Lyman Beecher (1775–1863), Harriet's father, was one of the leading clergymen of his time, and many of his sermons appeared in print. There were thirteen children in the family; the seven sons all became ministers and wrote and published, especially Harriet's nearest sibling, Henry Ward Beecher, he of the famous (or infamous) adultery trial. Her oldest sister, Catharine, was a noted educator and advocate for women's education and her younger half-sister Isabelle Beecher Hooker was an ardent suffragist and colleague of Elizabeth Cady Stanton and Susan B. Anthony.

I have tried to limit my collecting to the nineteenth century: Harriet was born in 1811 and died in 1896. As *Uncle Tom's Cabin* was for many years the second most reprinted book after the Bible, it seemed wise to have a cut-off date. At the beginning, I intended to collect only books by Mrs Stowe, but as I came across letters, manuscripts, *cartes de visite*, theatrical programs, ceramics, and more, well, like Topsy, the collection 'just growed'. The *Uncle Tom's Cabin* material has become the overwhelming bulk of the collection.

In 2002, the 150th anniversary of the publication of *Uncle*

Tom's Cabin, I was invited to prepare an exhibition for the Grolier Club, focused on the many faces of *Uncle Tom's Cabin* in print in an effort to demonstrate what an enormous impact it had in the broadening of American popular culture in the second half of the nineteenth century. I hoped to demonstrate not only how strongly

Mary Schlosser

the themes of *Uncle Tom's Cabin* seized the readers of its time, but also that there are few new publishing gimmicks out there, and that spin-offs of all kinds have been around for a long time. If only Harriet had had a good agent to handle the rights for all the foreign and translated texts, the figurines, card games, puzzles, toys, magic lantern slides, silver spoons, and *especially* the dramatic rights! Of course, I have had to collect examples of all of the above, including innumerable theatrical posters, trade cards, sheet music and theatre programmes, even an 1896 biscuit tin lithographed with scenes from the book.

Another aspect of collecting on such a particular subject in such a particular time period was an interest in the development of the trade publishing industry. The publishing industry at the beginning of the second half of the nineteenth century was in a state of rapid change. While still close to craftsmanship that allowed for variety in production at not too great expense, it was moving quickly to full mechanization where publishing could achieve great economies. Unfortunately, the trade editions which resulted were often made up of poor materials and unsound binding. Many more variants of each book could appear; many more readers could be served, but finding books from this period in fresh and excellent condition has been an ongoing challenge. In many cases, I have bought examples in less than perfect condition because they were the only ones I was able to locate, and with the eternal hope of 'improving' my copies. The issue of condition is especially difficult in the area of ephemera.

One of the most gratifying aspects of this collection has been the constant discovery of Uncle Tom material I never knew existed. On the other hand, when the Stowe volume of the *Bibliography of American Literature* came out in 1990, and I discovered that many of my 'first editions' were variants, sometimes later variants, it was enough to make one weep.

Copyright had a big influence on the publication history of *Uncle Tom's Cabin*. Since there was no international copyright law, dozens of foreign editions and translations were published, over twenty in England alone during the 1850s, and it was frequently re-issued abroad throughout the nineteenth century. This has been a difficult area to collect because other than the earliest editions, few foreign dealers are interested in this material.

United States law at the time of publication, begun serially in 1851, permitted twenty-eight years of protection to 1879, and could be extended for another fourteen years to 1893. Before the 1890s only a few variants of the original publication appeared in America, although the book was constantly reprinted. Starting in 1893, numerous American publishers entered the market with a flood of new editions, soon further inspired by Stowe's death in 1896 which seemed to call for a variety of 'memorial' editions.

This is apparently a bottomless pit of possible material. Again these books are of no interest to serious dealers, and must be found at second hand book shops, garage sales, or eBay. As this is also the period of wonderful decorated cloth bindings, it can be quite fun, although condition is a serious problem. I was thrilled to see at the recent V&A *International Arts and Crafts* exhibition a Charles Rennie Mackintosh design of about 1905 on Scott's *The Talisman* which the Glasgow publisher Walter Blackie also used on a copy of *Uncle Tom's Cabin* in my collection.

Happily, my area of collecting has not suffered the enormous inflation of prices that has occurred in so many other fields. Therefore, I can continue to indulge myself when something suitable appears. And aside from the thrill of the chase, one of the most enjoyable aspects of book collecting has been getting to know other book collectors, booksellers, and the many wonderful people involved in the book arts.

New York

'Little Eva reading the Bible to Uncle Tom' by Hammett Billings, wood-engraving from the first edition of *Uncle Tom's Cabin*, 1852 (Reduced to about 85%)

MARY SCHLOSSER

Dean A. Sewell

Gregynog Hall was the setting for my excusable drift into the world of private libraries, fine press and book illustration, and equine physiology my reason for being there. Around 1991, as a postgraduate research student nearing the end of my doctorate, I had been invited by a department at the University of Wales, Aberystwyth, to contribute to a lecture series for Masters students of Equine Science. In spare time, it took only a short while spent in the part of the building occupied by Gwasg Gregynog to draw me into the world of reading, feeling, touching, (even smelling!) books and bindings of quality, quality in the sense of content, typography, illustration, design and binding.

Why collect is a question that is often asked of me. Some of us seem to have the collecting and hoarding gene, and some of us not, and from stamps as a child, I have progressed to books as an adult. My collection is primarily of new books, though as the years pass, my interest in older books grows. I had, as a teenager, 'collected' the cricketer's bible. 'Collected' in reality meant that I bought, read (including at Grace Road when rain stopped play) and then kept the copies. Cricket books form only a small part of my interest. A 2005 Christie's catalogue of the library of the late E. D. R. Eagar is a fascinating one and puts my insipid collection of cricket books (perhaps excluding volumes of the *Wisden Almanack*) into perspective. Even my signed limited edition copy, (printed on hand-made paper), of Ranjitsinhji's *The Jubilee Book of Cricket* (1897) pales in comparison with the Eagar collected copy, signed by the 1902 Australians and the 1903 Philadelphians 'and extensively autographed throughout'.

On the theme of cricket, my joy of receiving a new fine press book reminds me of Rowland Ryder's description of his father's reading of Wisden. 'It was always a red letter day for me when our stock was increased by a new volume, and father announced "I've got the new Wisden!" with the same quiet pride that Disraeli – whom I eventually did get to hear about – would have announced that he had secured shares in the Suez canal' (*Wisden Cricketers' Almanack*, 1965). The famous Wisden woodcut is of course, the

Dean Sewell

work of Eric Ravilious, and a year or two ago I started to investigate aspects of this small, but memorable piece of Ravilious work. Though my day job as an academic physiologist, as well as family commitments, limit the time available for such hobby research, I hope to construct an essay on this matter sometime in the future.

DEAN A. SEWELL

So, to return to Gwasg Gregynog and that day that I naively wandered into the Press. I was happily left to peruse at my leisure the books recently produced and available for sale. I was struck by the magnificence of the Mrozewski wood-engravings in *Parzival* (unaffordable to me for some years) and the piquant poetry and simple drawings of Ormond in *Cathedral Builders* (affordable to me a year or so later having carefully saved).

Around this time I came to know of the Private Libraries Association – I am unsure how. After a few years of membership (though I know not when I joined, as our Members list, despite being chronological in terms of joining and surviving members, does not contain that information), I was lacking in sufficient judgement that I answered the call for a new Treasurer, on the retirement of Derek White from the position. I do, however, gladly continue in the role, despite subsequently moving to Scotland, and I thoroughly enjoy the acquaintance of the few members I know, particularly those who sit on Council.

After my introduction to Gwasg Gregynog, I began slowly to learn of other presses, of the private press movement, and of booksellers and book fairs. During a short, but enforced lull in my academic career in 1999, and having never previously travelled to the USA, I attended the Oak Knoll Festival. Having stopped off in New York and Philadelphia, I arrived in New Castle, Delaware, with a rambling spirit but misguided view that I would find accommodation easily. As luck would have it, I eventually stumbled on a guest house that had a cancelled booking, and fellow guests were Simon Lawrence, and John and Rose Randle. Having met the people behind these presses, I have since taken a greater interest in both The Fleece and Whittington, and have fallen for the thoroughly enjoyable and compulsive *Matrix*.

Appreciating that I was ignorant of the mechanics of fine press printing, in July 2000 I engaged in a workshop at the Alembic Press, and enjoyed the company of Claire and David Bolton and a small number of printing enthusiasts for a few days. Since then I've flirted with the desire to learn more about book binding, however, a full academic career, and family life, make the desire a goal to pursue in the future.

Carfraemill, Scottish Borders

DEAN A. SEWELL

Naseeb Shaheen

pre-King James English Bibles

Working as a professor at the University of Memphis I have for many years been collecting pre-King James English Bibles, now one of the largest collections in private hands. Included within it are some 115 copies of the Geneva Bible, besides numerous editions of the Bishops' Bible, the Rheims New Testament, the Douay Old Testament, and various editions of the Great Bible, the Matthew's Bible, and others.

The collection of pre-King James English Bibles began in 1968 when I was a graduate student at UCLA working on my dissertation on biblical references in *The Faerie Queene*. In spite of the hundreds of biblical references in Spenser's *magnum opus*, only one article had been written on the subject, published in 1926. An in-depth study of Spenser's biblical references was long overdue; it was a project whose time had come, requiring use of the Bibles of Spenser's day.

My first acquisition was a Geneva Bible of 1582, which I acquired in August 1968 from Alan G. Thomas. That edition was a small folio complete with the title-page. It cost £30 which at that time came to $74. It is still the edition I use whenever I quote the Geneva Bible in my publications.

The Geneva Bible, however, was not the Bible endorsed by the Church of England. The version authorized for use in the services of the Anglican Church during the reign of Elizabeth I was the Bishops' Bible, which first appeared in 1568. Since Spenser was a conforming Anglican, it is possible that Spenser may have been better acquainted with the Bishops' Bible than with the Geneva.

It was my good fortune that Alan Thomas had just acquired a Bishops' Bible, a huge second folio edition of 1572. Bishops' Bibles are considerably rarer than Geneva Bibles. Only eighteen editions of the complete Bishops' Bible were published (of which I have nine in my collection), in contrast to the more than 140 known editions of the Geneva Bible. That Bishops' Bible cost £100 or $240, a huge price in 1968 when the average university press book cost anywhere from six to ten dollars. I received the volume in November 1968.

As time went on I managed to acquire other important Bibles. In 1972, I purchased the first edition of the Roman Catholic Rheims New Testament, published in 1582. In November 1976, I received a rare Matthew's Bible, 1549. Two years later, I acquired the 1553 folio edition of the Great Bible. Of this edition we are told that 'Queen Mary is said to have destroyed the greater part of this impression'. I acquired my most valuable English Bible, the Coverdale of 1553, in 1980 while in London, again from Alan Thomas. Other acquisitions included early versions of Elizabethan Homilies, Prayer Books, later editions of the Douay Old Testament and Rheims New Testament, and many other Bibles.

Not until 1978 did I arrange my travel plans so as to be able to attend the antiquarian book fairs in London, especially the annual International Antiquarian Book Fair held that year in the grand ballroom of the Europa Hotel. Many other fairs were held in London at approximately the same time, especially the two International PBFA fairs where over 200 book dealers exhibit books for sale on two consecutive occasions. That initial 1978 trip was so productive that I have attended these London fairs every summer since then. Being there in person enabled me to acquire many volumes I needed for my research, volumes I would not otherwise have been able to acquire. These include – after I began work on Shakespeare's biblical references – not only many Bibles, but also the 1587 edition of Holinshed's *Chronicles,* the 1595 edition of Plutarch's *Lives,* and the 1600 edition of Philemon Holland's translation of Livy, the exact editions of these works that Shakespeare is known to have used as sources for his plays.

Although I have traded some of my Bibles for editions I did not have, none was acquired with a view to selling them for profit. I have used them only for study, producing three volumes of Shakespearian research between 1987 and 1993, revised and issued together in 1999, with a reprint in 2002, *Biblical References in Shakespeare's Plays*. I have also published over forty articles in various academic journals.

I may not have received royalties for any of these publications, but the manner in which they have been received and quoted by other scholars is a sufficient reward in itself.

Memphis, Tennessee

George Chapman Singer

Why Collect Books?

Book collectors, like heroes, are born not made. Book collecting technique can be acquired. Not so is the urge to collect, which is buried in the primordial ooze of our ontogeny. For some lucky victims it strikes late. For me it came early.

At age seven or eight my hoard of Big Little Books (10 cents then, 30 dollars today) were carefully arrayed on a shelf next to my bed. In high school I collected records, the old 78s, the Bluebird and the Okeh labels along with Columbia and Victor, and stacked those on the shelf as well. The albums wouldn't fit upright so, without parental permission, I bought a record cabinet. My parents were not amused, but one's collection must be displayed.

At Dartmouth, Herbert F. West, Professor of Comparative Literature, taught me the difference between accumulators and collectors. Herb was a dedicated teacher, author and collector. The founder of the Friends of the Dartmouth Library, he introduced me to Henry Miller and Robert Frost among other luminaries who visited the campus at his invitation. He is best known for *Modern Book Collecting for the Impecunious Amateur*, Boston, 1936. Reading it enabled me to self-diagnose a virulent case of bibliomania.

After graduation and marriage to Gloria, my long suffering but generally understanding partner of fifty-five years, my next step was the MBA program at Wharton. After some cajoling, my faculty advisor approved a scheme for my dissertation topic, an investigation into the marketing of rare books. *Marketing Methods and Channels of Distribution in the Rare Book Trade* was an original piece of research utilizing both primary and secondary sources. It was published serially in *The Amateur Book Collector* in 1955.

One of my sources was Marston Drake of James F. Drake and Co., a distinguished rare book firm in New York. Drake introduced me to John Carter who gave me a copy of *Taste and Technique in Book Collecting*, New York, 1948, with a delightful inscription. Another was Edwin Wolf who gave me a nearly com-

George Chapman Singer

plete run of Rosenbach Company catalogues dredged from the cellar archives at 1320 Walnut Street in Philadelphia.

In addition to a detailed questionnaire and personal interviews, I read everything available about book dealers, auctions and the business of selling rare books. One variant, wildly successful, had been used by an English collector who manufactured first editions and cleverly palmed them off to unsuspecting buyers. In many ways he was despicable, but no rascality could hide his one redeeming virtue – he loved books. Covered by his public persona as book collector and bibliographer, Thomas James Wise was actually a piratical publisher, a book seller and a forger.

After meeting in successive years with John Carter, the doyen of Wiseans, I was hooked and began buying the forgeries and related material, whatever my limited budget could afford. Michael Papantonio, the English literature half of the John Van E. Kohn / Papantonio partnership, dba The Seven Gables Bookshop, occasionally threw me a bone. One evening in 1953 Mike showed me a copy of *Sonnets from the Portuguese*, Reading, 1849. It was

GEORGE CHAPMAN SINGER

Wise's most successful forgery and is the star piece of any Wise collection. He planned to offer it to Maurice Pariser whose Wise library was rivalled only by the University of Texas.

Mike suggested I take it home on approval. It could be mine for $600. That was roughly a month's salary, and I had a wife and infant daughter to support. The book went back the next morning. At least I had held it in my hands for a while! When Alderman Pariser auctioned his collection in 1967, the *Reading Sonnets* sold for $1,680. John Carter's copy sold in 1976 for $3,492.

There was never a second opportunity. Did my failure to beg, borrow or steal the funds mark me a faux bibliomaniac? Would Sir Thomas Phillipps have hesitated?

Not as pricey as the *Sonnets,* my 'star piece' is bibliographically more interesting. *The Runaway Slave at Pilgrim's Point* was Elizabeth Barrett Browning's protest against American slavery. Although dated 1849, this modest pamphlet was actually printed in 1888 by Richard Clay & Son. The secret publisher was T. J. Wise.

While the stack of printed sheets were piled unfolded in Clay's shop, an inked forme containing a sheet of a legitimate publication, *Notebook of the Shelley Society*, London, 1888 was laid on top creating an imperfect set-off. The image is faintly visible across the sheet and incontrovertibly fixes the true publication date some forty years later. The story is detailed in *The Book Collector*, Spring, 1963. See also John Collins, *The Two Forgers*, Scolar Press, 1992.

A forty-five year pursuit of Wiseana resulted in a 350 item collection of forgeries, piracies, letters and mss. It was given to Dartmouth in 2000.

My current collecting is the serendipitous result of Gloria and me starting the Ashley Book Company in 1982. Private press and book club bibliographies, the materials of our reference library, became irresistible. At first it seemed that two or three shelves would be sufficient. Fifteen years later forty feet of shelf space is full and no end is in sight.

Bibliographies compiled by the owner and printed at the press are the most sought after, because they embody the character of the press and the proprietor's style. Heading the list would have to be St John Hornby's *A Descriptive Bibliography of the Books Printed at the Ashendene Press MDCCCXCV–MCMXXXV.*

Done with all the care, attention to detail and typographical skill that were the hallmarks of his press, it is an exemplar of Hornby's life work as a dedicated amateur. With 390 copies printed, it has never been a scarce book.

A Note by William Morris on His Aims in Founding the Kelmscott Press Together with a Short Description of the Press by S. C. Cockerell..., London, 1898, was the last book printed at the Kelmscott Press and retains all the flavour of Morris's 'typographical adventure'. Another appealing owner-generated history comprises the four bibliographies of Henry Morris' press, 21 *Years of Bird & Bull*, 1980; *Thirty years of Bird and Bull*, 1988; *Forty Years of Bird & Bull* (an expensive spoof), 1998; *Forty-Four years of Bird & Bull*, 2003.

An outstanding new one is *Hoi Barbaroi: a Quarter Century at Barbarian Press,* Mission, British Columbia, 2004. Assembled and beautifully printed by Jan and Crispin Elsted, the deluxe edition is presented in a magenta slip case containing a generous helping of press ephemera in a matching clam shell box. Just handling this book tells you much about Barbarian Press and its owners.

A degree less interesting, at least from a collector's standpoint, are the recent spate of commercially done checklists and bibliographies sponsored by The British Library and Oak Knoll Press. While they will be of unquestioned value to future researchers, several are marred by errors and careless editing. Even as reference books they are, to be blunt, less attractive than they have to be. Typography, design, illustration and binding have been trumped by cost.

For a book hunter, the smaller, unsung presses, whose output has escaped critical attention, are especially rewarding. Some make it into that invaluable PLA publication, *Private Press Books,* many don't. Some which flourished prior to 1950 were listed in Will Ransom's *Private Press Books,* New York, 1929 *et seq.,* but only the important ones. An offbeat item I found not long ago is an *Exhibition of Modern American Printing, a Catalogue,* compiled by T. L. Yuan and printed in Peiping, China in May 1935, under the auspices of the National Library of Peiping.

The ultimate challenge, though, is the early nineteenth century presses like Sir Egerton Brydges' *Lee Priory Press.* There were several checklists of the works printed at the Press – maybe some-day one will come my way. David Chambers' checklist and engaging history of this notable press appeared in *The Private Library*, Autumn, 2002.

Hundreds of small presses are out there. Alice and Bud Westreich in the sixth edition of the *International Directory of Private Presses (Letterpress)*, Sacramento, 1993, list some 1,100 private press printers from around the world. Many of them will leave a printed record of their activities. Perhaps it will be just a list of publications on a folded sheet, maybe something more elabo-rate. If it displays the output of a private press, it is fair game.

Burlington, Vermont

'Lee Priory', wood-engraving from
William Brown, *Original Poems*, Lee Priory Press, 1815

Thorsten Sjölin

Thorsten Sjölin

My first book (*Snow White*, I am reliably informed) was lost during a hospital stay in about 1941. The budding book collection then grew with roughly a book every Christmas and birthday from the age of six. Perhaps not a remarkable start, but there were public and school libraries nearby and I was never short of reading matter.

As I grew older I started to buy books fairly indiscriminately, mainly in the annual book sale (then held every February) and, once I moved to a bigger town, in the antiquarian bookshops which were a new discovery for me. Most of these books are long since gone as tastes, interests and knowledge of other languages changed and increased respectively. So, of course I had to specialise. For many years I collected books on shaving, beards, razors, hair and allied subjects. They were mainly acquired as research tools for a book which eventually was written, but remains in manuscript. The books on shaving, etc., eventually found their way to the Worshipful Company of Barbers in London and the ones on hair were donated to a museum library in Sweden.

A lot of my books were bought to help me understand the texts I had to disentangle during my many years as a translator and, as they have proved their usefulness over the years, I have retained many of them even after I stopped translating – they are invaluable for crossword and polymath puzzles. Over the years the family has found the answer to many a clue in our collection of reference books.

I cannot recall how I became interested in private press books. Maybe it was a chance meeting in an antiquarian bookshop in Sweden, where one of the customers produced a book from the Kelmscott Press. He always carried it with him in his rucksack in case anyone was interested. That was, incidentally, the same bookshop where I started to buy illustrated books more seriously. In the beginning I bought just about everything, but later concentrated on certain Swedish authors / illustrators, eventually contacted some of them, translated them (published by Incline Press) and visited them.

British illustrators also fascinated me, not least wood-engravers like Robert Gibbings and all these fantastic women engravers. I soon had a large collection of books with wood-engravings, but in the end had to restrict myself and so some of them had to go.

The number of private press books has also been reduced as I found that some of them were not what I would call proper private press, i.e. where virtually everything is done in-house. Instead I have concentrated on certain presses which interest me for various reasons.

As my interest in specific fields wanes, books have to be pruned out and new ones are acquired. Books by or about relatives and ancestors, books on windmills, books on lighthouses, books by certain authors have appeared during the last ten years. Perennial ones are authors like Doris Lessing (no Nobel Prize yet), Selma Lagerlöf (Nobel Prize 1909), half forgotten ones like Compton Mackenzie and the evergreen Joseph Conrad to mention just a few. Add to that metres (or yards if you like) of books on books, art, history, astronomy, Greek coins, topography and a number of other subjects. No wonder the house is filling up fast.

Some years back I suggested at a committee meeting of the Brooking Family History Society (on my wife's side) that we should start a library of books written by people with the name Brooking, Brookings, Brookin and other variant spellings including, of course, descendants on female lines plus spouses. This was agreed and I was given the rôle of Hon. Librarian. Without the internet and helpful members it would not have been possible to do this, but the Library now contains well over a hundred books – and what a varied collection it is: everything from academic papers to self-published poetry interspersed with sci-fi, religious tracts and autobiographies. I had never expected that many (and I keep finding new ones all the time) or that variety, especially on the American side of the family. It is a truly interesting library which I will treasure as long as I am in charge of it.

Darley Abbey, Derby

THORSTEN SJÖLIN

Ronald K. Smeltzer

The Physical Sciences

For more than twenty-five years I have been collecting publications in the physical sciences and related fields. The subjects of the collection include general physics and the 'experimental philosophy' since Newton; radioactivity and atomic physics; the historical development of scientific instruments; microscopy; science by women; selected topics in chemistry; spectroscopy; early modern digital computing; and scientific and technical works with special and unusual aspects of graphic design. The collection spans four centuries and encompasses many languages.

Many items in the collection fit more than one category in the list above, and I find it particularly interesting to consider the various themes around which any one book can be organized. During late 2004 through early 2005 an exhibition 'Four Centuries of Graphic Design for Science' from the collection was on view at the Grolier Club. The exhibition was organized around book design and techniques of illustration, rather than scientific subject. Items in the exhibition included nineteenth-century scientific publications with mounted photographs; scientific texts with colour illustration; publications with unusual examples of 'graphic invention' such as illustration in three dimensions; books to show interesting and attractive design, typography, and illustration; and prints and broadsides. An illustrated checklist was published to document the exhibition.

Scientific publication by women is another category for which examples can be drawn from a number of subject collections. A special interest is Madame du Châtelet, paramour of Voltaire and French translator of Newton's *Principia*. The collection includes most editions of her scientific works. With her works, both printings of the first edition of Voltaire's treatise on the Newtonian philosophy are included. English authors of scientific works represented in the collection include Margaret Bryan and Mary Somerville. Most of the publications of Marie Curie are included in the modern physics collection, which is primarily focused on radioactivity and atomic physics.

The modern physics collection begins with original materials associated with the discoveries of x-rays and radioactivity in 1895 and 1896, and extends through what is sometimes called the atomic age, *c.* 1945–1955. Just about every monograph, many single-issue serials in original wrappers, and some separata by the important researchers in radioactivity and atomic physics are in the collection. A paper 'Collecting Modern Physics' appeared in the *Gazette of the Grolier Club*, number 54, pp. 59–80, for 2003. On the subject of modern science, a paper 'Collecting Classics in Science' was the invited, lead-off presentation for a symposium on landmark chemistry books of the twentieth century during the 230th National Meeting of the American Chemical Society, August 28 – September 1, 2005.

Du Graphometre. 47

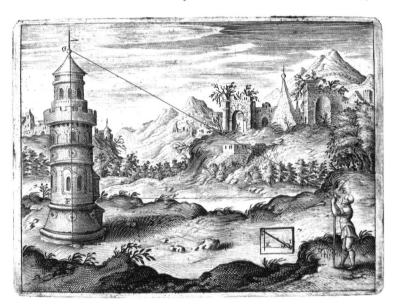

Engraving from Philippe Danfrie,
Declaration de l'Vsage du Graphometre, 1597

The collection focused on the historical development of scientific instruments includes Danfrie's book of 1597 on surveying instruments printed in a Civilité typeface, books with the text printed from intaglio plates, and many other publications, seventeenth century and later, with attractive illustrations. This collection is complemented by a small accumulation of eighteenth and nineteenth century scientific hardware, some of which is illustrated in the books. For this subject I try to obtain all new publications worldwide. Membership in the Scientific Instrument Society, which is the organization for those interested in the historical development of scientific instruments, keeps me in touch with developments in this subject. In the area of microscopy, the collection begins with Robert Hooke's *Micrographia* of 1665. The earliest German, Italian, and French publications on microscopy in the collection date from 1716, 1691, and 1718, respectively. From the nineteenth century, as early as 1853, the collection includes numerous scarce and little-known works with mounted albumen photomicrographs. This collection extends to the very early twentieth century.

The primary interest in chemistry books is colour illustration. During the nineteenth century a number of chemistry texts appeared in Germany, England, France, and the United States with remarkable colour illustrations achieved with printed colour in letterpress and lithography, hand colouring, and attached coloured specimens. Most of the books so illustrated and identified are in the collection.

The collection focused on physics and the 'experimental philosophy' since Newton includes many of the important works from the very early eighteenth century onward. Places of publication are England, France, the Netherlands, Denmark, Sweden, Italy, and Germany. Many of the publications illustrate early scientific apparatus, so there is a relationship to the interest in the historical development of scientific instruments. Included in this part of the collection are important publications on optics and electricity. As I now need, generally, very scarce publications, major acquisitions tend to be few and far between. But I continue to find items of interest in the book trade world-wide. Members of the PLA with specific interests or queries that relate to the collection described here are welcome to inquire.

Princeton, New Jersey

RONALD K. SMELTZER

Brian D. Stilwell

Brian D. Stilwell

Fine Printing

I grew up in a house with books. My father was a professional artist and a collector of illustrated books. He had a particular interest in Arthur Rackham. I started collecting in the late 1960s, purchasing examples of modern fine printing and illustrated books. Initially most of the items I acquired were from American or British presses. In the 1970s, I started to acquire examples of some of the major presses of the eighteenth and nineteenth centuries. In recent years the internet has permitted acquisition of many examples of continental fine printing. My collection today consists of several thousand items.

Examples of eighteenth- and nineteenth-century British fine printing include various Baskerville editions, as well as Hume's *The History of England*, printed by Bensley, in folio, and Milton's *The Poetical Works*, printed by Bulmer, in folio. Finely printed French editions include a number of the de luxe editions printed by François Ambroise Didot l'aîné and Pierre Didot l'aîné, such as the *edition du Louvre* of Racine in folio. I also have a considerable number of Bodoni productions, including editions of Longinus and Thomas à Kempis in folio.

Modern British press books include *The Four Gospels* produced by the Golden Cockerel Press, the Gregynog edition of Euripides in the George Fisher special binding, the seven volume Shakespeare produced by Nonesuch, and the sets of Chaucer, Froissart, and Spenser produced at the Shakespeare Head Press. There are also examples of the Ashendene Press, including the Cervantes and Thucydides, the Kelmscott Press, including the Voragine and *The Recuyell of the Historyes of Troye*, the Vale Press, including *The Parables* and *Julia Domna* on vellum, and the Doves Press, including Emerson's *Essays* in a Katharine Adams binding. There is much from the Rampant Lions Press, including the special issue of *The Story of Cupid and Psyche* by William Morris.

German fine printing includes such productions as Nietzsche's *Also Sprach Zarathustra* produced by Henry van de Velde, and the German private presses are well represented, including the Bremer Presse editions in folio of Homer, St Augustine, and Dante, the Cranach Presse edition of *Canticum Canticorum Salomonis*, the Rupprechtpresse editions in quarto of Spee, Spinoza and von Moltke, and the Officina Serpentis editions in folio of Dante (one of the twenty-five with hand-painted initials), Aeschylus, and *Parzival*. The Austrian private press of Robert Haas, the Officina Vindobonensis, is represented, including *Das Bergwerk zu Falun* by Hugo von Hofmannsthal. Books produced in the Netherlands present in the collection include those designed by Jan Van Krimpen, such as *Het Boeck der Psalmen*, 1928, and *The Book of Psalms*, Stichting De Roos, 1947, both printed by Joh. Enschedé en Zonen, and A. A. M. Stols, including his edition, in six quarto volumes, of Molière produced for La Compagnie Typographique. Private presses are represented in works of Heuvelpers and Kunera Pers. Czech fine printing is well represented in the collection. Examples of fine book production in Switzerland include Shakespeare's *The Tempest* printed at the Officina Bodoni and publications by André Gonin, Lausanne. Italian fine printing includes examples of work of the Officina Bodoni after its move to Italy, Alberto Tallone, and the editions produced in 1927, in folio, of Foscolo and Machiavelli by the Stamperia Della Officina Governativa Carte Valori di Roma.

Examples of American fine book production include the Grabhorn Press edition of Walt Whitman's *Leaves of Grass*, Victor Hammer's edition of Hölderlin's *Gedichte*, the Overbrook Press *Manon Lescaut*, and many examples of Bruce Rogers, including the limited edition of Homer's *The Odyssey* and Morison's *Fra Luca de Pacioli*.

Fine French productions include many examples of publications issued by the various French bibliophile societies and illustrated works, such as the edition of Longus illustrated by Maillol and printed by Philippe Gonin. Other French printers represented in my collection include the Imprimerie Nationale, Pierre Bouchet, Coulouma, Jean-Gabriel Daragnès, Maurice Darantiere, Féquet et Baudier, and Léon Pichon. Fine Spanish productions include works published in Barcelona in the early 1930s by La Cometa (Gustavo Gili).

Wayne, Pennsylvania

BRIAN D. STILWELL

Michael Taffe

Mandrake Press and other Fine Printing

By grade seven, instead of using school lunch money for its intended purpose I was investing the 10*d*. on such treats as Cassell's *British Battles on Land and Sea* and *Heroes of Britain*. By age fourteen, I had graduated to Charles Knight's *Imperial Shakespeare*. Our generational home is a cottage and I did try to keep boundaries accordingly. Over the past five years however I've discarded the cottage aesthetic and delight in at least some of the treasures I yearned for decades ago.

In my public service career I travelled, and lived elsewhere, and my boundaries broadened. In the 1980s I returned to the family home and commenced restoring its heritage listed garden. Collecting garden books in keeping with the theme of our new / old home, and building on my forebears' garden books was a permissible indulgence. As this collecting grew, I fell back into my old ways seeking wider fields, but by that time, retired and with student children, I could ill afford the books that I wished I had bought all those years ago. Despite this, I had my father's and grandparents' books that included some wonderful Victoriana.

Over many years of working life my interests were Australian art and decorative arts, especially porcelain. Over those years I built up a small collection of paintings and English ceramics and also a body of literature on art and antiques. In my school years I had seen photos of the great libraries and, maybe subliminally, felt the need to have books complemented by decorative arts, as many of my art books relate to those wider collections.

In much the same way, my involvement in garden history, horticulture and the teaching thereof, came to be reflected in the books I was collecting. I still look for specific horticultural treasures that relate to our garden and region. My local history and horticulture collections assisted in my research and publishing of *Exploring Ballarat's Heritage Gardens* in 1999. I have also had many journal articles published in relation to both history and garden history.

By the 1990s I had started collecting books simply to enjoy, not only for reading or teaching purposes, but also as artefacts. I adopted a collecting policy, hmm! In so far as I have followed

Michael Taffe

this I have aimed for a small niche, one particular fine press for a cabinet collection. Knowing that there were good academic collections of most fine and private presses, I decided upon The Mandrake Press, P. R. Stephensen's outgrowth from the better-known Fanfrolico Press. I believe that his worth as a book designer still remains undervalued.

One of the earliest Mandrakes that I acquired was Stephensen's *Bushwhackers*. Despite *Bushwhackers* literary shortcomings the collection was on its way. Over time I was fortunate in acquiring the Mandrake booklet series. I remember my delight when Melbourne antiquarian book dealer Kenneth Hince rang to advise me of a copy to hand, of the Right Honourable Erskine of Marr's *The Old Tribute*. I was away, and already slightly distracted with a wonderful first edition of Scott's *The Vision of Don Roderick* and *Rokeby* in contemporary regency binding. So home I travelled with both books in hand. I have managed to follow the Mandrake quest fairly faithfully but somehow other non-related material has crept in.

While waiting for some of the harder to find ephemeral items I have satisfied myself with connecting threads including some Kelmscott material such as *A Note by William Morris on His Aims in Founding the Kelmscott Press*, and the ultimate Australian private press production of *The Heemskerk Shoals* for which I am indebted to Melbourne dealer, Peter Arnold. Other private press productions seem to have muscled their way into the library. I now spend many hours enjoying not only the wonderful *Wyf of Bathe* and *The Book of Tobit* produced by Mandrake Press but the Fanfrolico connections of *The Tunning of Elynour Rummin* and *Gwenevere*. This latter work demands that I seek out the Kelmscott version that spawned it, and so it goes on.

The library has now outgrown its origins, and occupies every room in my Australian-Irish generational home so that it has become not my library but the library of *Hymettus*. Today I have almost fulfilled my Mandrake goal and am enjoying books for pleasant reading while building on my twenty-first century Australian private presses – and the occasional overseas productions such as Kickshaws or Old Stile Press.

Lake Wendouree, Ballarat, Victoria, Australia

MICHAEL TAFFE

G. Thomas Tanselle

Publishers' Imprints & Bibliography

I began collecting in a systematic way in the late 1950s, when I was writing a Ph.D. dissertation based on the Floyd Dell papers at The Newberry Library. Because Dell was involved in the so-called Chicago Renaissance during the years just before 1913 and then, for the rest of the decade, was a part of the radical and avant-garde literary community in Greenwich Village, I began assembling books by the writers associated with those movements, as well as books reviewed by them. I soon noticed that the same few publishers were responsible for many of these books, and I started picking up other titles they published as I came across them. Before long I was able to discern the character of each of these publishers and the distinctive contribution each had made to cultural history by disseminating work that was not generally acceptable to the major trade publishers. In this way I embarked on a collecting path that I have followed with enthusiasm and pleasure for half a century.

When I started, the idea of collecting the output of twentieth-century publishing firms was nearly unheard of. Private presses were of course a well established field for collectors, and some people were interested in the *fin-de-siècle* publishers like Stone & Kimball and Mathews & Lane. But dealers were continually surprised, as I pointed out in an essay for *The Book Collector* in 1970, to learn that the books I selected, published by commercial firms, were chosen not for their subjects or authors but for their publishers – though in the end the subjects and authors were essential to the story my collection was telling. I began with Mitchell Kennerley, B. W. Huebsch, and Boni & Liveright and moved on to the early Knopf, A. & C. Boni, Thomas Seltzer, and the American branch of John Lane. Several even smaller New York publishers, like Frank Shay, Egmont Arens, and Laurence Gomme and such little magazines as the *Masses*, *Liberator*, and *Mother Earth* also fell naturally within my scope. As the years went by, I added a number of other American publishers between 1890 and 1930 to my list, representing Boston, Chicago, and San Francisco as well as New York. The resulting collection now

G. Thomas Tanselle

contains some eight thousand volumes, both firsts and nonfirsts –
for in publisher-collecting it is important to show which titles required successive printings and how their appearance and texts
were sometimes altered. I thus have had the pleasure of owning
first printings of many major authors of the period and also of
placing them in the context of the other books that emerged from
the same firms at the same time.

G. THOMAS TANSELLE   *333*

Besides collecting imprints, I have assembled several thousand books in a series of bibliographical collections – histories of publishers and printers, descriptive bibliographies, works on book collecting and textual criticism, and writings by the principal bibliographical and textual scholars. These books are in one sense a working reference library, which has served me well in my own writing on these subjects. But the distinction between a 'collection' and a 'reference library' is an artificial one, and I approach my bibliographical collections with the same concerns that author-collectors focus on – paying attention, that is, to editions and printings, to the presence of dust-jackets, and to other aspects of condition. My friendship with some major bibliographical scholars, such as Fredson Bowers, John Carter, Ruth Mortimer, and Gordon Ray, no doubt accounts in part for my forming comprehensive author-collections of them. But another reason is that it is just as useful with scholarly works as with other works to know the biographical context, and it is certainly important when using those works for reference and quotation to be cognizant of the revisions made in different editions and printings. I have therefore collected many other bibliographer-authors, including Bradshaw, A. W. Pollard, McKerrow, Greg, Sadleir, Muir, Munby, Graham Pollard, and Gaskell.

Michael Sadleir, indeed, is a central figure for me because he was not only a publisher and novelist but also a bibliographical scholar and collector. When I had to select a single item from my collection for inclusion in the Grolier Club exhibition and catalogue entitled *The Grolier Club Collects* (2002), I chose the pamphlet form of his Melville bibliography (one of twenty copies, 1923) to suggest the affinity between his interests and mine. All of my collections have supported my publications; in fact, I do not distinguish between them as scholarly creations. My collecting and my scholarship are inseparable, and I cannot conceive of one without the other.

New York

G. THOMAS TANSELLE

Jim Thirsk

Autobiographies of Childhood

It was in the early 1930s that I first read books by Anatole France, published by John Lane in the 1920s, in those orange-coloured cloth-bound reprinted translations. Those which delighted me most were the four which tell in semi-fictional form the story of his childhood and boyhood: *My Friend's Book*, *Pierre Nozère*, *Little Pierre* and *The Bloom of Life*, all translated by a devotee, James Lewis May, who wrote a memorable account of his own childhood, *The Path through the Wood* (1930), which I have. I became more and more interested in books about childhood, particularly in the concept that 'the child is father of the man'.

So it was that during the war years, being at Bletchley, I had easy access to the second-hand bookshops of London, Oxford and Cambridge and since then, I have purchased many more books of childhood memories. My collection grew and now I have more than three hundred and fifty volumes. I also collected books on Shakespeare, English translations of Russian literature and essays on literature.

The most useful guide to the subject is a bibliography of some six hundred books on the 'Autobiography of childhood and adolescence'. This is an appendage to an article by Richard N. Coe, 'Reminiscences of Childhood' in *Proceedings of the Leeds Philosophical and Literary Society* (Volume xix, part vi, 1984). My collection consists mainly of autobiographies covering the period of childhood only. There exist, however, many autobiographies whose first chapters on childhood are so memorable that I have included them. I'm thinking of such books as Charles Chaplin's *My Autobiography* (1964), the early chapters of which tell of his unhappy childhood. Among my favourite books are Eleanor Farjeon's *Nursery in the Nineties*, Frank Kendon's *The Small Years* and Herbert Read's *The Innocent Eye* (1930).

One of my treasured foreign autobiographies is Maxim Gorky's *Childhood*, later made into a memorable film. Another treasure is Tolstoy's *Childhood, Boyhood and Youth* in the Maude translation.

Among modern French writers the memories of the film-maker

Jim Thirsk

Marcel Pagnol of his childhood in Provence are outstanding. Like Anatole France, he was a member of the French Academy. The four volumes of his *Souvenirs d'enfance* have been popular in England, especially the first two volumes, translated as *The Days Were Too Short* (1960).

It was inevitable I suppose that, having collected all these books – and I have not ceased buying yet – I should try my hand at the same sort of autobiography. For the benefit of my grandchildren I have published two books. The first, *A Beverley Child's Great War*, appeared in 2000. The continuation: *Boyhood in Beverley: a Mosaic of the 1920s*, followed in 2003. These are still in print.

Hadlow, Tonbridge, Kent

The young James Thirsk, from his
A Beverley Child's Great War, 2000

Martyn Thomas

My collection of around 2,000 books mainly comprises twentieth century UK private presses, fine printing and typography. I have yet to see a litho book that can match the best letterpress for the beauty of words on paper; the impression from metal type adds texture and contrast, and the inks appear richer in colour.

I have boundless admiration for four contemporary printers: John Randle (Whittington Press), Martyn Ould (Old School Press), Simon Lawrence (Fleece Press) and Sebastian Carter (Rampant Lions Press). I subscribe to the first three of these presses, so my collection of each is almost complete (indeed, I have inadvertently ended up with three complete sets of *Matrix*, including a set of the specials, so if any reader is looking for a set of the standard edition they should get in touch).

The Rampant Lions edition of T. S. Eliot's *Four Quartets* is a perfect example of letterpress printing – everything in its design and printing heightens the pleasure of reading without in any way intruding between the reader and the poems.

I have an extensive collection of books printed in the Fell types, particularly in Fell English and larger sizes. The types date from the sixteenth century and were largely the work of Robert Granjon of Paris, purchased for Oxford University Press in the seventeenth century by Bishop John Fell and supplemented by further faces designed and cut by Peter Walpergen, who also cut the music types. These types were brought back into use towards the end of the nineteenth century, largely through the interest of the printer Charles Daniel, provost of Worcester College, Oxford, and the Poet Laureate, Robert Bridges. Some of the finest letterpress books of the twentieth century were printed in Fell, by O.U.P., of course, but also by Daniel, by the Ashendene Press, and by Stanley Morison and Francis Meynell at the Romney Street Press. *The Fell Revival* (Old School Press, 2000) tells the story, and contains a comprehensive list of books printed in one or more of the Fell types.

I am pleased to own one of the original copies of Horace Hart's *A Century of Oxford Typography* that first catalogues the Fell types. My copy is number 97, presented to Christopher Halifax

Martyn Thomas

who was Oriental Reader at O.U.P. in 1900. It contains, loosely inserted, a set of 'Plates I–XI as used for the Controller's Article in *The Printing Art*, Feb 1904. Given to him by Controller's direction.' The note is signed by Hart himself.

My collection also includes a set of the four fascicules prepared by Stanley Morison, Harry Carter and John Simmons in preparation for what was to be Morison's last and greatest book, the monumental *John Fell*, published in 1963 on the eve of Morison's death. Each *fasciculus* was printed in fifty copies only, for private circulation to those who (it was vainly hoped) would be able to contribute scholarship to the project. My copies were bought from the printer, Charles Batey, by Robert Elwell, and contain his bookplate inside a purpose-made, Oxford blue box.

It is a great luxury to be able to reach for precisely the reference book one requires to check a fact or pursue a line of thought, and I consider myself very fortunate to have such a wide collection of catalogues, autobiographies and bibliographies covering twentieth century printing. When I was writing *Harry Carter, Typographer* (with John A. Lane and Anne Rogers, Old School Press, 2005) I could draw on Barker's *Stanley Morison*, Francis Meynell's *My Lives*, J. H. Badley's *Bedales*, *The Curwen Press Miscellany*, various articles in *Matrix*, and many books by Harry Carter himself and others, all without leaving my study.

Harry Carter was an extraordinary man, whose quiet modesty denied him the fame and honours that surrounded Stanley Morison. Yet Carter was the greater scholar; Morison preferred the large picture rather than the detail, and *John Fell* benefited hugely from Carter's meticulous additions and corrections of Morison's text. Carter had done everything in printing: he had designed types, cut punches, struck matrixes, cast sorts and printed letterpress; he had designed books and commercial catalogues and managed a publishers; he had handled and catalogued the historic typographical materials at O.U.P. and the Plantin Moretus Museum: his eye for detail was scientific and rarely mistaken.

Carter's writing was direct and witty. I strongly recommend his two volume notes on the Edward Clark Library which is frequently seen in bookdealers' lists and usually inexpensive. His *View of Early Typography* has recently been republished with an introduction by James Mosley (Hyphen, 2002), and is necessary reading for students of typographic history.

There are many gaps in my collection that I must fill if I am to really understand the people who made the early part of the twentieth century such a fertile period for typographic development and fine printing. There are unsolved puzzles (why did the bookbinder Sarah Prideaux buy a sizeable font of Fell around 1903? Did she print anything with it? What happened to the two cases of Fell English that Francis Meynell bought for his Romney Street Press? Why was there so little contact between the circles of Leonard and Virginia Woolf and those of Francis Meynell, Stanley Morison, Oliver and Herbert Simon, and Harry Carter?). I am still collecting, reading and, I hope, learning.

Bath

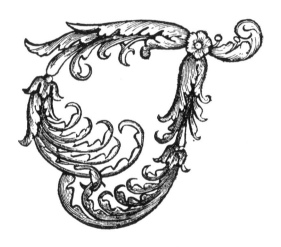

Dutch bloemen initial
used in Wood's *Hist. et Antiq.*, from
John Fell's Sheldonian Press, 1674

Philip A. Truett

Golfing Books

Playing golf as a boy at Littlehampton Golf Club (founded 1888), my friends were not interested in the old golf books in the pine-panelled dining room. This lack of interest was shared by the membership generally, because, arriving down one Spring in the late 60s, that lovely old dining room had become the Mixed Bar and the Club's library had disappeared. I discovered it in the cellar, beside the dustbins, to be taken away the following Monday. I made sure I was there before the dustmen and carried away this small, but very choice, Library in two large suitcases. That was the start of my golf library.

I was still living at home at the time and the small bookcase in my room was just large enough to house my new library. However, upon buying my own home in 1972, I was able to house more books, although this was as much for decorative purposes, as it was to satisfy my interest in the history of golf.

Getting married in 1973 and having many new outlets for my meagre finances, and on the basis of not beating them but joining them, I decided to become a part time golf book dealer. I felt that the catalogues produced by others could be greatly improved upon, by way of description and condition. This book dealing lasted for ten years until 1983, when I got a much busier job at Lloyd's. I remain proud of the twelve catalogues that I produced and have the satisfaction of knowing that anyone who bought a book off me has something that is now worth considerably more than when they bought it. With hindsight, my mistake was to sell anything.

The defining moment, concerning this decision to join the dealers, was asking the proprietor of the Bognor Regis Bookshop, if he had 'got any others?' – In those days there was always a selection of early golf books at any decent bookshop and this visit had been no exception, so I'm not sure what prompted this question. 'Yes', he said and, in a few moments, I was shown two magnificent golf books, the likes of which I did not even know existed. There was the De Luxe Library edition of the Rev. John Kerr's *Golf Book of East Lothian* of 1896, limited to 250 copies, signed by the author with its half leather binding and gilt edges for £35

Philip A. Truett

and the only slightly less magnificent *Chronicles of the Blackheath Golfers* of 1897 by Hughes for £25 . . . and I had never paid more than a pound or two for any golf book.

But I had to have them . . . and I did.

My grand plan, from the outset, was to collect everything published before 1920. To this extent, I should think that my golf library is as complete as any private collection this side of the Atlantic and, perhaps, both sides of the Atlantic, with one major exception – my friend in Cleveland, Ohio. Indeed, as my 'wants' list has diminished and the wanted have become scarcer, I have concentrated on acquiring antiquarian books (pre-1850) with just a reference to golf. The earliest of these, the Scottish Acts of Parliament book of 1566, contains the first printed reference to the word when the act 'utterly cried down' the playing of golf (and football). Asking very superior booksellers at book fairs if they have any golf books and getting a response that suggests this is a subject that is somewhat beneath them, I enjoy pointing out that the first edition Robbie Burns on their shelf includes reference to the game, as do, say, Allan Ramsay's poems and the novels of Sir Walter Scott. We usually finish up by having an interesting chat . . . and they've learnt something new.

Post 1920, I collect only those books that interested me. These include histories of the game and of particular UK golf clubs – these alone amount to about 1,200 volumes – golf course architecture, ladies' golf, selected biographies / autobiographies and those books written by Bernard Darwin and other great golf writers. Whereas I have stuck to my self-imposed book rules, my golf collecting interests have broadened to include post cards, cigarette cards, programmes and early printed ephemera.

The display of my books is very important. Perhaps they should be in alphabetical order by author, but aesthetically this does nothing for me – arranging them neatly, like soldiers on parade, gives me a lot more satisfaction . . . and, anyway, I'm the only one who ever has to find a book.

I also like the whole idea of recreating the Victorian gentleman's library, so to complement the books, my library has pictures, display cabinets, silverware, bronzes and even stuffed birds (killed by golf balls) in glass cases. All these items are, of course, golf related.

344   PHILIP A. TRUETT

My golf library has given me, and will continue to give me, great pleasure. Likewise, the thrill of the hunt is still there – only at a recent book fair, I came across the previously unrecorded *Up Country Golf in India* (Bombay, 1947) . . . Almost as exciting as my Bognor discovery thirty-two years ago. Never give up looking!

Croydon, Surrey

PHILIP A. TRUETT   345

Norman Waddleton

Colour-printed Illustration

This collection of books with colour-printed illustrations has been formed by Norman Waddleton, and is gradually being transferred to the Cambridge University Library. His aim has been 'to assemble and record all books having colour-printed illustrations or decorations up to 1893 when the processes known as three-colour halftone and three-colour plus black were introduced'. Thus the collection includes few examples of hand-colouring, which is covered by the collection formed by the late John Harley-Mason, now also in the Library.

Norman's interest in colour began when he came up to Cambridge. In his second year at Emmanuel College he joined the Thomas Young Club (Young was the first to develop the theory of colour sensation which as modified by Helmholz is accepted today). Work, the war years and a growing family intervened until in the early 1960s whilst working in Lincoln's Inn Fields he used to wander around the monthly Book Fairs that were held in various local hotels. During his lunch hour he would browse all the different book stalls to see what he could pick up. At one of these Book Fairs he met Gavin Bridson and Geoffrey Wakeman of the Plough Press. Gavin Bridson was Secretary of the Linnean Society of London. Together they published *A Guide to Nineteenth Century Colour Printers* in 1975 which described as many colour printers as they could find. He also got to know Ruari McLean and his wife who would visit him at home in the Chilterns. He had by now found a new treasure trove of books at Weatherhead's, an Aylesbury bookshop. He was a regular weekly visitor leaving the shop each time with an armful of books. He also visited Book Fairs that were regularly organised in Cambridge and other towns in England, sometimes even when he was abroad. Whenever he and his wife were out and about he would disappear for an hour or so, saying 'I'm off to look for books'.

At first he concentrated on collecting all the books listed in the 1910 publication by Burch and the 1972 publication by Abbey. After writing a bibliographical description for each book, concentrating on the colour printer and the colour printed element of the book, he decided to publish these, and in 1979 the first edition of the Waddleton *Chronology* appeared containing all the books collected to date. As more books were added, five new editions were published up to 1993. In 1984 Gavin Bridson and Geoffrey

Norman Waddleton

Wakeman published *Printmaking and Picture Printing* and stated that the Waddleton *Chronology* was undoubtedly the fullest list of English colour-printed books. Six supplements were later published for the newly collected books.

He was extremely fortunate in that when it was decided to house the books at Cambridge University Library, Chris Sendall helped him to convert his records into electronic data by scanning his typed records. Without this invaluable help right at the beginning he would not have had the head start that was needed later on when he decided to create the Bookartworld database, with some help from his family, which is now available on line for anyone to search his collection, including the colour printer list. As from *Supplement* 7 the additional books have only been added to this database and no more supplements were published.

There are essentially four methods of printing which have been used to produce colour illustrations during the period covered by the collection: woodcut, which appeared in the printing of incunabula before 1501; wood-engraving, a similar technique except that the medium was the end-grain of a hardwood, typically boxwood; intaglio printing from copper or steel plates into which the image had been engraved; and chromolithography, a planographic process using specially-prepared blocks of limestone. Of these, the woodcut was the first to be used, followed by intaglio, used from the fifteenth century for monochrome images and developed in the late seventeenth century for colour work. Wood-engraving and lithography were introduced at the end of the eighteenth century, the former by Bewick and the latter by Senefelder. Examples of all these methods can be found in the Waddleton collection.

Because the *raison-d'être* of the collection is the printing method employed, the subject coverage is extremely diverse: gift-books with coloured engravings stand next to a catalogue of floor-tiles, an illuminated breviary is followed by a chapbook of Tom Thumb. Nevertheless certain categories stand out; there are naturally many bird and flower books, works on the history of architecture, furniture and ceramics, pattern books for decorators, and a considerable number of children's books, mostly in English (including a significant collection of the so-called 'toy-books'), French, German or Dutch. Some of the books, mainly French, are included because of the colour-printing employed on their bindings. The geographical spread is also very wide; British material predominates, but there are substantial French, German, Dutch, Spanish and American holdings, as well as lesser amounts from eastern Europe, Scandinavia, Australia and New Zealand, and Asia.

At present the majority of the non-British items in the collection have been added to the Library's online catalogue (http://www.lib.cam.ac.uk); the British material (which to a considerable extent duplicates items already in the Library's other collections) is mainly still to be catalogued.

The Norman Waddleton collection of books containing colour printed illustrations now has a well illustrated website where you can search the chronology by a variety of search terms. This website is at http://www.bookartworld.com/waddleton.

Nicholas Smith for Norman Waddleton,
   Lee Common, Great Missenden

Philip Ward

I began collecting books as soon as I could read and have never stopped broadening my horizons. My library (often pretentiously, I feel) aims to become a repository of world civilization in books, journal articles, press cuttings, photographs, recordings on cassette, vinyl and DVD, with albums of autographs and signed photographs in such fields as music, opera, ballet and dance, art, theatre and film, radio and TV and signed programmes in the above fields.

By career I have been an international librarian in England, Libya, Egypt and Indonesia; with parallel lives in publishing (having founded The Oleander Press in 1960; now acquired by Dr J. P. Toner and still active in Cambridge), poetry (a dozen volumes published, the latest being *His Enamel Mug*), travel (sixty-four countries visited for thirty-four travel books, particularly four on India and three on Bulgaria), reference books such as *The Oxford Companion to Spanish Literature*, *A Dictionary of Common Fallacies* and *A Lifetime's Reading*. The PLA was founded in 1956 following a letter I wrote to *The Observer* in May of that year.

The library has grown up around these many areas of interest and is divided principally into five areas, inspired by the late Dr Reinhold Regensburger, founder President of the PLA, a refugee from Germany like so many other seminal figures of the postwar period such as Dr Ernst Gombrich, Dr Aby Warburg, and Dr David Diringer whose Alphabet Museum began in Cambridge. These too had a vision of global knowledge and wisdom based upon a sound personal library not bounded by language, creed or prejudice.

My East Room begins with China and the civilizations which have learned from the Middle Kingdom and its streams of Confucian, Taoist and Buddhist thought, being particularly strong on Indonesia, Japan, India and Sri Lanka. My many years in the Islamic world both working and travelling have yielded a rich harvest. We have a home in Malta which feels comfortable because of its union of Arabic and Italian in its language, and its rich prehistoric Roman and other Mediterranean cultures.

Philip Ward, 1982

My West Room begins with Greece and its possessions in the Eastern Mediterranean, Byzantium and Hellenistic life, then Rome and Vulgar Latin spreading into the Romance languages, with a very good Italian department based on Dr Regensburger's envelope system for individual towns and villages and authors (I studied Italian in Perugia), then Portugal (I studied Portuguese in Coimbra), France and Benelux.

My Art Dept covers the history of art following the same pattern as the above: China and the East; Greece and the West, with envelopes for each artist including photos, articles and obituaries, in A/Z order for 1900 onwards, and by country for earlier artists.

My General Room covers subjects without a topographical slant, such as history and geography in general, science and technology, the card catalogue and accessions registers, and journals such as *National Geographic, Geographical Magazine, Encounter* and *London Magazine*.

My Spanish and Latin American Dept is strong in literature and travel, but weaker on history and politics.

Lastly, none of this would have been possible without my ever-patient and tolerant wife Audrey, who has suffered books and papers everywhere. On my first day of work at the National Central Library (now the British Library) in 1955 she was asked if she would take the newcomer Philip under her wing, and I am thrilled beyond words that she has done so ever since.

The continued success of the Private Libraries Association following my departure for Libya in 1963 (I gave up editing *The Private Library* in 1964) is due in great part to David Chambers, and his willingness to shoulder my burden then, and continue right up until now, requires a massive vote of thanks from all past, present and future members. He is the real hero of the PLA.

Cambridge

Oleander Press Device

PHILIP WARD

Len Weaver

1936–2006

My interest in book collecting started over 50 years ago during my National Service in Kenya (the Mau Mau Emergency) when I became fascinated by the turbulent history of East Africa, and particularly Kenya. I now have a collection of over 2,000 books on the region comprising classic accounts of early explorers such as Livingstone, Stanley, Burton, Speke, Grant and Baker; memoirs by early settlers and Colonial Administrators; accounts of the East African Campaign in WWII and the subsequent Mau Mau insurgency; and an extensive range of commentary by historians and politicians.

Whilst my fascination with Africana has remained unabated for over half a century my other collecting interests have waxed and waned and have included various themes, single authors and private presses. Of these I have found that the collection of single authors is the purest form of bibliophily requiring patience and single-minded dedication over an extended period!

I built up comprehensive collections of two authors – Winston Churchill and Siegfried Sassoon. I started collecting Churchill in the late 1950s receiving much help and encouragement from Sawyer's (then in Grafton Street) and Joseph's. Over a period of some fifteen years I established a substantial collection of his works mostly in outstanding condition and with the rarer items preserved in black morocco bound boxes. Sadly I was eventually unable to resist what then seemed to be a spectacular offer for the collection. (Oh. if only . . .)

I collected the works of Siegfried Sassoon for some twenty years aided and abetted by a number of dealers but particularly by Anthony Rota of Bertram Rota and Bill Lent of Maggs. I was despairing of ever finding some of the early and very rare privately printed items when Christie's auctioned the Sassoon library in June 1974. I was outbid by Lew Feldman of the House of El Dieff on all the rare items but that evening I bearded him at the Westbury Hotel and managed to negotiate the purchase of all the outstanding ones thus completing one of only three virtually complete Sassoon collections: one is in the Humanities Research

Len Weaver

Center at the University of Texas and the other, in King's College, Cambridge, was collected by Sir Geoffrey Keynes (Sassoon's bibliographer). My collection, with the rarer items preserved in maroon morocco bound boxes, now resides in the McFarlin Library at the University of Tulsa, Oklahoma. My single author collecting is now on a rather more modest scale and is confined to G. A. Henty, James Lees-Milne and Bernard Cornwell.

Private press books have been another enduring field of interest. I initially compiled an extensive collection of the Nonesuch

Press which included virtually mint sets of the Dickens and the Shakespeare as well as a superbly bound copy of *The Nonesuch Century* from the library of J. R. Abbey. However, I eventually found that collecting the works of a single private press was not particularly satisfying and I disposed of that collection in favour of acquiring select items from a variety of different presses. Over the years I have acquired some books from virtually all the major private presses and also from the less well-known ones such as the Eragny, Essex House, and Daniel.

I collect press books which appeal because of their typography, binding or illustration. For example, some years ago I did an M.A. in the History of the Book at London University and my thesis was on early illustrated Italian books. I was so entranced by these remarkable illustrations that my library now also includes books from a number of other presses – Officina Bodoni, Shakespeare Head and the Limited Editions Club as well as two Roxburghe Club publications – which contain reproductions of those superb fifteenth century Florentine woodcuts. My favourite press book, which I once proudly owned, is the vellum edition of the Ashendene *Ecclesasticus*.

Over the past few years my approach to book collecting has changed in that I have not been influenced by list or bibliography or fashion and I have collected only those items that really appeal. Having indulged such catholic and eclectic tastes means that I now have a large and varied library spread over several rooms which also includes such diverse fields as nineteenth century literature, bibliography and cricket (well over 1,000 books).

I am now gradually culling my various collecting interests and am building up a collection of those books which, in my view, have made a significant contribution to man's thinking in the twentieth century. In the foreseeable future I intend to concentrate on this fascinating and, as yet, none too expensive, field which can perhaps be best described as the application of the *Printing and the Mind of Man* concept to the twentieth century. This is a comparatively new collecting venture of mine but I will readily admit that it is as absorbing and satisfying as any other field that I have ploughed during a long and diverse book collecting career.

Leatherhead, Surrey

LEN WEAVER

Bryan Welch

I had read all the Dr Dolittle books except for *Gub Gub's Book*. It had not been reprinted and the local library did not have a copy. When I saw the first edition (1932) for sale at 7*s*. 6*d*. in Bredon's Bookshop in Brighton I persuaded my parents to buy it for my ninth birthday. This was my first rare book.

Bryan Welch

Books which are rare as texts interest me more than rare editions of common books. In the following forty years I have acquired about 5,000 books but I have only intermittently been a collector. I have collected Baron Corvo, Sir Osbert Lancaster, books on death and cemeteries, Montague Summers, the 1890s, T. E. Lawrence and travel and some modern firsts. Books on cemeteries and travel have illuminated my own travels and visits to cemeteries, and I have published some brief accounts of interesting

356   BRYAN WELCH

cemeteries in the Czech Republic and Japan amongst others. My Corvo collection is the largest, and as a collector I persisted in collecting Corviana after the desire to read the books had tailed off. With modern firsts I have collected long enough to find out what poor paper many reputable publishers used. Mostly I have bought books that interested me to form a library: finding that one book endlessly suggests another. As a result I have a varied library with many curiosities and have not formed a single minded and possibly splendid (or even important) collection. When I scan my shelves for something to read, I recall a speaker at the opening of the London Antiquarian Book Fair some years ago. He said that one should buy books to read in seven years time. A good principle. In fact as well as restarting on Baron Corvo I am currently reading some of my university texts (*c.* 1966) for the first time.

London

Trevor Weston

Illustrated Books

I suspect that my collecting must have started as a pre-natal activity. Certainly, for as long as I can remember, I have been of an acquisitive bent; and by no means only in a commercial sense. For what initially appealed to me most – to my parents' horror – were the things that other people had abandoned; detritus for which nobody else could find a use. I have never regretted this or found it an occasion for shame – they have all, sooner or later, found a usefulness to me. Indeed, a bent nail file I once picked up on a station platform literally saved my life only a few hours later. This penchant for the discarded has greatly influenced my book-buying. Not only do I not reject – or even grimace at – a soiled, coverless and generally distressed volume that turns up on a book-shop shelf or at an auction viewing; I seem positively to seek them out. Not just because they are ragged and likely to be cheap – although that is certainly an added incentive – but because I have not infrequently found great treasure within them.

For me – perversely, I am assured – their very poverty belies a rare richness, the sheer persistence of their survival a charm that is sometimes greater and more satisfying than could be afforded by owning the finest copy of the same work. For what you hold is also a unique, an unrepeatable example and has the same text and illustrations – even if soiled and grubby. Its unsung provenance a damp, rat-infested cellar of some German monastery ravaged during the Thirty Years War rather than an armorial pedigree. Miracle one is that it has managed to cling on to life without the benefit of a sound binding or a luxurious library. Miracle two is that it has fallen into your hands and offered you the honour (and the pleasure) of saving it from the final bonfire. Miracle three is that you know a restorer / binder in the shadow of the church of Our Lady of the Forsaken (how appropriate; and how tender is the Spanish word – *desamparados*) in Valencia who will use it to teach his students about what makes a book good and then return it to you lovingly and delicately revived; and fit for another 400 years' adventures.

Apart from the distracting luxury of befriending *desamparados*,

Trevor Weston

my chief interest for the past sixty years has been in book illustration and the placing both of text and pictures on the page and of pages in the book. There are no rules for this – it is, I think, an intuitive, arcane, magical skill possessed by very few – and 'design' is a too self-conscious term that doesn't convey what I mean. In the rather haphazard pursuit of this interest I seem to have assembled a posse of books that contain examples from most periods and personalities in book-making both in England and the rest of Europe. I am particularly fascinated with what I call 'comparative book illustration' – the response of different illustrators to the same text. The 120 or so recorded renderings of *The Song of Songs* are of particular interest to me and I vainly tried to persuade the Royal Academy of Arts to put on an exhibition of them. I am hopeful that the British Library will be more receptive to the idea.

Some ten years ago feeling, after half a century of revelling in illustrated books, that it would be interesting to add something contemporary to the pile, I set up a small publishing company called Clarion. The idea was to commission new poetry and short stories from both known and unknown authors and then to arrange for different types of illustration, medium and format to go with them; thus creating a kind of round-up of contemporary British book illustration. It was great fun and at least gave me the satisfaction of adding two very different treatments of *The Song of Songs* to the 120 mentioned above – a very sensual one by the inimitable Anita Klein and a somewhat more spiritual one by the late, greatly lamented Henry Fuller.

Holybourne, Alton, Hampshire

David Wickham

Austin Dobson

(Henry) Austin Dobson (1840–1921), principal clerk in the Marine Department, Board of Trade; 'man of letters', poet and historical essayist, lifelong friend of Sir Edmund Gosse.

Unlike several of my sub-libraries, my Austin Dobson collection began less in a fit of absence of mind and more in the desire not to miss a bargain. In August 1976, in St Martin's Court, London, I bought the three volumes of his *Eighteenth Century Vignettes*, 1892, 1894, 1896, R. S. Garnett's signed copies, for £4 the lot. The style seemed familiar and I discovered that I already owned fourteen books written or edited by him, the first acquired not later than 1961.

Dobson's interests were wide. His *Collected Poems* appeared in 1897 and enjoyed eight more editions and two further impressions. He edited Jane Austen. He wrote lives of Hogarth, Fielding, Steele, Goldsmith, Richardson, Bewick, Horace Walpole, and Fanny Burney. His edition of Goldsmith's *Poetical Works* began to appear in 1906 and lasted for decades. He edited and / or provided learned introductions for many classics: Boswell's *Johnson*, 1901, *The Diary and Letters of Madame D'Arblay*, six volumes, 1904, *Evelyn's Diary* with notes, three volumes, 1906, and so on.

There were numerous reprints of many of his works, American editions with altered titles, re-issues in Everyman's Library, World's Classics, and Temple Classics. He was illustrated by Edwin Abbey, Hugh Thomson, and Herbert Railton. A reasonable number of his books appeared in large paper and limited forms. They were often sumptuously rebound. Many of Dobson's essays and poems were first published in magazines. He occasionally had items privately printed in small numbers as gifts or to secure copyright. Some of his verses were to be set to music and printed. He was a soft touch for warm dated inscriptions in his ornately mannered hand, once seen, never forgotten.

The 'completist' circle widens. I own examples of most of such items, but also the copy of Dobson's *Evelyn's Diary* annotated by E. S. de Beer for his own definitive edition. I even have a small bound collection of engravings by Daniel Chodowiecki,

David Wickham, in his Old Library, standing beside
the main section of his Austin Dobson collection

The Berlin Hogarth, first treated by Dobson in an essay in the
Magazine of Art in 1885, then reprinted in the second volume of
the *Vignettes*. The basic items bear repetition: another trio of
Vignettes is / are so tight in their bindings that the volumes might
be fresh off their original shelves and a third trio preserves the
immaculate tissue wrappers.

Dobson's family collection is in University College Library,
London. Three bibliographies enable me to boast that I probably
have the best Dobson collection in private hands in Britain,
perhaps in the world, since another collection was apparently
presented to an American University. I now own about one thousand Dobson items, including over one hundred autograph letters
and cards, a portrait in oils, and, my latest acquisition and a very
rare bird indeed, one of his autograph books of notes and sources,
this example for Matthew Prior.

Belvedere, Kent

DAVID WICKHAM

Graham Williams

Passing by Arthur Ransome and Enid Blyton's adventures of the imagination I arrive at *Amelia*. Some part of those children's books nevertheless remains important, for looking at natural things and country ways still appeals more than city life. I was eight when *Amelia* came into my life, with loose boards and long ſes. I bought Henry Fielding's novel in our village jumble sale, from the white elephant stall. I wasn't looking for books but for false teeth. A jeweller to whom I took all the silver bits I found in junk shops introduced me to Victorian false teeth, some of which had platinum pins holding the teeth on. Pocket money was better earned with silver and platinum than empty jam jars.

Back home I sat on my favourite stair and soon found that the long ſ was easy to read and the story began to unfold. I was captivated by this book and I still have it, sporting a new full calf binding. I doubt it has value, published in 1766 it is the third edition of the *Works* of Henry Fielding, volume ten, with the 'Life of the Author'. I couldn't read the 'Life' as it was in another volume. I found out that this man so long ago had written about things that he knew. He was a magistrate and maybe knew of cases when maids mistakenly were taken off the streets, whether or not they were rushing for help for their pregnant mistress. This was better than boats on the Broads, I thought.

Chance plays such an enormous part in life and looking at my books I see the outcome of chance that has directed me in several ways. My father was a compositor, a hand comp, on the *Daily Mail* in Tudor Street. Just a stone's throw away my mother had worked as a reader in the Co-operative Printing. When I grew up I wasn't going to be a printer, I wanted to be an artist; my parents thought I would be a doctor, and I let them think so. I set out to find a job in London, naturally going to Blackfriars and Fleet Street where eventually I was employed, in a commercial art studio.

Printing must have been a part of me though, for geometry at school was sometimes done in picas which fitted the paper better than inches and were conveniently on the ruler, the type gauge, which my Father had given me when I started at grammar school.

Graham Williams

Accidents took me to St Bride's and the Printing Library. A chance took me for interview at the Folio Society and by the time I was twenty-one I was deep in books, soon with a hand press that I borrowed from Walter Tracy. I looked at original prints as well and amongst them came some modern proofs from Thomas Bewick's blocks and my first acquaintance with Iain Bain and David Chambers. All that came together and I was sucked into the engraving and printing of wood blocks as assuredly as if they had been a vacuum cleaner.

Seeking the three dimensions that I knew Thomas Bewick had engraved into the blocks led me to the old printers' manuals, in the library or as reprints. I bought the new edition of Moxon and devoured it and the new scholarship of Davis and Carter. I found out how the lowered blocks might be printed and books accumulated around me – printers' manuals including the colour printing of William Savage and Jackson, manuals of wood-engraving and volumes of Bewick's work.

In a picture framing shop I rescued a volume of Bewick's *Birds*, the cuts without text, that was destined for the knife and framing. From that first volume of Bewick's work others joined and with them scores of Bewick's original wood blocks, many of them for his Aesop. Chance again fired my interest in the Aesop till now I can sit down and read about half the text of the book in Thomas Bewick's own hand. Touching the manuscript of 1814 is to touch history, to discover Thomas writing his text, often on Sunday as the dates give away.

Picking up Moxon in its original serialised parts of 1683 and settling with a glass of wine into a winged chair I found a friend I could not find in the modern, scholarly printing. Here Moxon chatted to me, discussed techniques I had found for myself or clearly saw the need for. *Amelia's* long ſ still holds no barriers.

Biddenden, Kent

Wood-engraving signed TB,
possibly engraved by Luke Clennell,
from *The Sportsman's Cabinet,* 1803,
reproduced from an impression
taken by Graham Williams from the
original block in his collection

Ray B. Williams

History and Bibliography of Biology

A first glance at my books reveals that this is most definitely a working library rather than a 'collection'. Chaos reigns, but I convince myself that I know where everything is; this I achieve largely by having multiple copies of the most regularly consulted books spread about so that if I can't find the particular copy I was originally seeking, the chances of stumbling across another are reasonably high. Shelf space ran out many years ago, and there are now more books in boxes and in heaps on the floors of literally every room in the house than on the lovingly constructed shelves that I installed in my original 'proper library'. There is a serious danger that during a restless night I might accidentally bring the stacks of books that tower some four feet over our bed crashing down upon my wife and me! It is perhaps reasonable to enquire how this somewhat unusual situation arose.

By training I am a zoologist, having two parallel occupations, one as a parasitologist (for money), and the other as a marine biologist (for fun). My passion for books arose from the necessity of having essential marine science texts at my fingertips; I reasoned that it would be cheaper to buy the books I constantly needed, rather than to spend money on train fares visiting specialized academic libraries up and down the country with the further disadvantage of having to use valuable holidays to do it. It seemed to make sense at first, but subsequent financial calculations would certainly no longer support the hypothesis! However, it's too late now – bibliomania has taken hold. And because the medical libraries that I visited for professional purposes did not satisfy my desire for completeness, parasitological works soon began to join the marine books.

The core of my library comprises academic text books and monographs on the biology and descriptions of parasites and marine animals, published from the eighteenth to the twenty-first century, as well as runs of scholarly journals and countless separate offprints. Inevitably, however, various specialities have evolved during the last thirty-five years or so. The first emerged in order to determine the precise dates of publication of works in

Ray Williams in 2005, with shelves of Van Voorst books behind, holding Anne Bullar's *Domestic Scenes in Greenland and Iceland* and Edmund Sharpe's *Architectural Parallels*.

which previously unknown animals were described. This is an essential prerequisite for establishing nomenclatural priority when the same species is mistakenly described and named by different authors, often widely separated geographically and temporally. The necessary tools are hugely varied: histories of science; encyclopaedias; indexes of zoological names; library catalogues; booksellers' catalogues; contemporary English and foreign dictionaries; descriptive and analytical bibliographies of authors, subjects and publishers; studies of bibliographical methods; works on printing and binding practice; histories of printers, publishers and publishing practice; biographies of authors – all these, and more, contribute to the publication history of a book or journal.[1]

This immersion in the history of zoological publications quite naturally awakened a fascination with the lives of those who had gone before in my fields of interest, for example, the parasitologists Theodor Eimer, Alphonse Labbé and Ernest Edward Tyzzer; and the naturalists John Ellis, Edward Forbes, William Yarrell and Philip Henry Gosse. The full list is enormous, and the temptation to trace all the publications of my favourites proved irresistible. Books, journals, offprints, reprints, engravings, and where possible original drawings, photographs and letters were eagerly sought. Anything by or about these eminent scientists is constantly being added. If I live long enough, there is enough material for several short biographies! In the interim, this second speciality has provided the tools for over forty short articles on the history and bibliography of biology, published since 1981, mostly in the *Newsletter of the Society for the History of Natural History.*

However, priority is currently given to my third speciality, the life and work of the Victorian publisher John Van Voorst (1804–1898).[2,3] The accumulated materials for this project now threaten to overwhelm the rest of my library. I am certainly not alone in my admiration for the publications of Van Voorst; indeed I know several collectors of his works, on account of the high quality of his well printed books with beautiful illustrations. But as far as I know (and fervently hope), I am alone in undertaking an academic study of the man, his career and complete publishing output. This sprang from my early work on zoological taxonomy and the nomenclatural priority of scientific names. Besides Van Voorst's publications, I have an archive of letters, legal documents and ephemera, including the remarkable collection relevant to Oliver Goldsmith's *Vicar of Wakefield*.[4]

Van Voorst sometimes issued scientific monographs in a series of parts, often over a period of two or more years, the last part often being timed to capture a Christmas market when the completed volume in boards was simultaneously issued. So that the new work would not seem already old by the following month (January of the succeeding year), the title-page issued to subscribers in the last part and also appearing in the completed volume(s) would typically give the publication date as the next year. Hence, without knowledge of the original parts and their publication dates, one would be totally misled by the spurious title-page date, resulting in serious errors when attempting to establish nomenclatural priorities.[5] When I discovered that many professional zoologists were not aware that certain important taxonomic monographs were published in parts, I decided to trace the publishing history of all Van Voorst's zoological works. A few moments' consideration persuaded me to include his botanical publications as well, before I convinced myself that I should also cover all the geological and physical sciences; and then why not all of his remaining disparate output of architecture, fine arts, poetry, juvenilia, angling, religion, law, etc? Naturally, all editions and issues would have to be included; and to complete the work, surely a biography of this doyen of Victorian publishing could not be omitted. My fate was sealed!

Although the subject range of Van Voorst's output (between 1834 and 1886) is fairly wide, about two-thirds of it comprises the sciences, primarily zoology, botany and geology. The physical form of his publications ranges from sheets bearing the scientific names of birds or insects for labelling specimen collections to huge tomes of architectural plans. Besides some single sheets and pamphlets, perhaps his smallest cased book is Anne Bullar's *Domestic Scenes in Greenland and Iceland* (1844), measuring 13.4 × 9.0 cm, and his largest is the large paper issue of Edmund Sharpe's *Architectural Parallels* (1848), measuring 61.7 × 47.0 cm, and weighing some 17 kg. Books were available in up to four different paper sizes; maybe with paper covers, paper-covered boards, cloth-covered boards or leather bindings. Some special examples, such as heavy bevelled boards, Yapp bindings and 'tuck' bindings (a kind of wallet) also exist. Illustration methods are equally varied; steel and wood-engravings, lithographs, Baxter-process prints and actual photographs are all to be found. For some titles, coloured or plain plates were available. A very unusual example is the plaster of Paris relief map of the geology of the Isle of Wight by Levett Ibbetson (1849). Sometimes illustrations from books were also available separately, such as the steel engravings from the *Cabinet Holy Bible* (1834), and the geological map from John Salmon's *Flora of Surrey* (1863).

However, the most fascinating items are those books and journals surviving in original parts with printed paper wrappers. Some parts contain important text on leaves that were later cancelled, and were therefore missing from the complete volume when issued.[5] There may be bibliographical information in a prospectus or advertisements on separate leaves tipped in or loosely inserted, or printed on the wrappers. Or one may find ephemeral primary text, printed on wrappers of journals and books, that was never reprinted in the definitive volumes.[6] But, of course, the crucial information on wrappers is the publication date of each part, bringing us back to the whole *raison d'être* of my Van Voorst work, which is to provide as nearly as possible a complete publishing history of every title issued.

Tring, Herts.

1. Williams, R. B. (1990). 'Who, what, where, when and why: the elements of history'. *Archives of Natural History*, 17: 263–282.
2. Williams, R. B. (1988). 'John Van Voorst – patron publisher of Victorian natural history'. *The Private Library* (4th series), 1: 4–12.
3. Williams, R. B. (2004). 'John Van Voorst'. In *The Dictionary of Nineteenth-Century British Scientists* (ed. B. Lightman), volume 4, pp. 2063-2066. Thoemmes Continuum, Bristol.
4. De Beaumont, R. (1992). 'Some new light on the 1843 Vicar of Wakefield'. *The Private Library* (4th series), 5: 4–19.
5. Williams, R. B. (1981). 'The authorship of the family name Metridiidae (Coelenterata: Anthozoa)'. *Bulletin of Zoological Nomenclature*, 38: 156–7.
6. Williams, R. B. (2005). 'Three unrecorded publications by Philip Henry Gosse, with notes on primary text on wrappers of journals and books, and a proposal for the bibliographical description of wrappers'. *Archives of Natural History*, 32: 34–40.

Jonathan Wood

To the Memory of my Mother

I began collecting in 1982 aged twenty-two, using some of my first pay packet to begin the foundations of a collection. It has been invaluable to live and work in London with easy access to the Charing Cross Road, Cecil Court and the PBFA and ABA fairs, especially during that golden era of choice and price – 1984 to 1994. Most weekdays, I drop into what's left of Any Amount of Books, ever on the lookout. It is a far cry from my childhood attempts at collecting, when I formed a small but precious (to me at least) collection of cheap leather bound volumes of Poe, worth no more than a few pounds for sure, but which opened up the world of bindings, tissue guards and the printed page. I was fool enough to lend them to a school chum; they came back to me in pieces, of course and in some cases minus covers – once bitten!

Book collecting has been a consummate delight over the years and my interests have taken me down many by-roads, from single authors like Graham Greene and E. M. Forster to significant periods / movements like the 1890s, the War Poets, the English short story tradition of the 30s and 40s, Bloomsburyana – through my mother's great interest, the Powys Bros, to the esoteric idiosyncrasies of Arthur Machen, Aleister Crowley (a lover and exploiter of private press as evinced by Timothy d'Arch Smith's *The Books of the Beast* in 1987) and latterly that modern master Iain Sinclair, as well as the unique treasures of English and American private press and bibliography. I shall never forget the electric thrill of purchasing a pristine copy of Crowley's *Moonchild* in its wonderful Beresford Egan dustwrapper at £48 at the PBFA's Hotel Russell fair in 1984 (I shall refrain from mentioning the dealer's name), a mint copy of Leonard Green's *Dream Comrades* for £1 in a bookshop near a suburban railway station down from Waterloo, and a signed crisp copy of *The Grande Trouvaille* by Arthur Machen from Rupert Cook (sadly now deceased) from Lusitania Books, and the elusive *The Cosy Room*, courtesy of my father's expert eye for a bargain.

I am at that point in my collecting life where I can slow the pace and attune my pocket to avoid the fevered inflation of the

Jonathan Wood

market place. I am standing back, taking stock, cherry picking when opportunities arise (a recent purchase of an Andrew Block, found it inscribed to the dealer / collector Harry Spilstead), relishing what I have and what encounters I have experienced over the years with dealers, writers, collectors and characters. I delight in the underdog author like John Gawsworth and publishers like R. A Caton and his deeply prolific Fortune Press; the Vine Press of Victor B. Neuburg down in Steyning – *Larkspur*, *Swift Wings*, *Songs of the Groves* etc. – with their rough-hewn antique paper and satyrs dancing on each colophon, the simplicity of the wood-cut illustrations by Dennis West and the frequency of the author inscriptions and those elusive hand-coloured editions. Likewise, the Redlynch Press of Phyllis Taunton Wood – a wonderfully obscure war-time private press of the 1940s, residing in London W5, with its combination of Blakeian spiritual texts and woodcuts, offsetting and smudging almost a necessity in their production. Also, Ralph Chubb's *Songs of Mankind*, *Woodcuts*, and

A *Fable of Love and War*, forgotten visionary gems in a tarnished new world. The works and literary activity of Father Brocard Sewell opened up a whole new vista for me, when I chanced upon them in 1985 – the *Aylesford Review* (surely the most eclectic and liberated literary periodical of the 1960s and possibly of all time) the catalyst for me collecting Corvo and Summers – having also devoured Woolf's and d'Arch Smith's respective bibliographies. Also, through the *Review*, the poets Penelope Shuttle and Frances Horovitz, Beardsley and the 1890s, Hilary Pepler, Joseph Delteil, John Gray, Henry Williamson *et al*. Ephemera, prospectuses, mimeographed letters from Sewell and by some miracle, that finest and rarest of all Sewell private press items – a copy of *The Thing* produced by him and Edward Walters – of course only one issue was ever produced. Another Sewell treasure – a signed and inscribed copy of *My Dear Time's Waste* festooned with the jottings and tipped-in minutiae of the collector Stanley Scott. Mention of Henry Williamson takes me back to Clearwater Books in Dean Street and then Great Pulteney Street and the seeds of my collecting and that of my father – who developed his own collecting habits from a visit paid to Stephen Clarke's shop back in 1984 or thereabouts. Shelves of gleaming copies of *A Chronicle of Ancient Sunlight*, *The Flax of Dream* and the signed *Tarka* abounded amidst that sadly now long gone atmosphere of the collector's bookshop; the chance meetings, the dust, the wonderful gems fairly priced, the friendships made and nods given. Stephen died in 2004 after a short illness but his legacy lives on through his catalogues – now collectors' items – and his impact upon Williamson collecting and bibliomania in general.

I am a sucker for printed ephemera too, especially prospectuses and hand-bills announcing works by various presses – works of art in themselves – and those treasured items behind the acronyms a.l.s, t.l.s and a.p.c etc. I found an a.l.s in a battered old Clifford Bax book from Bax to Aleister Crowley asking him to come to tea to meet Margaret Maison. Another is from Beresford Egan inviting a cricket lover to peruse some of his works for possible sale. It is decorated with a wonderful Egan image.

It is also a joy to collect the catalogues of the great private dealers and fine opuscule producers – George Sims, Anthony d'Offay, Timothy d'Arch Smith to name but three. George Sims –

what catalogues. It is a bibliographical education to read them.

The web of correspondence and good fortune grew with membership of various literary societies and of course, the Private Libraries Association – with so many diverse members with diverse interests – and the PLA's eagerly awaited and sometimes irregularly appearing journals. It would not be the same if they weren't. The greatest kernels of knowledge have here been imparted – I was looking the other day at a past issue – Spring 1979, on the Polish printer Stanislaw Gliwa. A wonderful essay by R. T. Risk on the real trials and tribulations of Gliwa's life and his delicate craft, cited as living in south-east London – it bowled me over to read it again and to recall how it gave me another instant entry point for my interests. Although not in a financial position to purchase items of those grand presses like Corvinus, Ashendene and Kelmscott etc, the information afforded to collectors in *The Private Library* about these giants has been of the highest order, challenging the reader and collector to see beyond the sometimes limiting impositions of their own collecting desiderata. Likewise, exposure to the more obscure or diminutive presses has been highly innovative. I am proud to be mentioned in Paul Nash's article on Joel Biroco's Herculaneum Press (Summer 1998), having mentioned its genesis in my own fatalistic sun-dog of a journal, *Netherwood* (Kosmopoli, 1990). It's a nice feeling to have some connection. My own Biroco collection remains with me intact. It is a highly treasured collection of books, letters and ephemera from a fertile period in late Twentieth Century underground publishing. *The Private Library* editors have been kind enough even to give space for mention of some of my own offbeat and licorice literary pursuits. My own imprint, the Arbor Vitae Press is certainly more small press than private press, but again, it has been influenced by the delights of the printed page and the lure of the limited edition.

I have managed over the years to purchase treasures from such private presses as The Old Stile, Tragara, Priapus, Sceptre, Durtro, Tartarus, Tern, Perpetua, Strawberry and The Kemble Press, the latter with its strange volume called *Haunted Ground* by Michael Oakley lovingly printed in 14pt Perpetua in 1955. Also, a real obscure gem – the apocalyptic *After the Fall* from The Aldham Press (1968) set in 10pt italic Times New Roman with poems by

Peter Dale and David Blackmore, printed on Oxford paper with striking anonymous linocuts. My copy has an inked '39' on the colophon, but there is no limitation set down. What more could one want but some mystery? Also, newer presses like The Teitan Press of Chicago run by Martin P. Starr, the world authority on Aleister Crowley, producing the most exquisite editions of Crowley's works, some bound in very limited editions by Sangorski and Sutcliffe to the haunting tune of Crowley's own original specification; instructions echoing down the years to the present – worthy of an article in itself. I have learnt many things from *The Private Library* – not least to appreciate the love and dedication and toil of those craftsmen and women who had the vision to unite image and word through wondrous techniques into such printed excellence.

Finally, it is a delight when the June bookfairs happen each year and characters like Martin Stone appear from out the ether on the Charing Cross Road as if by magick and collectors, dealers and runners talk nothing but books. Only Driffield's shade is absent. Last year, I came away with a signed John Fowles, books on Henry Moore and Derek Jarman – poet of the eye. It is great to be a part of the PLA and to receive *The Private Library*. It has moved successfully with the times. It is a unique society with a unique journal, its volumes residing proudly in my collection next to other unique items – which will remain my secret.

London

JONATHAN WOOD

John Rutter's library, bookshop and
printing office, Shaftesbury, Dorset.
Wood-engraving by William Barnes,
reproduced from *William Barnes,
The Dorset Engravings*, 1986.
*Courtesy, Trustees of the
Mansel-Pleydell Trust.*

CONTRIBUTORS

G. Thomas Tanselle, 332
Jim, Thirsk, 335
Martyn Thomas, 338
Philip A. Truett, 342
Norman Waddleton, 346
Philip Ward, 350
Len Weaver, 353

Bryan Welch, 356
Trevor Weston, 358
David Wickham, 361
Graham Williams, 363
Ray B. Williams, 366
Jonathan Wood, 371

RETAIL PRICE INDEX

Inflation over the past fifty years has been so substantial that some reference needs to be made to the Retail Price Index if earlier figures are to be related (aproximately) to current values.
£1 in June 1956 would thus be equivalent to £17.26 in June 2006.

Table of inflation, as at June each year:

Year								
1906	1.00							
1916	1.59	1.00						
1946	2.22	1.40	1.00					
1956	3.51	2.21	1.58	1.00				
1966	4.73	2.98	2.12	1.35	1.00			
1976	12.07	7.60	5.42	3.44	2.55	1.00		
1986	29.87	18.81	13.40	8.50	6.32	2.47	1.00	
1996	46.72	29.42	20.96	13.30	9.88	3.87	1.56	1.00
2006	60.60	38.17	27.19	17.26	12.82	5.02	2.03	1.30